T0330256

Economic Policy and Climate Change

NEW HORIZONS IN ENVIRONMENTAL ECONOMICS

General Editor: Wallace E. Oates, *Professor of Economics, University of Maryland*

This important series is designed to make a significant contribution to the development of the principles and practices of environmental economics. It includes both theoretical and empirical work. International in scope, it addresses issues of current and future concern in both East and West and in developed and developing countries.

The main purpose of the series is to create a forum for the publication of high quality work and to show how economic analysis can make a contribution to understanding and resolving the environmental problems confronting the world in the late twentieth century.

Recent titles in the series include:

The Economics of Environmental Protection
Theory and Demand Revelation
Peter Bohm

The International Yearbook of Environmental and Resource Economics
1997/1998
A Survey of Current Issues
Edited by Henk Folmer and Tom Tietenberg

The Economic Theory of Environmental Policy in a Federal System
Edited by John B. Braden and Stef Proost

Environmental Taxes and Economic Welfare
Reducing Carbon Dioxide Emissions
Antonia Cornwell and John Creedy

Economics of Ecological Resources
Selected Essays
Charles Perrings

Economics for Environmental Policy in Transition Economies
An Analysis of the Hungarian Experience
Edited by Péter Kaderják and John Powell

Controlling Pollution in Transition Economies
Theories and Methods
Edited by Randall Bluffstone and Bruce A. Larson

Environments and Technology in the Former USSR
Malcolm R. Hill

Pollution and the Firm
Robert E. Kohn

Climate Change, Transport and Environmental Policy
Empirical Applications in a Federal System
Edited by Stef Proost and John B. Braden

The Economics of Energy Policy in China
Implications for Global Climate Change
ZhongXiang Zhang

Advanced Principles in Environmental Policy
Anastasios Xepapadeas

Economic Policy and Climate Change

Tradable Permits for Reducing Carbon Emissions

Paul Koutstaal

Netherlands Energy Research Foundation ECN

NEW HORIZONS IN ENVIRONMENTAL ECONOMICS

Edward Elgar
Cheltenham, UK • Lyme, US

Published by
Edward Elgar Publishing Limited
8 Lansdown Place
Cheltenham
Glos GL50 2HU
UK

Edward Elgar Publishing, Inc.
1 Pinnacle Hill Road
Lyme
NH 03768
US

A catalogue record for this book
is available from the British Library

Library of Congress Cataloguing in Publication Data

Koutstaal, Paul, 1960–
     Economic policy and climate change : tradable permits for reducing
carbon emissions / Paul Koutstaal.
     (New horizons in environmental economics)
   Includes index.
     1. Emissions trading—European Union countries. 2. Greenhouse
effect. Atmospheric—Economic aspects—European Union countries.
   I. Title. II. Series.
   HC240.9.A4K68 1997
   338.94—dc21   97–14357
                                                                           CIP

ISBN 1 85898 634 6

Printed and bound in Great Britain by Hartnolls Limited, Bodmin, Cornwall

Contents

Figures

Tables

Acknowledgements

I have received much help during the writing of this book for which I am very grateful. I want to thank the Dutch Ministry of Economic Affairs and the Dutch National Research Program on Climate Change for the financial grants which have made this book possible, and the Institute of Ecology and Resource Management of the University of Edinburgh for their hospitality.

I am heavily in debt to Andries Nentjes from the University of Groningen, whose comments have considerably improved this book. Others who have been helpful in different ways include Hermann Meyer, René Paas, Annick Teubner and Herman Vollebergh. The omissions and errors that remain are of course my own responsibility. To my wife Annick I owe my warmest thanks of all.

Paul Koutstaal

Strasbourg
May 1997

1. Introduction

On the agenda of environmental problems, the enhanced greenhouse effect has nowadays acquired a prominent place. Although there is still much uncertainty about its extent and its consequences, there is an important rationale for addressing the possible problem of climate change now: whatever the specific consequences may be, they are to a large extent determined by the actions we take (or do not take) today. Emissions of greenhouse gases will determine the atmospheric concentrations of these gases for centuries to come. Because of the increase in anthropogenic CO_2 emissions, starting with the industrial revolution and the rise in the use of fossil fuels which it caused, the concentration of CO_2 in the atmosphere has risen by 25 per cent since 1750. If we want to limit the increase of CO_2 concentrations, action must be taken now.

Within the broad area of research on climate change, one specific strand of economic research has focused on the problem of how to reduce emissions of greenhouse gases, especially carbon dioxide, which is the main greenhouse gas. Taking as a starting point the assumption that a CO_2 emission reduction target has been set, the objective of these studies is to determine the optimal way of reducing these emissions.

From the start, it has been pointed out by environmental economists that economic instruments are suitable for implementing a policy of reducing emissions of greenhouse gases. With economic instruments, emissions will be reduced in an efficient manner, according to the theory. This has been argued and illustrated in a large number of studies which deal with economic instruments such as taxes or charges and tradable emission permits (see, for example, Barrett 1992; UNCTAD 1992; OECD 1992a and 1992b; Smith 1992). In this study, the instrument of tradable carbon emission permits (TCPs) is studied in more detail. The central issue is the design of a feasible system of TCPs and the study of the consequences of implementing such a system.

Up till now, the focus of research in this area has been predominantly on the efficiency of reducing CO_2 emissions by means of tradable emission permits or taxes. Less attention has been paid to the design of such a system, which is the subject of Chapter 2. In this chapter the outlines are sketched of a feasible system of tradable emission permits for the European Union. The

1

proposed system is in essence a system of (carbon in) fuel rationing with tradability of quotas between citizens. Points under consideration include the characteristics of the fuel permit; the distribution of the permits (whether the government sells them or gives them away free); the market allocation of the permits; the time path by which the number of available permits is reduced; monitoring and enforcement of the system; and the possible consequences of a system of tradable emission permits for business location choice. Moreover, we consider whether a system of TCPs can operate on a national base in one member state of the European Union or should be implemented at the European level. Last, the requirements of an EU-wide system are sketched.

A study of the implications of reducing CO_2 emissions by means of TCPs (or any other instrument) cannot be complete without considering the economic consequences of such a system. In order to predict some of the consequences of introducing an instrument such as TCPs to an industry, a microeconomic approach is necessary in which the influence on one or more facets of economic behaviour can be studied in detail. For example, attention has been given to the potential misuse of market power in the permit market (see Tietenberg 1985; Hahn 1984). On the other hand, hardly any attention has been paid up to now to the possible effects of tradable emission permits on entry into industries. This is especially interesting because it has been the practice to grandfather permits to existing sources while new sources, potential entrants, have to buy them. Many people, even economists, feel that this system of grandfathering erects barriers against potential entrants, but that a system of auctioning permits to all firms, both established ones and new entrants, would not have such an impact, or at least would reduce the negative effect on entry. In chapters 3 and 4 I analyse how far this idea is true. The question is addressed whether, how and to what extent a system of tradable permits might create barriers to entry in the product market. Several forms of entry barriers which might be caused or increased by tradable permits are identified and analysed. Subsequently, I study whether these forms of entry barriers are likely to occur in the system of TCPs which is outlined in Chapter 2. An effort is made to determine to what extent entry will be affected when entry barriers are raised by to the TCP system.

These questions are important, not only from a static but also from the dynamic point of view. If a TCP system for reducing CO_2 emissions raises entry barriers, it will influence the whole economy, affecting long-term industry dynamics. This in turn could diminish research and development efforts and reduce economic activity and the efficiency of the whole economy in the longer run. The approach taken here is to study the microeconomic consequences of a system of tradable carbon permits with respect to entry barriers, both with grandfathering and with auctioning of CO_2 emission permits. The results will be compared with the results achieved under two other instruments: taxes and standards. The possible occurrence of entry barriers is analysed both theoretically and empirically.

A salient feature of the greenhouse problem is that it occurs worldwide, irrespective of where CO_2 and the other greenhouse gases are emitted. While this facilitates the design of a TCP system considerably (see Chapter 2), it does pose the additional problem of coordination of policies. It is important to examine whether and in what ways countries cooperate to reduce emissions, and what the role of taxes and tradable permits can be in an international setting. This is the subject of Chapters 5 and 6.

The approach is more general than in the earlier chapters. The model used 'pictures' the whole economy but in a very simplified way. The economy is assumed to consist of one representative consumer who can consume two goods, one of which causes pollution when it is consumed (the pollution represents CO_2 emissions). In addition, the consumer chooses how much of his time he will spend working (and earning an income) and how much leisure he will take. The consumer does not take this pollution into account when he makes his consumption decision, therefore the government has to use instruments such as taxation (or TCPs) to limit emissions. In the first sections of Chapter 5, the optimal levels of CO_2 emission reduction are not taken as given; instead, they are a result of the analysis. In addition to reducing pollution, the government also has to raise an exogenously given amount of revenue. The government maximizes a (social) welfare function which includes damage from pollution under constraint of its revenue requirement. Its instruments (the variables in the model) are the taxes it can levy on the two goods; labour is not taxed. The taxes must serve two purposes: reducing pollution and raising revenue. This reflects the complicating factor that fossil fuels, the main source of CO_2 emissions, are already taxed in most countries. In this model it can be determined how an emission reduction policy should be combined with these existing taxes, as was originally done by Sandmo (1975).

Our approach differs from earlier literature on the subject by extending the model to an international context. The extended model includes two countries which are assumed to be equal in all respects except in the damage suffered from pollution and the amount of revenue which has to be raised. The object of the analysis is to answer the following questions:

- How will the tax structure in both countries change when they cooperate to reduce emissions and use taxes as instruments of coordinated emission reduction?
- What is the consequence of such cooperation for the welfare level (or,

put another way, for the economy) and the level of pollution in both countries?

- Can coordination be improved (made more efficient) and total emission reduction increased by allowing for joint implementation; that is, by allowing one country to pay another country which, in return, increases its emission reduction by raising its tax on the polluting good? In our model side payments have to be raised by taxation on the two goods, which further complicates the analysis.
- How are the tax structures and the pollution levels affected by this form of joint implementation?

In addition to the formal analysis, a less general functional form is used in simulations to get more specific answers to the questions posed above.

Instead of a damage function from which the optimal level of pollution is derived, an exogenously determined emission ceiling can be used. This better reflects the current practice of CO_2 emission reduction policy. In Chapter 6 the model is modified to include such emission ceilings instead of damage functions. I study how different government budgets and different initial emission quotas influence the tax structures in both countries when they cooperate.

It might be an interesting exercise to determine the optimal tax structures when countries coordinate pollution control policies; it is also important to determine which institutional arrangements and instruments can be used to achieve the optimal conditions. I consider whether international agreements have to specify in detail the level of taxes which each country should levy or whether it is sufficient to agree on emission limits and side payments and leave it to individual countries to set taxes. Moreover, I analyse which role TCPs can have in international agreements to limit CO_2 emissions. Conventional wisdom is that trade in emission quotas between countries will lead to a cost-efficient and welfare-maximizing solution. I consider whether this is also the case in our model in which governments have to reduce emissions and raise revenues at the same time.

A last question which is addressed is the role of grandfathering. Selling the permits will raise revenue for the government while grandfathering means that taxes have to be used to meet the government's budget constraint. The question arises whether grandfathering and auctioning have the same welfare effects or whether they differ in their consequences.

In the outline sketched above, two themes are recurrent. First, the choice between grandfathering and auctioning of permits. This is a central element in the design of a system of tradable emission permits. Experience with tradable emissions shows that up till now it has been practice to grandfather permits to existing sources, whereas new sources have to buy the permits they need. A main reason for this policy is that grandfathering permits reduces resistance from (industrial) polluters considerably as compared with auctioning the permits or imposing emission charges. The outlays of polluters on permits can be large compared with their abatement costs when they have to buy permits to cover their remaining emissions. While this does not mean that the use of the permits is costless (the firms forgo the opportunity to sell the permits, therefore they bear the opportunity costs), receiving the permits free is equivalent to receiving a lump-sum capital transfer. However, while grandfathering is attractive from the point of view of existing sources, it might be a drawback to entrants. This possible negative effect of grandfathering is considered in Chapter 3, on entry barriers. Furthermore, in Chapter 6 the role of grandfathering is analysed in a model in which governments have to reduce pollution ánd raise revenue at the same time. The welfare implications of grandfathering are compared with those of auctioning of permits (Chapter 4).

The second recurrent theme is the comparison of the instrument of tradable emission permits with other instruments: a charge on CO_2 emission (the so-called carbon tax) and the command-and-control type of regulation such as emission standards. This comparison is made (a) in order to highlight the peculiarities of tradable emission permits *vis-à-vis* other policy measures; and (b) because carbon taxes have received much attention in the current debate on CO_2 emission reduction, both from policy-makers and scientists. The different consequences for entry barriers between, on the one hand, TCPs and, on the other hand, taxes and standards are studied in Chapters 3 and 4. In Chapter 6 the role of taxes and TCPs in international agreements on CO_2 emission reduction policies are compared.

2. Designing a System of Tradable Carbon Permits for the EU[1]

2.1 INTRODUCTION

At the United Nations Conference on the Environment and Development in Rio de Janeiro in 1992 the Framework Convention on Climate Change (FCCC) was signed by the representatives of over 150 countries of the world (UN 1992, 1994). It was ratified by an initial 50 countries in late 1993 and came into force on 21 March 1994. The parties that have signed the climate convention agree that emissions of the so-called greenhouse gases resulting from human activity are the cause of a rising global mean temperature and climate change and that steps must be taken to curb emissions. Stabilization of emissions at the 1990 level by the year 2000 is mentioned as a first target of a global climate policy. The convention leaves the countries free in the way they choose to fulfil their promises. For a time it looked as if there was a political consensus that a tax on emissions of greenhouse gases, in particular a carbon tax to curb CO_2 emissions, would become the major instrument for implementing the climate convention. However, the initial postponement of such a tax by the Council of Environment Ministers of the then European Community (now the European Union, EU) in December 1994, and its eventual demise, and the pressure on US President Clinton to avoid an increase in taxes have scuppered the hope of an early introduction of a carbon tax.[2] The political discussions about the now defunct carbon tax made it quite clear that a large and probably decisive obstacle to the introduction of such an economic instrument is the political resistance that any proposal to impose a new tax on a specific interest group calls forth. This has, for example, been shown by the activities of the Union of Industrial and Employers' Confederation of Europe, a European business lobby based in Brussels, which has been a strong opponent of the carbon/energy tax (SkjÆrseth 1994, p. 28). For that reason it makes sense to look for instruments that do not have the disadvantage of raising the tax burden or changing the existing tax structure but yet leave emitters more flexibility than the direct regulation of emission or carbon use would do. In this chapter we shall discuss such an instrument: tradable carbon permits. Section 2.2 provides

6

a short survey of the most important properties of tradable emission permits (TDPs) in general and of the experiences up to this date with tradable permits. Section 2.3 considers the effect of TDPs on business location choice and makes a comparison with taxes. Section 2.4 then sketches the outlines of a system of tradable carbon permits (TCPs). Special attention is given to the design and feasibility of a system of TCPs for the European Union.

2.2 TRADABLE PERMITS

Tradable permits in environmental policy are a relatively new instrument, in theory as well as in actual policy. The idea was developed by J.H. Dales in 1968. The basic concept – the rationing of production and the handing out of coupons to consumers, who are allowed to trade coupons among themselves – has a much longer history. During the period of scarcity caused by the Second World War and its aftermath, the system was applied in many European countries. As an instrument of pollution abatement policy, tradable permits were first brought into use from 1975 by the US Environmental Protection Agency (EPA) in its Offset Program for air pollutants (among others, sulphur dioxide, carbon monoxide and nitrogen oxides).[3] The main reason for the introduction of the permit system was to create a means by which new firms could enter areas in which no new sources of emissions were allowed because of high pollution levels. New sources could start operating on condition that they acquired emission permits from established firms. This was called the offset policy. In addition, firms could use netting, bubbles and banking. Essentially, netting and bubbles are methods which allow firms to exceed emission standards in some of their operations as long as they compensate with others in which emissions fall below regulatory standards. In banking, emission reduction credits (as the permits are called in this program) are saved for later use or sale.

While the EPA program has undoubtedly reduced abatement costs (bubbles and netting has resulted in an estimated cost reduction of $700 million, Dwyer 1992), it has fallen short of expectations (Hahn and Hester 1989). In particular, the number of trades between various firms has been far less than was expected. Three main reasons can be mentioned (Klaassen 1996): regulations which restricted the number of potential trades; high transaction costs which reduced the attractiveness of trade; and uncertainty about the future value of the permits which made them less attractive to purchase.

In 1973 a programme started in the US to reduce the lead content of gasoline (see Nussbaum 1992). Standards were reduced in a number of phases. The programme allowed trade in lead rights and banking. The number of trades was large: in 1987, up to 60 per cent of the total number of lead rights available (Hahn and Hester 1989). This can be explained by the modest administrative requirements and by the fact that the refineries already dealt with each other in a number of markets, keeping transaction costs low.

In 1995 an emission trading programme started in the US to reduce sulphur dioxide (SO_2) emissions from fossil fuel fired power plants (see Klaassen and Nentjes 1995, Klaassen 1996 and Kete 1992). Emissions are being reduced from a level of 19 million tons in 1980 to about 9 million tons in 2000. The permits are defined as a sulphur allowance which allows a source to emit 1 ton of SO_2. They are grandfathered to the established generator companies on the basis of average fossil fuel consumption in the period 1985–7 and an emission rate. To ensure a sufficient supply of allowances for entrants to the power-generating sector and to provide a price signal, permits are auctioned each year. The permits to be auctioned are provided by taking 2.8 per cent of those grandfathered to the established power generators. In addition, firms can also offer their allowances to be auctioned. The revenue of the sale of the special reserve of 2.8 per cent is returned to the established firms from which the reserve was taken (hence it is called a zero-revenue auction). As well as the auction, firms can trade directly with each other.

Trade in this programme started in 1993. The first available overviews (Klaassen 1996) indicate that the volume of trade at auction is lower than expected while trade in the secondary market exceeds expectations. Transaction costs on the secondary market appear to be small, with brokerage fees at around 5 per cent.

The Montreal protocol on the reduction of ozone-depleting substances like chlorofluorocarbons and halons (CFC) is implemented both in the US and in the EU through a system of trade in CFC (see Klaassen 1996, Stavins and Hahn 1993, and Peeters 1992 for more details).

With the exception of the trading allowed under the Montreal protocol there has been little experience of full-blown tradable permit systems for pollution control outside the US, although there has been some experience with schemes which allow firms to offset emissions from one source by another within the firm. In the Netherlands and in Denmark bubbles are introduced for the power sector for SO_2 and nitrogen oxides (NO_x) (Klaassen and Nentjes 1995, and SEP 1991). There is some experience of comparable systems in other policy fields. In New Zealand (and in the European Union) tradable quota systems are used to limit the amount of fish which can be caught, and there exists a salmon quota system in the Atlantic in which trades have taken place. In the EU, overproduction of milk is tackled with a tradable quota system (Oskam *et al.* 1987, and Schuurman 1992).

From this short overview of TDPs the essentials of a system of tradable pollution permits can be derived. A full-blown system of TDPs consists of the following elements:

- on national, or if necessary regional, level the acceptable total release of a pollutant is determined and expressed in a homogeneous unit of measurement, for example tons of carbon dioxide;
- permits that entitle their owner to release pollutants are issued either free or in exchange for payments. The total of pollution quota distributed in this way equals the pollution ceiling mentioned in the first point;
- the pollution permits can be traded.

It should be noted that permission to pollute without payment is usually a part of existing environmental policies in developed countries. The innovative element is the possibility to transfer the entitlement to pollute.[4] In principle the tradable pollution permit is an attractive instrument: it is effective, efficient and stimulates the development of cleaner technologies. Furthermore, by giving out permits free to pollution sources the excess burden that is typical of (pollution) charges can be avoided.

Tradable permits are effective because the number of units of released pollutants they represent is limited and is determined by environmental policy targets. Consequently, the total amount of pollutants emitted cannot increase. Individual sources may increase their emissions and new sources may be established, but this has to be compensated by reductions in released pollutants elsewhere. The total level of emissions permitted can be reduced in the course of time as environmental necessity dictates.

The efficiency of tradable permits arises from the ability to trade permits. Those who can reduce emissions at low cost will do so and sell their permits to emitters who could reduce emissions only at very high costs. Consequently, the opportunity to trade permits opens up the possibility to reallocate emissions and emission reduction in such a way that the total costs of emission reduction are minimized. In a perfect market, trade would take place and reallocate pollution abatement in such a way that all sources reduced their emissions at equal marginal costs; total costs would be at a minimum and the reduction of emissions would be allocated efficiently (see Tietenberg 1988, ch. 14).

Emitters are obliged to obtain permits for every ton of a regulated pollutant that they emit. Since the permits have a price (even if they are handed out free, they have an opportunity cost), there is an incentive to search opportunities to reduce emissions and to invest in the research and development of new, cleaner technologies. In other words, tradable permits are a dynamically efficient instrument (Downing and White 1986; Nentjes and Wiersma 1988).

The last, and certainly not the least, attractive feature of tradable permits (from the viewpoint of existing emitters) is the possibility of distributing permits free to the emitters (Dijkstra and Nentjes 1994, p. 203). This form of distribution is known as grandfathering. As a basis the environmental authority can take the 'historical rights' of established polluters: existing sources receive a number of permits relating to a given percentage of their emissions in a reference year. Compared with a system of pollution charges, polluters can make considerable savings, since the individual source need pay only for any additional permits required, whereas under the charge system a price must be paid for every unit of pollution released. Taken as a group, permit-holders who receive permits free will only have to bear the abatement costs. Compare this with the cost impact of a charge. If within a given period the emissions of CO_2 are to be reduced by 10 or 20 per cent only, the expenditure on charges for the residual emissions of CO_2 would be a multiple of the abatement costs. Even if the increase in tax revenue for the government were returned to taxpayers in the form of a lower rate for other taxes, it would not be possible to perform such an operation neutrally from a distributional point of view (see, for example, Pearson 1992). Those who would benefit from tax reductions would not fully coincide with those who bear the charge. Consequently, the resistance of industry, especially of the pollution-intensive sectors, can be overcome more easily with a system of tradable permits with grandfathering than with a charge.

Tradable pollution permits are a suitable instrument for reducing several forms of pollution as long as the market for pollution permits works well. The conditions are the usual ones for developed markets, such as sufficiently large numbers of buyers and sellers in order to induce 'workable competition' (Hahn 1984), certainty of entitlements, and frequent transactions (which implies reasonably low transaction costs). Competition (anti-trust) policy would apply to permit markets just as to other markets.

Another important question with regard to the permit is whether grandfathering can create barriers to entry for new firms. This issue, which has received scant attention in the literature, is addressed extensively in Chapter 3.

A last point concerns the grandfathering of permits. Usually, the number of permits an emitter receives is based on emissions in a reference year. Therefore, the greater the emissions in the past, the more permits are received. This favours emitters who have done the least to diminish their pollution. One way to overcome this injustice is to limit the total number of permits an emitter can receive by choosing as a point of reference, not the actual emissions in a reference year, but the emissions that would have resulted if the firm had complied with a given (minimal) emission standard. This is the practice in the sulphur allowance trading system introduced in the US which we mentioned on page 8.

2.3 GRANDFATHERING, RELOCATION AND COMPETITION FROM ABROAD

Given the differences in overall costs for polluters between a tax and TDPs, the question arises whether the economic consequences differ between the two instruments. The negative economic consequences of ill-designed environmental policies can be considerable (see, for example, CPB 1992). In the now defunct European carbon/energy tax proposals, energy-intensive industries were exempted because these sectors are open to competition from outside the EU. It was feared that, if other regions did not impose comparable carbon-reduction policies, these industries would shrink, emigrate or close down if they were subjected to the tax (Minne and Herzberg 1992). If, instead of a tax, TDPs were grandfathered and overall costs reduced, would this change the competitive position of the industry *vis-à-vis* competition from abroad and would it affect firms' decisions about relocation to countries with less-demanding environmental policies? On the one hand, it can be argued that grandfathering reduces expenditures for industry and therefore might reduce the incentive to move. On the other hand, relocation has the added advantage that the grandfathered permits can be sold.

A simple static model is used to clarify the issue. There are two regions in which firms can produce. In one region, denoted D (domestic), an emission-reduction policy is implemented, either in the form of a tax or through TDPs with grandfathering. In the other region, F (foreign), there is no policy for reducing emissions. Apart from the difference in environmental policy, it is assumed that there are no differences in production costs between the two regions. Furthermore, it is assumed that relocation is costless. Consider first the situation in which emissions are reduced by way of a tax on emissions. Let π^t_D be the profits earned when a firm produces in a domestic location (the superscript t denotes tax):

$$\pi^t_D = \max \ p \cdot q - (c(q) + t \cdot E(q)) \qquad c_q, c_{qq}, E_q > 0 \qquad (2.1)$$

where:

p	= product price
$c(q)$	= production costs
$E(q)$	= emissions
t	= emission tax

Without loss of generality, it can be assumed that abatement has higher costs than acquiring permits. Producing in the other region would yield profit π^t_F:

$$\pi^t_F = \max \ p \cdot q - c(q) \qquad (2.2)$$

Domestic profit π^t_D will be smaller than the profit earned when production is located abroad because of the expenditure on emission taxes. Therefore, there is an incentive for firms to move to regions which have no emission reduction policy.[5]

Next, assume that TDPs are used to reduce emissions. Assuming that the same emission reduction target is achieved, the permit price P_P will be equal to the tax t. Let G be the number of permits grandfathered to the firm (each permit covers 1 unit of emissions E). His profit is (the superscript p stands for permits):

$$\pi^p_D = \max p \cdot q - [c(q) + P_P(E(q) - G) + P_P \cdot G] \qquad (2.3)$$

The firm does not have to buy the permits which have been grandfathered to it, therefore its expenditure is lower than with the tax (second term within the brackets). However, using the grandfathered permits in its production process means that they cannot be sold. In other words, the grandfathered permits have opportunity costs which must be taken into account in determining net profits (third term within brackets). Consequently, the net profit earned when production takes place at home under TDPs equals the profits earned under a tax regime: $\pi^p_D = \pi^t_D$. Moving to the other region and selling the permits that have been received would yield profit:

$$\pi^p_F = \max p \cdot q - c(q) + P_P \cdot G \qquad (2.4)$$

Consequently, its profits will be higher by the value of its grandfathered permits compared with emigration under a domestic tax regime (equation 2.2). If net profits are considered, a TDP scheme with grandfathering provides an additional incentive to relocate because in that case the grandfathered permits that have not to be used can be sold. This is not the case under a tax regime.

However, in addition to the differences in net profits, the differences in the change in net assets (net worth) should be considered as well. It is assumed that initially a firm has no net assets. First, consider a tax. At the end of the period, net assets have increased by the retained earnings. If production takes place abroad, net assets will equal net profit π^t_F. If the firm produces at home, assets will be π^t_D. The increase in net assets therefore equals net profit when emissions are reduced by means of a tax, both domestic and foreign.

Next, assume that emissions are reduced by means of TDPs. The retained earnings at the end of the period when production is domestic are $\pi^p_D + P_P \cdot G$. Although opportunity costs have to be taken into account when the net profit is calculated, they are not actual costs which the firm has to incur. Compared with a tax, a firm sells the same quantity of goods and earns the same gross revenue, but it does not have to bear the tax burden because it has received permits free. Producing abroad yields retained earnings of π^p_F. Compared with a tax, these are higher by $P_p \cdot G$.[6] Table 2.1 summarizes the results for the net worth of the firm.

Table 2.1 Change in net assets

	domestic	foreign	foreign - domestic
tax	π^t_D	π^t_F	$\pi^t_F - \pi^t_D$
TDPs	$\pi^p_D + P_p \cdot G = \pi^t_D + P_p \cdot G$	$\pi^p_F = \pi^t_F + P_p \cdot G$	$\pi^t_F - \pi^t_D$
TDPs − tax	$P_p \cdot G$	$P_p \cdot G$	0

Grandfathering permits is equivalent to bestowing a capital gift on firms. Net worth is therefore higher by the value of the grandfathered permits when TDPs are grandfathered compared with a tax regime (or the sale of permits). Obviously, this is more attractive for industry and therefore a TDP scheme is politically more acceptable. The difference in net assets between producing domestically or in a region which has no emission reduction policy is the same under both instruments. As regards the change in net worth of the firm, grandfathered TDPs provide no additional incentive to relocate compared with a tax (but neither is the incentive less). This contrasts with net profit; producing abroad yields a higher profit with TDPs. We could reconcile this difference as follows: the cash flow from 'normal' production is equal to that earned when a tax is in force (both domestic and foreign). In addition, under TDPs there is the gain of the capital gift of the grandfathered permits. In this view, whether permits are grandfathered or whether there is a tax makes no difference to the incentive to relocate business.

2.4 OUTLINE AND FEASIBILITY OF A SYSTEM OF TRADABLE CARBON PERMITS

In this section, a system of tradable carbon permits is described. In particular, the question is whether and how such a system would work in the context of international common markets like the European Community. Attention is given to (a) the definition of the permits; (b) the issue of permits over time;

(c) the initial distribution of permits; (d) the permit market; (e) compliance with the system; and (f) the EU dimension of TDPs.

Definition of the Permits

For the time being fuel saving and fuel substitution are the major and almost the only economically feasible options for reducing emissions of CO_2. For that reason and also for reasons of administrative efficiency and enforcement it makes sense to implement a policy of restricting CO_2 emissions by the use of tradable carbon permits. The use of carbon contained in fuel that is allowed in total can be calculated from the CO_2 emission targets of the government. On this base a limited number of tradable carbon permits is issued. A carbon permit is equivalent to 1 ton of carbon: one carbon permit allows the use of a quantity of fossil fuels which contains 1 ton of carbon. The permits are not limited in any way as regards the period or the place where they can be used. This property arises from the fact that the greenhouse effect is a consequence of the accumulation of gases like CO_2 in the atmosphere and is independent of the place where CO_2 is emitted. Since the carbon permit can be used at any unspecified date, it will retain its validity until the moment it is 'used up'; that is to say until the time the carbon is released to the atmosphere. Consequently, permits are a homogeneous good that can be easily traded, at low transaction cost, among a nationwide or even larger public of potential carbon users. The importance of these properties is illustrated by the experiences with the EPA emission trading programme: trading was restricted to the geographical area in which the permits originated and every single deal had to be approved by the authorities. Transactions costs were high and the future value of permits was uncertain. These limitations have seriously restricted the number of trades and, by the same token, also the efficiency gains (see above, p. 7).

When permits are grandfathered, firms receive a number of permits each year free (a number which will decrease when the overall emission limit is reduced). The right to receive these gratis permits during an indefinite number of future years may be termed a quota. In addition to trading permits, firms can also trade quotas. For example, a firm which stops producing can sell its right to receive a number of free permits to another firm, which consequently is assured of a supply of free permits each year.

Issue of the Permits

Fossil fuels are an essential resource to keep the economy going. Therefore a steady supply at a reasonably stable or steadily changing price is a necessary condition for economic stability. A system of tradable carbon permits comes very close to a system of fuel rationing. Such a system must have enough flexibility to allow the economy to adjust smoothly to changing circumstances. A system which rigorously limits the number of permits available in each single year can lead to large price variations, with negative consequences for the economy.

Therefore, special care should be exercised to avoid unnecessary bottlenecks caused by a temporary lack of permits. One of the ways to increase flexibility in the supply is to maintain a permanent stock of permits which can be drawn upon, for example, in an extremely harsh winter which drives up fuel consumption. Such a permanent stock can be created when the system is launched. Instead of permits being issued for only one year, they could cover expected use for four or five years. During the first years this stock of permits would be adequate to meet exceptional demand variations. The permits intended to cover the next period could be issued in advance in order to maintain a reserve stock of permits. For example, permits for the second five-year period could be issued at the start of the last year of the first five-year period. Such mechanisms would ensure that there are always permits available to meet changes in demand due to exceptional circumstances. It should be noted that such a system does not mean that the number of available permits exceeds the emission limit. The reserve is created exclusively through the timepath used for issuing the permits.

In addition, it is important that the permit system allows the authorities some flexibility in setting its future emission targets, because the problem of global warming is beset with uncertainties. Care must therefore be taken in issuing permits to avoid committing policy to a specific emission limit for a long period. However, this might conflict with the requirement for the supply of permits to be known in advance for a sufficient number of years. Given a known supply of permits, economic subjects can anticipate future demand and therefore form expectations about the development of the permit price. This is important not only for the development of a well-functioning permit market, but also for firms which have to make long-term investment decisions in which the permit price is a factor. For example, investments in the electricity-generating sector will be influenced by the current and future permit price. As these investments are made for periods of up to 20 years, it is important that there is some idea about the future price of permits. In order to reduce uncertainty for fuel users and at the same time to allow the government some flexibility with regard to future emission targets, a scheme can be used in which the government's emission targets are set for a certain period, during which they should not be changed. The emission limit for subsequent years need not be precisely specified. Instead, the government could announce an upper and lower limit for its planned distribution of permits, with a gradually increasing gap between the two for the more distant future. Within these margins, the authorities have room to set the exact number of permits made available, taking into account new insights into the enhanced greenhouse effect. The exact number of permits to be issued must be announced sufficiently in advance of the year in which they are distributed to assure a well-functioning market.

In addition to these schemes, the development of a forward market in tradable carbon permits will add further opportunities for risk-averse fuel users to shift uncertainties to those who are willing to bear them.

Distribution of the Permits

In a system of tradable carbon permits, both grandfathering and auctioning can be used side by side, according to political expediency. Since fuel-intensive industries in particular would have to incur large expenditures if they had to obtain carbon permits in auctions it can be politically expedient to hand out permits free to firms in this category. A practical dividing line for the Netherlands would be between, on the one hand, industry, horticulture and possibly freight transport as sectors which are fuel-intensive and for that reason benefit from grandfathering and, on the other hand, consumer households, services and (personal) transport as sectors which fall under the auction regime.

The objective of grandfathering permits to energy-intensive industries is to exempt them from the additional financial expenditure of buying permits for their full fuel use. For example, reducing CO_2 emissions in the Netherlands by 10 per cent from the 2015 level would require a charge which would raise 33 billion Dutch guilders (about 16 billion ECUs, 1 ECU = 2.09 Dutch guilders). The abatement costs are only 2.3 billion Dutch guilders, or 7 per cent of the revenue of the charge (Koutstaal 1992). According to calculations of the Dutch Central Planning Bureau (CPB 1992), reducing emissions in 2015 by about 10 per cent by means of a unilateral tax on fossil fuels would result in energy-intensive industry being wiped out almost completely in the Netherlands. The proposed system of grandfathering tradable permits would cost industry only a fraction compared to a charge. Firms would still bear opportunity costs for the permits grandfathered (see section 2.3) but their total expenditure would be far less.

The carbon permits needed for the emissions of CO_2 by the less energy-intensive sectors and consumer households are auctioned by the government. It would not be efficient for consumer households and small enterprises in the service sector to have to buy the permits at the auction themselves because transaction costs would be huge. The alternative is for distributors of fossil fuels, such as gas distribution and oil companies, to buy permits at auction. Subsequently, they can sell fossil fuels to customers, putting a mark-up on the fuel price which is equal to the price of the permits. This will motivate small fuel users to reduce their consumption (or to switch from fuels with a high carbon content, like coal, to fuels with a low carbon content, like natural gas).

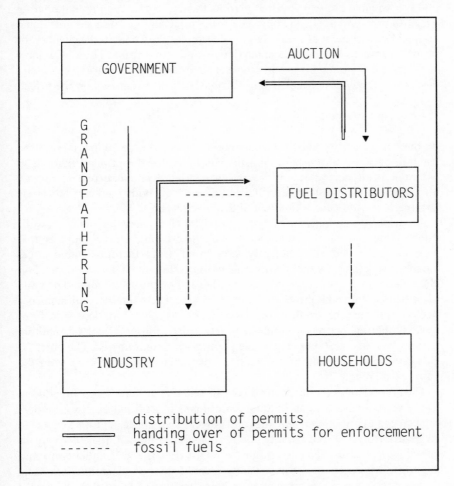

Figure 2.1 Operation of the system of tradable permits.

It should be noted that in such a system it would not be consistent to hand out permits free to the distributors because they would be able to collect the scarcity rent without incurring any costs for reducing carbon use, because only their customers can reduce CO_2 emissions.

Figure 2.1 shows schematically the way in which the system functions.

Permits are distributed by the government, both through grandfathering (to industry, horticulture and transport) and by auction (to distributors of fossil fuels). Distributors deliver fossil fuels without a mark-up on the fuel price to those who have already acquired permits themselves through grandfathering (for example, industry); the buyer pays the price and transfers permits equal to the carbon content of the fuel to the distributor. The other trade channel for distributors is to buy permits at auction or from other firms. Those who have not acquired permits in one way or another (for example, consumer households) buy fossil fuels from distributors with a mark-up on the price.

The Permit Market

In the system outlined above two markets can be discerned. First, there is the auction of some of the permits. This can be called the primary market. In addition, firms can trade permits between themselves on the secondary market. In theory, the permit price will be the same on both markets; otherwise arbitrage would occur which would equalize prices.

An important condition for a system of TDPs is the development of a well-functioning (secondary) market. A well-functioning market implies that permits are traded in sufficiently large numbers to facilitate stable price-making. Whether this will be the case in the system of TCPs will depend on the number of potential actors in the market and on the supply of and demand for permits. Table 2.2 provides data for the Dutch economy on emissions per sector, the number of firms per sector and average emissions per firm. Grandfathering permits to industry, refineries, transport and horticulture implies that about 50 per cent of the permits are grandfathered. The other 50 per cent would be sold at the auction, guaranteeing a large supply on the primary market.

The number of potential actors on the secondary market is large. In industry alone there are more than 45,000 sources and in addition energy suppliers such as gas distribution companies and power generators can also be expected to trade.[7] However, presumably not all industrial firms will trade actively on the market. Transaction costs might be relatively large for smaller firms and for those whose energy costs are only a small fraction of production costs. Instead, these firms can arrange with their suppliers of fossil fuels to supply them with the fuels they need and to acquire the permits which these firms might need in addition to those they received through grandfathering (and presumably pass on the price). The suppliers might also get a mandate to sell permits which firms do not need. In essence, suppliers would take on the role of a broker, bringing together supply of and demand for permits.

The potential for trade depends not only on the number of actors but also on the supply of and demand for permits and relates to differences in

Table 2.2 CO_2-emissions, Dutch economy, 1989.

sector	CO_2 emissions [mln. ton]	number of sources	average emissions [1000 ton/source]
Food and beverages	3.9	7258	5
Textiles	0.3	1515	2
Paper	1.5	362	41
Fertilizer	6.6	12	5500
Other chemicals	3.8	838	44
Building materials	2.2	684	32
Base metal	8.8	119	740
Other metal	1.8	14563	1
Other industries	0.5	21358	< 1
Refineries	12.1	7	17285
Power companies	36.8	88	4182
Transport	26.4		
Households	19.3		
Horticulture	6.4		
Others	11.3		
Total	141.7		

Source: Koutstaal 1992, p.74.

abatement costs. The larger the differences, the larger is the potential for trade because the gain from trade increases when cost differences increase. Studies indicate that the costs of reducing CO_2 emissions differ considerably between various sectors (see Velthuijsen 1995; Blok *et al.* 1990). Consequently, there are sufficient incentives for trade.

A last point concerning the permit market is the form which the secondary market will take. Ideally, permits are traded on an exchange similar to stock markets or exchanges for raw materials or agriculture products. However, this will only be possible if the volume of trade is large enough. Given the potential for trade and the number of actors, such an exchange might develop in time in the TCP system. Until then, trade can take place through brokers, a role which might be filled by suppliers of fossil fuels. In the CAAA sulphur-trading scheme, brokers facilitate trade on the secondary market (Klaassen and Nentjes 1995). In the EU tradable milk quota programme, a number of firms of solicitors which were already active in agriculture have specialized in milk quota brokerage (personal interview, Scottish Agricultural College dairy test farm 1993).

Monitoring, Enforcement and Administrative Costs

As has been shown, distributors acquire permits for the fossil fuels they sell to consumer households and other small CO_2 emitters. The permits industry receives through grandfathering can be handed over to the distributors in exchange for the carbon contained in the fossil fuels they buy from the distributors (see Figure 2.1). In this way, all permits will end up in the hands of the distributors, who to a large extent are the same as the producers and importers of fossil fuels. Those distributors who do not produce or import fossil fuels themselves can in turn hand the permits over to their suppliers. In the end, all permits will land up with the producers and importers. This property of the system can be used to set up an efficient system of monitoring and enforcement. Producers and importers of fuel are placed under the obligation once a year to turn over to the environmental authorities carbon permits for the carbon contained in the fossil fuels they have sold on the market (see Figure 2.1). They have either received the permits from their clients or bought them at auction.

The advantage of supervising compliance with the tradable permit system in this way is that it fits in with existing institutions for levying excise duties on fossil fuels, which exist in most western countries. In the Netherlands, traders and suppliers of mineral oils must have a licence. They are obliged to report each month how much they have supplied to the market and turn over the excise tax to the authorities. This administrative system of self-reporting is supplemented by occasional physical checks. The system operates satisfactorily (Dutch Parliament 1991, nr. 21368, p. 21). Instead of handing over the excise, suppliers and producers of fossil fuels hand over permits, as described above. In addition, suppliers of other fossil fuels, such as natural gas and coal, should be brought into the system.

In addition to the administrative monitoring system, other sources of information could be used for double checking. Victor (1991) mentions four other sources of information:

* *direct monitoring of emissions* This might be an option for some large stationary sources. However, it is not practical for smaller and mobile sources.

- *data from other reports by either the source itself or from third parties*
  For example, data reported to the fiscal authorities from buyers of fossil
  fuels.
- *data from environmental annual reports* Reports of this kind, which are
  sometimes verified by accountants, are published by an increasing
  number of companies.
- *data generated by modelling exercises* Starting from known input data,
  estimates can be made of emissions. These data are probably not very
  accurate, but they might serve to detect large-scale frauds.

One way of direct monitoring is by the use of tamper-proof metering
devices fixed to machinery and pipelines (Cnossen and Vollebergh 1992).
Using the excise system will guarantee a high level of compliance and will
make a system of TCPs just as feasible as a carbon charge as far as
compliance is concerned. Only the limited number of firms producing or
importing fossil fuels has to be checked. In the Netherlands, for example,
there are between 40 and 50 such firms.

Not only must there be an effective system of monitoring, enforcement must
also be assured. For effective compliance two elements are of importance.
First, sanctions should be such that the expected costs of fraud exceed the
costs of sticking to the rules.[8] Second, the environment should not suffer
from fraud. Consequently, in addition to a fine, firms which have failed to
supply permits for the fossil fuels they have used should be forced to acquire
permits to cover these emissions (this is the approach taken in the tradable
sulphur allowance scheme; see Kete 1992).

The administrative costs of the system of TCPs will consist of several
elements. The two main cost factors are the costs of monitoring and
enforcement and the costs of registration of the ownership of permits.
Furthermore, data will have to be collected for determining the quota which
firms receive when permits are grandfathered. This will also entail costs
which, however, only have to be incurred once. Last, a yearly auction will
have to be set up. The first cost factor, monitoring and enforcement, will be
comparable with those of implementing a charge on carbon in fossil fuels.
They will not differ very much from the costs of the current system for
levying excise duties on fossil fuels. In Allers (1994, pp. 71–75) the
administrative costs of existing environmental taxes in the Netherlands are
given. The environmental taxes which are levied under the WABM law *(Wet
algemene bepalingen milieuhygiëne)* consists mainly of a tax on fossil fuels.
In 1990, the administrative costs ran to 40.5 million guilders, about 20 million
ECU. Compliance costs of this environmental tax are difficult to ascertain due
to the fact that only data on compliance costs for all environmental taxes in
the Netherlands are available (Allers 1994, p. 179).

Registration of the ownership and trade in permits is characteristic of TDPs; no comparable arrangement is necessary when a charge is levied or standards are applied. The most efficient way to register ownership is probably to use a giro system comparable to those used to register ownership of and trade in shares and certificates traded on stock exchanges. In the Netherlands, NECIGEF (the Dutch central institution for trade in shares by giro) registers the ownership of shares. Yearly operating costs of the institute were 9.5 million guilders in 1990 (4.6 million ECU) (NECIGEF 1990, p. 29). The daily average number of trades registered in that year was 4,532. It is not to be expected that trade in CO_2 permits will exceed this number, therefore the costs of this institution serve as an example of the costs of registering the carbon permits.

A rough estimate of the yearly operating costs of the system of TCPs described here is about 50 to 70 million guilders if implemented in the Netherlands: around 29 million ECU. In addition costs must be incurred to grandfather permits (which, however, will only happen at the start of the system) and an auction must be set up.

In the next sub-section, compliance at the European level in a EU-wide system of TCPs will be addressed.

EU Dimension of Tradable Carbon Permits

An important question is whether a system of TCPs would have to be confined by national boundaries. The Member States (MS) of the EU have delegated part of their power to the European Union. Consequently, the freedom for independent policy is restricted by primary legislation (the Treaty of the EU) and secondary legislation (e.g. directives and regulations).[9] A national system of tradable carbon permits restricts the use of carbon contained in fossil fuels. Consequently, TCPs imply a restriction on the quantity of fuel that can be produced at home and imported from abroad. It might therefore be seen (by the European Commission) as a restriction of the free movement of goods between MS and consequently as a violation of article 30 EG. Art. 30 EG states that trade in goods between MS may not be restricted. In a system of TCPs the import of fossil fuels is restricted by the total amount of carbon permits available and therefore it might be contrary to the article.

However, there are exemptions on article 30 EG (Pisuisse and Teubner 1994, p. 97). Restrictions of imports are allowed under article 36 EG and under the 'rule of reason'. The rule of reason applies if the following conditions are met:

1.   There must be no Community measure regarding the policy area in

which the MS wants to implement the policy measure which could restrict free movement of goods.

2. The proposed policy measure must apply to domestic and imported products alike.

3. The proposed policy measure must justify certain interests which are accepted by the Court of Justice. Examples of these interests are environmental protection and consumer protection.

4. The policy measure must be reasonable and is subject to the proportionality test. This means that trade between MS must not be restricted any more than is necessary to achieve the policy purpose. Moreover, there must not be another policy measure which would be as effective (and efficient) but which would not restrict trade to the same extent.

Concerning the first condition, there is currently no substantial greenhouse policy in the European Union. There has been considerable discussion in the last five years on the use of a EU tax to limit carbon dioxide emissions. However, on 15 December 1994, the Council agreed that no Community tax measures will be taken (Europe Documents no. 1918, 6 January 1995).[10] Instead, it was agreed that those MS which wish to do so may introduce a CO_2/energy tax themselves. Such unilateral carbon taxes should follow a Community framework which would be developed in further discussions by ECOFIN (the Council of Finance Ministers). They have asked the Commission to develop a proposal for such a framework, which will probably consist of minimum levels of excise duties on a number of fuels. It is not clear by what time the framework will be developed and implemented. However, it will probably leave room for MS to use other additional policy measures to limit CO_2 emissions like TCPs. In the mean time, it seems plausible to assume that as long as there is no Community policy nor a proposal for a regulation, MS can take their own policy measures.

The tradable permit scheme described above does not discriminate between fossil fuels sold by national firms and firms from another MS. For all fossil fuels brought on to the market, regardless of their country of origin, carbon permits have to be acquired. The second condition is therefore fulfilled.

Environmental protection has been recognized as an interest which justifies a restriction of free movement of goods, therefore a system of TCPs meets the third condition.

A system of tradable emission permits is both an efficient and effective instrument to control CO_2 emissions. Other instrument types are either not as effective (for example, a carbon tax) or not as efficient (for example, emission standards). The last condition appears to be met as well.

Another question regarding the possibility of implementing a system of

TCPs in one country in the EU is the issue of enforcement. As long as differences in excise taxes are allowed, the administrative system which is used to enforce the system remains in place.

Enforcement might also become more difficult when national frontiers within the EU are abolished. A start has been made in the Schengen agreement, which abolishes border controls between seven countries of the EU. Without such border controls, fraud is more difficult to discover. End-users could import fossil fuels directly from suppliers in other MS without procuring carbon permits and without running the risk of discovery at border controls. However, this problem should not be overstated. Large-scale evasion of the obligation to acquire permits will remain difficult because of the properties of fossil fuels: movement of fossil fuels is by bulk transport which, moreover, needs large installations for unloading. The obligation to acquire permits will be hard to evade for large quantities of fossil fuels because it will be difficult to escape detection.

It can be concluded that it is probably possible to implement the national system of TCPs sketched in this chapter in one MS of the EU. A system of TCPs might conflict with free movement in goods within the EU but it will probably fall under the rule of reason which allows exemptions to article 30 EG. One possible problem is that there will be no room for other instruments once it is decided that MS can introduce a carbon/energy tax unilaterally. However, it is not yet clear if and when such a decision will be taken and how it will be formulated. Enforcement might become more difficult when border controls are abolished. However, fraud on a large scale will still be difficult.

Although TCPs might be realized within one country, it would be preferable to introduce a system across the whole of the EU; it would be more effective to limit emissions in all MS of the EU instead of only one. Moreover, the problem of firms in MS which have implemented TCPs being at a disadvantage *vis-à-vis* firms from MS without CO_2 reduction policies is avoided.

As a first step in the introduction of the system the Council of the EU will have to decide on: a time path for total carbon use within the EU; the sectors that are selected for grandfathering; and the basis on which permits are grandfathered. Another question to be decided at EU level is whether and how the available permits should be distributed among the different MS. Permits can be grandfathered and sold at EU level or they can be allotted to the MS which in turn distribute them. With regard to this last option, it should be realised that MS would not be allowed to use their permits to support specific sectors or firms by grandfathering permits in excess of those allowed by the rules for grandfathering. Such behaviour would be contrary to articles 92 – 94 EG. These articles prohibit governments from supporting sectors if this would reduce competition and obstruct trade between MS. Furthermore, a member state would not be allowed to sell the permits exclusively to firms registered within its own borders, thereby favouring its own industry, as this would be discrimination. Hence, the only rationale for allotting quotas to MS would be as a method of distributing the revenue generated by the auction of (part of) the permits among MS. The other option is to decide on an allocation rule for the revenue and to auction the permits centrally.

When the system is introduced, a distinction must be made between the activities which should be undertaken at the central EU level and those which can be delegated to the MS. For the execution of the various tasks, a Brussels bureau should be set up (or alternatively the European Environmental Agency in Copenhagen could perform the task) as well as a network of national bureaux. The tasks of the national bureaux include:

- registration of the ownership of the permits;
- grandfathering of permits to designated sectors;
- monitoring and enforcement.

One of the tasks of the national bureaux is to set up and operate a giro system for registration of the permits (see p. 22). Furthermore, they should implement the rules on the grandfathering of permits to industry. For this purpose, the national bureaux must draw up a list of all firms eligible for grandfathering and issue to them each year their allotted quota.

An important task of the bureaux is to enforce the tradable carbon scheme. They should collect the permits handed in by importers and producers of fossil fuels (see p. 20) registered in their MS. In addition, the national bureaux should make periodical inspections to check whether firms accurately report the amount of fossil fuels they have brought on to the market. The task of the Brussels bureau would be threefold:

- to supervise (the performance of) the national bureaux;
- to act as a clearing house for transactions between permit owners registered at the various national bureaux;
- to evaluate the programme.

The Brussels bureau should supervise the national bureaux on a number of points, the most important of which is enforcement. The Brussels bureau should check with great care whether all the national bureaux enforce the carbon permit scheme equally accurately and collect all the permits due. If some MS do not enforce the system an EU-wide system of tradable carbon permits would suffer from lacunae which would detract from its effectiveness (and efficiency). This would also be true of any other instrument (charges or regulation) that had to be applied under such awkward conditions, but there is one difference: under TCPs, firms which operate in a MS without adequate enforcement can emit carbon dioxide without handing over permits. Consequently, they can sell their permits to firms in other MS and, as a result, pollution would increase in these other MS. When taxes or regulation are used, firms which defraud cannot sell permits to sources in other countries. With these instruments pollution only increases above the allowed level in the country in which enforcement is inadequate. In a European system of TCPs insufficient monitoring and enforcement in one or more MS will lead to higher overall pollution levels compared with instruments like charges or regulation.

As has been described above, MS are not allowed to favour specific firms or sectors by allocating them more permits than is allowed under the grandfather rules. The implementation of these rules should therefore be monitored at the European level. This task could be delegated to Directorate General IV of the European Commission, which deals with competition. Another field for supervision is competition between firms: firms would not be allowed to use carbon permits to limit competition (see Chapters 3 and 4 for an evaluation of the use of permits to limit entry). This task can also be undertaken by DG IV.

The evaluation of the programme can be made in the form of an annual report. Subjects to be dealt with are, among others: the number of permits issued and permits used; the volume of trade; and the occurrence of fraud.

2.5 CONCLUSIONS

Tradable permits are an instrument of pollution control that can be used to tackle a large class of pollution problems. It is particularly suitable if the problem is created by emissions from a large number of sources and the pollutant is spread more or less evenly throughout the environment. This is the case with emissions of CO_2; the greenhouse effect occurs worldwide and the pollution sources range from large stationary sources like power plants to small mobile ones like cars. With such a large number of different sources, it will be impossible to reduce emissions in a cost-effective way by means of direct regulation. The instrument of tradable permits has the important advantage that emission reduction will be cost-effective.

TDPs have other attractive features. The instrument is effective in the sense that emission targets are realized: the total amount of polluting emissions is limited by the number of permits issued. With regulation and taxes, the level of emissions can increase, although it has not been planned: for example, as a consequence of economic growth or sectoral shifts. Furthermore, permits can be grandfathered to polluters. This will considerably reduce their costs compared with the auction of permits or with emission charges; they will only have to bear the abatement cost. Especially in the energy-intensive sectors of industry, expenditure on permits would be several times larger than abatement costs. Therefore, tradable carbon permits would be politically more acceptable than a tax.

Even though grandfathering reduces the overall cost burden for industries, this does not necessarily mean that the incentives for industries to relocate to regions with less exacting environmental policies is less than with a tax. Because of the opportunity costs of the grandfathered permits, net profit will equal the net profits firms make under a tax. However, from the point of view of the net worth of firms, they are better off under TDPs. Presumably, the incentive for firms to move will be the same under either instrument.

In this chapter we have studied in detail how a system of tradable carbon permits should be designed. Elements on which the analysis has focused are: the definition and the issue of permits; the distribution of permits; the permit market; monitoring and enforcement; and the specific characteristics of an EU-wide system of TCPs. As regards distribution of the permits, it seems most practical to grandfather permits to industrial sources and to sell the permits which cover the other emissions. As it is not practical to compel consumers to buy (and trade in) permits themselves, a government agency can sell these permits to their suppliers of fossil fuels, who can subsequently mark up their prices by the price of the permits.

Compliance in a national system of TCPs does not pose greater problems than compliance with a carbon tax. Under both instruments producers and importers of fossil fuels can be obliged to hand over either the tax payments or the permits for the carbon contained in the fossil fuels which they bring on to the market. The existing mechanism for levying excise duties on fossil fuels can be used to levy the carbon tax or carbon permits. In addition, other information sources can be used to supplement monitoring, such as periodical checks and data on other taxes. The administrative costs do not have to be excessive as long as a giro system is used for the registration of trades and the ownership of permits.

So far there is no concerted EU policy on carbon dioxide reduction. There has been much discussion about introducing a European carbon/energy tax but in the end it was decided to leave it to individual countries whether to introduce a tax or not. In the absence of a European policy, it seems possible for one MS to introduce a national system of TCPs. Although a national system might be seen as a restriction on the free movement of goods within the EU, it will probably fall under the 'rule of reason' which allows exemptions to article 30 EG which deals with the free movement of goods. The disappearance of border controls within the EU might make enforcement more difficult, but this does not seem to be a large problem, due to the bulk character of fossil fuels.

Although a system of TCPs can probably be introduced in one MS, it would be preferable to implement it at the European level. The instrument would be much more effective and there would be no consequences for the competitiveness of firms in different MS. Within a European system of TCPs all MS would have to use the same grandfathering rules. They would not be allowed to use the permits to support specific sectors or firms. Special care must be given to enforcement within an EU-wide system. TCPs would not be effective (or efficient) if firms could evade the system in one or more MS. Although a system of TCPs might be just as sensitive to fraud as other instruments such as standards and taxes, the consequences for the overall pollution level are greater under TCPs because firms which can evade the obligation to hand over permits can sell them to firms in other countries. As a result, pollution would increase not only in the MS where enforcement is not adequate but also in the other MS.

NOTES

1.   This chapter is based on Koutstaal (1992) and Koutstaal and Nentjes (1995). See also Koutstaal *et al.* (1994).
2.   Instead of introducing an EU-wide tax, it has been decided that 'Those Member States which want to do so may introduce, on a unilateral basis, a CO_2/energy tax' (*Europe Environment*, no. 445, 20 December, 1994, p. 2).
3.   A short overview is given of systems of tradable pollution permits which have been implemented up to the present. For a comprehensive overview of past experience, with full references, see for example, Tietenberg 1985, Peeters 1992, OECD 1992a and Klaassen 1996.
4.   A second important difference is that no additional permits are made available for new sources, as is the practice under direct regulation.
5.   In reality, there are many more factors, apart from differences in environmental policy, which influence business location decisions. Environmental costs are generally only a small part of total production costs, differences in environmental policy do not seem to be that important (see, for example, Komen and Folmer 1995). As our interest is in the effects of different forms of environmental policy, the focus is exclusively on the consequences of environmental policy for location decisions.
6.   If the permits are not sold, net assets would also increase with the profit π^p_F. The difference is that in the first instance the cash flow includes the revenue from selling the permits, in the second case net assets increase with the value of the grandfathered permits which have been neither used nor sold.
7.   In a European-wide system of tradable carbon permits the number of (potential) actors on the market would be much larger.
8.   The expected costs of fraud equal the chance that fraud is discovered times the level of the sanctions.

9. For an overview of European Law, see Pisuisse and Teubner 1994 and Teubner 1993. The discussion of TCPs in European law is based on personal communications with A.M.M. Teubner (1995).
10. At the Essen summit the heads of state already decided that there would not be a Community carbon tax.

3. Entry Barriers and Tradable Permits: Overview and Transaction Costs

3.1 INTRODUCTION

Permit markets might fail to coordinate pollution control decisions efficiently if opportunities existed for abuse of market power in the permit market, or if a tradable permit system created barriers to entry on the product market. The first possibility was researched by Hahn (1984). He studied the strategic behaviour of a firm which has market power in the permit market (it is a price-maker rather than a price-taker) and uses this power to minimize its abatement costs and expenditure on permits. The main conclusion of this study is that, in the case of market power, abatement costs for the industry as a whole can be higher than is necessary. The extent of the inefficiency is related to the number of permits allocated initially to the dominant firm. The more the number of allocated permits deviates from the number the firm will use in equilibrium, the less efficient is abatement. This holds both when the firm does not receive enough permits, in which case he will act as a monopsonist on the permit market, and when it receives more permits than it will use, in which case it behaves as a monopolist. In an empirical example which simulates trade in sulphates in the Los Angeles area (where an electric utility was a large emitter and therefore would have had market power on the permit market), Hahn studied the extent of the possible abatement cost inefficiency. The result was that total abatement costs would only rise significantly above the minimum level when the initial allocation to the dominant firm was sufficiently large. Otherwise, abatement cost efficiency would be affected only to a minor extent.

There are other studies of the effect of market power on abatement cost efficiency. Hanley and Moffat (1993) analyse a potential tradable emission permit scheme for controlling biological oxygen demand discharges in the Forth estuary (near Edinburgh, Scotland). The data suggest that market power might be a problem in this scheme (which at the time of writing – Spring 1995 – is being considered for implementation).

Pototschnig (1995) has studied the possibility of using tradable permits for controlling acid rain in England and Wales. The permit market would be

30

dominated by two firms (both electricity generators), which would account for about 85 per cent of the demand for permits. Consequently, these sources would have market power and therefore might influence the permit price.

Overlooking the theoretical and empirical evidence, the problem of misuse of market power which might lead to higher abatement costs does not seem to be a large problem in the system of tradable carbon permits described in Chapter 2. It is essential that a firm does exert influence over the permit price. Given the size of the carbon market, it is not likely that one firm can exert much influence on the carbon permit price (see section 3.6).

The second possible source of market failure, entry barriers, is a relatively neglected problem in the literature on tradable permits. Tietenberg (1985, p. 140) mentions the possibility of entry barriers, stating that: 'In general, the new source bias inherent in forcing new, but not existing, sources to purchase offsets to cover any emissions is probably a more serious barrier to entry than the existence of market power.' At first sight it makes sense intuitively that tradable emission permits might lead to entry barriers. When permits are grandfathered free to existing firms, this might disadvantage new entrants to the product market: they have to buy the permits and therefore their costs seem higher. Another possibility is that firms might try to exclude entrants from the market by limiting their access to the permits, as has been described by Misiolek and Elder (1989; see also Chapter 4).

In this chapter and the next we shall concentrate on this second form of market failure: entry barriers. The question is addressed whether, how and under what circumstances a system of tradable permits might create barriers to entry in the product market or might strengthen existing barriers. Both grandfathering and the sale of permits to incumbent firms are addressed. In this chapter an overview is given of the theory of entry barriers (sections 3.2 and 3.3) and the connection between transaction costs and entry barriers is studied in detail (sections 3.4 and 3.5). In the next chapter two other barriers are examined: capital costs and exclusionary manipulation.

We focus on the specific consequences of the instrument of tradable emission permits for entry barriers as compared with other instruments such as taxes and command-and-control regulation. Therefore, we ignore the possibility that entry barriers are created or raised due to the fact that firms have to bear abatement costs when an emission reduction policy is introduced; these would also occur with other policy instruments.

3.2 THE THEORY OF ENTRY BARRIERS

In discussing entry barriers, the natural point to start with is Bain's *Barriers to New Competition* (1965). In this treatise, Bain was the first to look systematically at potential competition as opposed to competition from existing rivals; or, in other words, he studied the entry of new firms into industries and the conditions that discourage entry. Bain (1965, p. 3) viewed barriers to entry as being determined 'by the advantages of established sellers in an industry over potential entrant sellers, these advantages being reflected in the extent to which established sellers can persistently raise their prices above a competitive level without attracting new firms to enter the industry'. Subsequently, other authors have come up with their own definitions. Like Bain's definition, most of them focused on the asymmetry in the costs of production between incumbent firms and entrants (see Stigler and Baumol & Willig; both quoted in; Gilbert 1989, pp. 476–8). In contrast, von Weizsäcker (1980, p. 400) also includes the welfare effect in his definition: 'a barrier to entry is a cost of producing which must be borne by a firm which seeks to enter an industry but is not borne by firms already in the industry and which implies a distortion in the allocation of resources from the social point of view'. A barrier to entry is defined here as *a cost which only firms entering an industry have to bear, making it possible for the existing firm(s) to enjoy a rent derived from incumbency* (see Gilbert 1989, pp. 476–8). A cost advantage in itself is not necessarily a barrier to entry; it must also confer an advantage on existing firms, such as the possibility to reap higher than competitive profits as in Bain's definition. If such an entry barrier occurs, welfare will be adversely affected. The incumbent will charge a price higher than his minimal average costs. Resource allocation will be inefficient and welfare reduced. Therefore, the entry barriers identified in the remainder of this study will imply that long-term industry efficiency is impaired and that therefore welfare is reduced.

What types of entry barriers exist and which types might apply to tradable permits? The basic identification and classification of categories of entry barriers was made by Bain (1965, pp. 14–16). He distinguished three categories; each of which will be briefly discussed:

1. absolute cost advantages;
2. product differentiation;
3. large-scale economies.

Absolute Cost Advantages

Absolute cost advantages appear in several different guises. Existing firms may possess cheaper production processes than the potential entrants. Consequently, they can outprice them and therefore keep them off the market. There are several possible reasons for this cost advantage such as learning by doing and research and development. The fruits of R&D might be protected by patents which deny use of the superior process to entrants.

Another form of absolute cost advantage exists when established firms can buy input factors at lower prices then entrants can. This is also applicable to capital markets. When capital markets do not work perfectly, it might be more difficult, or in other words more costly, for new firms to acquire the necessary capital than for existing firms. Consequently, entrants have higher production costs than existing firms. This form of entry barrier has been referred to as the 'deep pocket' or 'long purse' theory and is associated with predatory pricing. Predatory pricing can be used by incumbents who possess larger (financial) resources than entrants to drive these new firms off the market whenever they try to enter. Predatory pricing will not be possible when capital markets work perfectly, because entrants can borrow indefinitely on the capital market. But if capital markets work imperfectly new firms have to incur higher costs when they borrow money (see Tirole 1992, p. 377; and section 3.5 of this chapter). Consequently, there will be a cost advantage for established firms which have larger resources and therefore do not have to bear the costs of borrowing.

An extreme form of imperfect input markets occurs when existing firms control the supply of a strategic production factor and therefore have the ability to deny entrants access to this input. By excluding them from the use of this input factor, they force them to use inferior and more expensive alternatives, driving up their costs.

In all the cases discussed above, the entrant faces higher costs than the incumbent. Consequently, the incumbent will be able to charge a price which is higher than his average costs and make a profit, without having to be afraid of entry as long as the price he charges is lower than the average costs of the entrant. He thus reaps a benefit from the fact that entry is difficult, or, as the definition states, he enjoys a rent derived from his incumbency.

Product Differentiation

The second type of entry barrier that Bain identified was product differentiation. By differentiating, firms can to a certain extent set their product apart from other products in their market. These products are not viewed as perfect substitutes by the customers, and therefore it is difficult for a new firm to induce them to switch. This makes entry more difficult. There are several ways in which a firm can differentiate its products, for example, design differences as compared with products of other firms, customer service, dealer systems and advertising. Especially in the consumer good industries, advertising is an important form of product differentiation (Bain 1965, p. 123, Table X). Advertising can induce brand loyalty and make it seem less attractive for customers to switch to other brands. This raises the entry barrier for potential entrants because it is more difficult for them to acquire a viable market share.

Economies of Scale

When there is systematic economy of scale in producing and selling such that firms of the efficient size provide a significant portion of demand, entrants are at a disadvantage. In order to produce at minimum costs, an entrant has to produce on a considerable scale. Selling this amount means that the market price of the product drops and as a result the entrant is not able to cover his costs. Consequently, the incumbents are able to set a price which is higher than their average costs without having to fear entry. There is a limit price, higher than the competitive price, which still deters entry, while at any higher price entry will occur.

Since Bain's seminal work on entry barriers, the issue has been explored in more detail. A form of entry barrier which has received much attention (and which will be relevant to the discussion of tradable emission permits and entry barriers, see section 3.4) is the limit pricing model, a form of economies-of-scale entry barrier. In the basic form of the limit pricing model (the Bain–Sylos–Labini–Modigliani model, see Gilbert 1989, pp. 480–93), the established firm chooses the quantity which he wants to produce before the entrant enters the market. Given the quantity produced by the incumbent, the entrant decides whether or not it will be profitable to enter. At a certain level of output by the incumbent, the limit output, the profits of the entrant firm will be zero and therefore it will not enter. The associated price is the limit price. In this model, the incumbent acts as a Stackelberg leader while the entrant acts as a Cournot follower. The limit pricing model has been further developed by Spence (1977) and Dixit (1980). These developments are described in section 3.4.

The next step is to go further into the different types of entry barrier and to look in more detail at the developments of the theory and their relevance to tradable permits. The short survey presented above gives us the opportunity to indicate which of the three main types of entry barrier might be relevant. As regards the second type of entry barrier, product differentiation, there is no obvious relation with the way tradable permits might raise entry barriers. Product differentiation hinders entry because the product of an entrant will not be a perfect substitute for the product of the incumbent. Tradable permits, however, do not create a difference between the product of the incumbent and the product of an entrant although they might create a difference in the conditions under which both products are made. Both products will remain the same in consumers' eyes, regardless of how the necessary pollution permits are acquired.

The absolute cost and economies of scale (the limit-pricing model) types of entry barrier do appear to be relevant in the case of tradable emission permits. In the next sections, these cases will be discussed extensively.

3.3 ENTRY BARRIERS AND TRADABLE EMISSION PERMITS: OPPORTUNITY COSTS

At first sight, it might appear obvious that grandfathering permits to existing firms and selling them to newcomers raises entry barriers, because entrants seem to have an extra cost (buying the permits) which incumbents do not have. However, this naive conception of cost is mistaken. The permits owned by established firms are for them an opportunity cost which is as much a part of the cost of a firm as permits that have to be bought from others. Therefore the entrants' cost for input pollution is equal to the incumbents' cost. If there are no other cost differences, the cost functions are equal. The lowest price both can charge without making a loss is therefore also the same. At every price above this minimum price, the entrant can enter and make a profit. Therefore, grandfathering does not in itself raise entry barriers.

Land property provides an illustrative comparison. New firms have to buy land on which to establish themselves, while existing firms possess land. Even if established firms have completely written off their land, they still take into account its opportunity costs. These opportunity costs are equal to the price at which they can sell it. The fact that new firms have to buy land therefore does not create an entry barrier.

An example of the opportunity costs of permits are taxi medallions or permits which are needed in order to operate a cab in certain municipalities. When these medaillons are traded on a market, the opportunity costs to established firms of using their licences are equal to the price of the licenses on the market (Demsetz 1982). Another example is the milk quotas introduced in the European Community. Dairy farmers get a guaranteed price for their milk only as long as they do not produce more than their quota.[1] Quotas were grandfathered to established farmers when the scheme was introduced; new dairy farmers who started later had to buy them from the established farmers. The milk quotas have opportunity costs for the farmers. When they stop producing they can sell them. In fact, there has been a fair amount of trade in quotas and, additionally, quotas have been leased. In the latter case, a quota is let for one year to another farm. The price at which quotas are sold is roughly ten times their one-year lease price (Schuurman 1992).

For tradable pollution permits, the case is the same. Even though established firms receive their permits free while new firms have to buy their permits, they must take into account the opportunity costs of the permits. Therefore grandfathering permits does not necessarily raise entry barriers.[2]

Taking opportunity costs into account does not mean that using the instrument of TDPs will never raise entry barriers. The opportunity costs of assets are determined by their value in their next-best use. Generally, this value is given by the price at which the assets are traded on the market. A prerequisite is that there is a well-functioning market for the assets which conveys the value of the assets in their next-best use to their current owners. With systems of tradable pollution permits, this condition is not necessarily fulfilled. Most of the systems of tradable pollution permits implemented up till now have suffered from the defect of a thin and poorly functioning market (see Atkinson and Tietenberg 1991). In section 3.4 the consequences of imperfect permit markets for the occurrence of entry barriers will be examined. Furthermore, even though markets for pollution permits function well and firms do take the opportunity costs of their grandfathered permits into account, there is still a difference between incumbents and entrants: incumbents do not have to raise the money necessary to buy permits as entrants have to. When capital markets are not perfect this could lead to entry barriers, as is argued by predatory pricing and the 'deep purse' theory. The relevance of predatory pricing and imperfection of capital markets in the context of TDPs is explored in the next chapter. Also in the next chapter we consider the possibility of manipulating the permit market in order to raise rivals' costs, a subject discussed by Misiolek and Elder (1989).

3.4 TRANSACTION COSTS AND THE LIMIT-PRICING MODEL

Introduction

The first use of tradable pollution permits as an instrument to curb harmful emissions, the emission trading programme of the US Environmental Protection Agency, did not live up to expectations with respect to the cost savings predicted. The main explanation for this shortfall is generally considered to be the weak market performance of the market for pollution rights. About 80 per cent of the 'trades' have been within firms instead of between different firms. Several reasons can be adduced for the poor performance of these permit markets. New firms which enter an area do not only have to acquire the necessary permits, they also have to conform to stricter limits on their emissions thereby restricting the possibility of trade. Another cause of limited trade was the behaviour of some local authorities. In order to reduce emissions they confiscated some of the permits which firms had banked for future use or for selling. Such behaviour does not provide an incentive to firms to reduce their emissions in order to be able to sell permits (Dwyer 1991). The transaction costs associated with trading could be high. In the South Coast Air Management District, the costs of finding a seller, inclusive of the necessary engineering studies and of securing approval for the trade from the authorities, have been estimated at between $15 000 – 30 000 per trade. For average trades amounting to about $200 000 – 300 000, this amounts to 10–30% of the total costs (Dwyer 1992, p. 17). In the Bay Area District, transaction costs seem to have been less important. One reason is that brokers emerged who significantly lowered the costs of finding sellers and securing approval by the authorities. However, even with brokers firms still have to bear transaction costs, albeit lower than they would be without brokers. Hahn and Hester (1989) report that the costs of hiring a consultant to help identify possible sellers can be as high as several thousand dollars.

However, in more recent examples of tradable emission permit schemes transaction costs appear to be lower. In the late 1970s and early 1980s, a lead trading programme was established in the US for phasing out the lead content in petrol. At the close of the scheme, refineries were no longer allowed to use lead. In this programme, there has been a large number of trades (about 20 per cent of the total amount of lead permits have been traded between refineries) (Nussbaum 1991). The good performance of the permit market in this example can be explained by its large size, the lack of regulatory constraints on trading and the low transaction costs: the refineries did not have to incur large search costs to find trading partners because the potential sellers or buyers were well known to each firm and because they already dealt with each other in other markets.

The last example of tradable emission permit schemes is the CAAA sulphur trading programme for electricity generating companies. This scheme officially started in 1995 but trading started before then. The first experiences with this programme indicate that transaction costs are small. Brokerage fees are around 5 per cent (Klaassen and Nentjes 1995), considerably lower than those in the EPA tradable permit scheme described above.

Given the occurrence of transaction costs on permit markets, we shall analyse how transaction costs might influence entry. Following Stavins (1994), transaction costs are defined as the margin between the buying and selling prices of a commodity in a given market. Transaction costs consist of the search cost of finding a party with which to conclude the deal and the costs of reaching and implementing of an agreement. Regardless of who pays the direct transaction costs (the buyer or the seller of the permits), the effect will be that the price received by the seller of the permits falls while the price paid by the buyer increases.[3] In the remainder of this chapter, transaction costs are presented as an additional cost which increases the price buyers have to pay, thereby creating a positive margin between the buyer's and the seller's permit price.

How will transaction costs affect the costs of incumbents and entrants? When permits are auctioned by the authorities to both incumbents and entrants, their costs increase with the price which they pay for the permits (plus transaction costs[4]). In that case, costs for both incumbents and entrants are the same.

When permits are grandfathered to established firms, two cases can be discerned. First, the incumbent firms do not buy more permits than they have received free.[5] In that case, their cost function includes the opportunity costs of the permits. These opportunity costs are equal to the permit price minus at part of the transaction costs which the incumbent would have to bear if he sold permits. The entrant would have to pay both the permit price and the buyer's part of the transaction costs. The difference between their costs is therefore equal to the total transaction costs. The second possibility is that the established firm buys more permits than have been grandfathered to it (because this is less expensive than reducing emissions). It will have to pay for its additional permits ánd incur the buyer part of the transaction costs.

A last point must be mentioned is that transaction costs can take two forms: they can be once and for all costs which firms must bear whenever they make a transaction, regardless of the amount of permits traded. In that case, the transaction costs are fixed costs. The other option is that the transaction costs are in some way related to the amount of permits traded and therefore are variable costs. For example, a firm which needs many permits may not be able to acquire them from only one seller, so would have to look for more potential sources of permits and therefore its transaction costs would be higher. When firms employ brokers, this might also result in variable transaction costs if the broker's charge is a percentage of the value of the transaction.

Firm behaviour

Having established the characteristics of transaction costs and their consequences for the cost functions of incumbents and entrants, the next step is to analyse the effect of transaction costs on entry barriers. Whether or not transaction costs impose entry barriers will depend not only on the form the transaction costs take, but also on the form of behaviour of both incumbent and entrant and on the existing market structure. In a perfectly competitive product market, the cost difference caused by transaction costs between the established firms and potential entrants (in the case of grandfathering when incumbents do not buy additional permits) does not mean that the established firms will be able to enjoy a higher rent derived from their incumbency (see the definition of entry barriers on p. 32). Because they operate on a perfectly competitive market, established firms cannot charge a higher price, even though they have a cost advantage *vis à vis* the entrants: increasing their price would mean that they would lose their market because of competition from the other established firms.

In the next section, the consequences of transaction costs, both fixed and variable, for entry barriers will be analysed in the context of the limit-pricing model in which there is one established firm. Two cases are distinguished. In the first case, it is assumed that the incumbent has been grandfathered all the permits it needs. In the second case, the incumbent buys additional permits and therefore has to pay transaction costs as well.

Fixed Transaction Costs

One form of entry barrier which has received much attention in the literature is limit-pricing. Known in its original form as the Bain–Sylos–Labini–Modigliani limit-pricing model, it states that by producing a certain output, the limit quantity, a dominant firm or cartel might be able to prevent entry. The ability to forestall entry depends on the fact that production exhibits increasing returns to scale over at least some range. In the limit-pricing model, the incumbent chooses the quantity it will produce first and the entrant subsequently chooses its own quantity, assuming that the incumbent will not change the quantity initially chosen. The equilibrium in this sequential game is usually called the Stackelberg equilibrium, after the author of the original article dealing with this kind of behaviour.[6]

An important point to stress is that the incumbent must have some means of committing itself to the quantity chosen in the first period of the firm. If there is no commitment, the incumbent could change the quantity produced in reaction to the quantity chosen by the entrant in the second period. In that case, its profit-maximizing behaviour would be the same as in the one-stage Cournot game. In the absence of commitment, the optimal strategy in the second-period subgame for the incumbent is to accommodate entry and act as a Cournot competitor. The threat to stick to the quantity produced in the first period is not credible; in game theory terminology, it is not a subgame perfect Nash equilibrium (see Gilbert 1989, p. 487).

One form of commitment has been described by Spence (1977) and Dixit (1980). By investing in the first period in capacity, a firm commits itself when its investment costs are sunk. In that case, it cannot recoup its investments costs by selling part of its investments and therefore it prefers to use the capacity already installed. This model will be analysed in more detail below in the section on variable transaction costs and limit pricing. First, it will be shown how fixed transaction costs can influence the outcomes of the limit-pricing model.

The consequences of fixed transaction costs for entry barriers in the limit-pricing model are explained with the aid of a simple model (borrowed from Tirole 1992, pp. 314–17). In the next section, which deals with variable transaction costs, the issues introduced here are considered in a more general model. It is assumed that both the incumbent and the entrant have the same profit function:

$$\pi^i(q^i,q^e) = q^i(1 - q^i - q^e) - f \tag{3.1}$$

$$\pi^e(q^e,q^i) = q^e(1 - q^i - q^e) - f \tag{3.2}$$

In equations (3.1) and (3.2), profit is equal to revenue minus costs. Revenue is the quantity sold times the price (the inverse demand function is $1 - q^i - q^e$). The total costs f are assumed to be fixed and equal. In this way the role of sunk costs is incorporated in the model.

The model assumes that in maximizing profits the entrant will consider the quantity of the incumbent as given and that the incumbent is informed about the entrant's behaviour and maximizes its profits taking into account the expected reaction of the entrant. In the first stage of the game, the incumbent can commit itself to a quantity that it will produce in the second stage, when the entrant enters (or not). For a given level of q^i, the entrant will maximise π^e in the second stage with respect to q^e. This yields the reaction function of the entrant:

$$q^e = R^e(q^i) = \tfrac{1}{2}(1 - q^i) \tag{3.3}$$

Substituting equation (3.3) in (3.1) gives the profit function of the incumbent as a function of q^i. Maximizing this yields the Stackelberg equilibrium in which $q^i = 1/2$, $q^e = 1/4$, $\pi^i = 1/8 - f$, $\pi^e = 1/16 - f$.

The Stackelberg equilibrium may not necessarily be the optimal choice of output q^i for the incumbent. It might be able to increase its profits by preventing entry completely. The entry-barring level for q^i (denoted q^i_b) is at the point where the entrant's best response yields a profit of zero. Substituting (3.3) in (3.2) and setting $\pi^e = 0$ yields $q^i_b = 1 - 2\sqrt{f}$. Deterring entry is attractive for the incumbent if with deterred entry the profit of the incumbent exceeds the profit in the Stackelberg equilibrium. Therefore, deterring entry is attractive when:

$$2\sqrt{f}(1 - 2\sqrt{f}) > 1/8 \tag{3.4}$$

When the Stackelberg game yields a higher profit than the entry-barring game, entry is *accommodated* (in Bain's terminology), while in the other case entry is *deterred*. Another possibility is that at the monopoly level of q^i (which in this model is $q^i = 1/2$) the entrant will not be able to make a positive profit and therefore will not enter at all (termed *blockaded* entry by Bain).

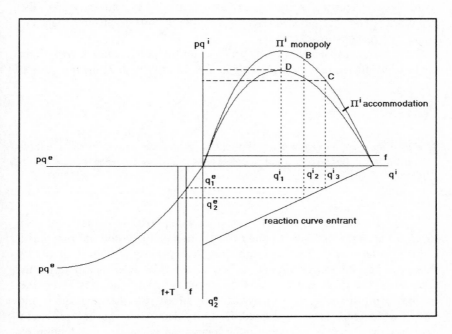

Figure 3.1 Fixed transaction costs and entry barriers

Figure 3.1 illustrates the case of entry accomodation. In the north-east quadrant, the x-axis gives the quantity produced by the incumbent, the y-axis gives his gross profits, the revenue. The south-west quadrant shows gross profit of the entrant (x-axis) as a function of the quantity produced (y-axis). The reaction curve of the entrant is shown in the south-east quadrant. First consider the incumbent. The curve 'π^i monopoly' is the gross profit earned by the incumbent when there is no entrant, that is when it is a monopolist. Its fixed costs are shown by the line f, net profit equals gross profit minus fixed costs f. Profit is maximized at q^i_1 (in the model used here at $q^i = \frac{1}{2}$). The curve 'π^i accommodation' shows the profit when the entrant is also in the market. Profit is maximized when the entrant is accommodated at q^i_1, the Stackelberg equilibrium.

The gross profit earned by the entrant is given by pq^e in the south-west quadrant. Given fixed costs of f for the entrant, the incumbent will accommodate the entrant, produce q^i_1 and make a gross profit of D. Deterring entry is not attractive; he must produce q^i_3 to keep the entrant out; at this point the entrant will produce q^e_1 as we can see from the reaction curve in the south-east quadrant. At q^e_1 profit of the entrant is zero: gross profit equals fixed costs. Deterring entry by producing q^i_3 is less attractive for the incumbent than accommodating entry because its gross profit C on the monopoly curve is lower than D.

The occurrence of fixed transaction costs on the permit market will affect the profit of the entrant by increasing its fixed costs f with T, the transaction costs:

$$\pi^e = q^e(1 - q^e - q^i) - f - T \tag{3.5}$$

This will increase the probability that entry deterrence is more attractive than accommodation because the entry-deterring level of q^i decreases:

$$q^i_b = 1 - 2\sqrt{(f + T)} \tag{3.6}$$

This is illustrated in Figure 3.1. The transaction costs shift the fixed cost curve of the entrant leftward to line $f+T$. Consequently the entrant's net profit is zero at level q^e_2. The corresponding (entry-deterring) level of q^i, as determined by the reaction function, is q^i_2, which is lower than q^i_3. At this level of q^i the gross profit which the incumbent will make is B on the monopoly profit curve. This entry-deterring profit is higher than the profit earned when entry is accomodated, D. Entry-deterrence can become more attractive than accommodation for the incumbent when the introduction of tradable permits raises the entrant's costs with fixed transaction costs.[7]

Above, it was assumed that the incumbent does not have transaction costs. However, the situation changes when the incumbent also buys permits and therefore also has to bear transaction costs. Consequently, its profit level will fall. The optimality conditions of the Stackelberg game are not affected when transaction costs are fixed, but profits will fall at the level of q^i at which it starts to buy permits, that is at the level corresponding with the amount of permits received through grandfathering. Its profit function becomes:

$$\pi^i = q^i(1 - q^i - q^e) - f \qquad q^i \leq G \tag{3.7}$$

$$\pi^i = q^i(1 - q^i - q^e) - f - T \qquad q^i > G \tag{3.8}$$

in which G is the quantity q^i produced by the incumbent and just covered by grandfathered permits. At higher levels, it has to buy permits and pay transaction costs.[8] The consequence is that entry-deterrence might not be attractive any more. This can be the case when G is larger than $q^i = 1/2$ (the Stackelberg equilibrium) and when G is lower than the entry-barring level q^i_b. In this case, the profit the incumbent makes when it deters entry is lower by the transaction costs T, while the profit it makes when entry is accommodated remains at $1/8 - f$. Consequently, the profit made when it accommodates entry $(1/8 - f)$ might be higher than the profit under entry deterrence with transaction costs for the entrant, even though the incumbent can deter entry at a lower level of q^i.[9] This is illustrated in Figure 3.2.

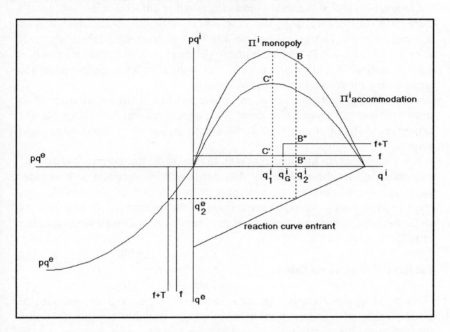

Figure 3.2 Fixed transaction costs for both entrant and incumbent

With tradable permits and fixed transaction costs on the permit market, the entrant's fixed cost curve shifts leftwards to line $f + T$ and the entry-deterrence quantity is as explained in the former section. If the number of permits grandfathered is equal to q_G, the incumbent will also have to buy permits if it produces more than q_G. Therefore, its fixed costs increase beyond this production level with T to line $f + T$. Net entry-deterrence profits decreases from BB' to BB". Because q_G is higher than q_1, the profit which the incumbent makes when it accommodates entry, CC', does not change because it does not have to buy additional permits. BB" is less than CC', therefore accommodation is preferred over deterrence.

When the incumbent also has to buy permits in the Stackelberg equilibrium, that is when G is lower than $q^i = \frac{1}{2}$, its profit in the Stackelberg equilibrium is $1/8 - f - T$. The necessary condition for entry deterrence for the incumbent (equation (3.4)) is:

$$\pi^i_b(q^i_b, 0) = 2\sqrt{(f+T)}[1 - 2\sqrt{(f+T)}] - f - T > 1/8 - f - T \quad (3.9)$$

Because the transaction costs occur in both the deterrence profit (left side of the inequality) and in the accommodating profit (right side of the inequality), there is no difference from the case where only the entrant had to bear transaction costs. Deterrence becomes more attractive when there are fixed transaction costs in a system of tradable permits, both in the situation where only the entrant faces transaction costs and in the case where both entrant and incumbent have to bear transaction costs.

If instead of grandfathering the incumbent would have to buy all his permits and therefore pay transaction costs, the same situation would apply. The existence of fixed transaction costs would make entry deterrence more attractive.[10]

The conclusion from this section is that if only the entrant has to bear transaction costs, the probability that entry will be deterred or blockaded increases *ceteris paribus*. This impact is moderated when grandfathered permits do not fully cover the production of the incumbent. In that case the incumbent might have to make fixed transaction costs as well when it deters entry.

Variable Transaction Costs

In this subsection, a more general model will be used to analyse the consequences of variable transaction costs of tradable permits for entry barriers in the limit-pricing model. First, variable transaction costs will be introduced graphically with an adapted version of the simple model used in the former subsection on fixed transaction costs. Subsequently the more general model is used to analyse accommodation of the entrant by the incumbent.

Graphical illustration of variable transaction costs

In the model in the former subsection, variable transaction costs can be represented in the entrant's profit function, where t is the (constant) transaction costs per unit of output:

$$\pi^e = q^e(1 - q^e - q^i) - f - t\, q^e \quad (3.10)$$

The entrant's reaction function is:

$$q^e = R^e(q^i) = (1 - q^i - t)/2 \qquad (3.11)$$

The incumbent's profit function is (equation (3.1)):

$$\pi^i = q^i(1 - q^i - q^e) - f \qquad (3.12)$$

Substituting q^e from equation (3.11) yields:

$$\pi^i = \tfrac{1}{2}\, q^i(t + 1 - q^i) - f \qquad (3.13)$$

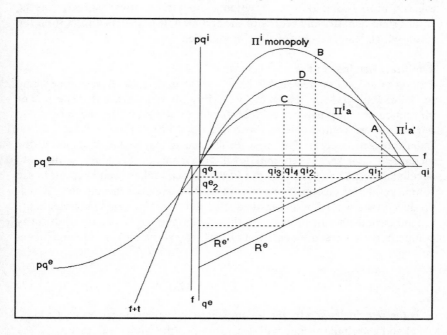

Figure 3.3 Variable transaction costs

Figure 3.3 shows the effect of variable transaction costs for the entrant. Curves π^i monopoly, $\pi^i a$, $\pi^i a'$, R^e and π^e present the situation without transaction costs (the π^i curves represent gross profit). Transaction costs shift the reaction curve of the entrant from R^e to $R^{e'}$. In the southwest quadrant transaction costs have been added to the (fixed) production costs, curve $f + t$. As a result the level of q^e at which the entrant's profit is zero increases from $q^e{}_1$ to $q^e{}_2$. The entry-deterring level of q^i, the level of q^i at which the entrant's profit is zero, decreases from q^i_1 to q^i_2. The profit which the incumbent will make when it deters entry increases from A to B. Therefore entry-deterrence becomes more profitable for the incumbent. At the same time, the transaction costs increase the profit earned by the incumbent when it accommodates the entrant: its profit curve shifts upward from $\pi^i a$ to $\pi^i a'$ and profit under accommodation shifts from C to D. Consequently, accommodation also becomes more profitable. Which effect dominates depends on the values of f and t.

It should also be noted that in the case where accommodation is the most profitable strategy for the incumbent, the impact of variable transaction costs is to raise the quantity produced by the incumbent (from q^i_3 to q^i_4) and to raise his profits compared to a situation without transaction costs, whereas the equilibrium quantity and profits of the entrant will fall. This differs from the result which was derived for fixed transaction costs.[11]

The limit-pricing model
The more general model used is based on the extension of the limit-pricing model of Bain–Sylos and Spence by Dixit in his seminal article 'The role of investment in entry deterrence' (1980). The strategies of the incumbent and the entrant are comparable to those described in the former subsection on fixed transaction costs. The main difference is that in the first period the incumbent chooses the optimal level of a strategic variable, taking into account the effect on the behaviour of the entrant in the second period. In the simple model discussed above, the incumbent chooses the quantity it will produce in the second period instead of the level of a strategic variable. In the second period, the incumbent and the entrant compete as Cournot quantity competitors (if the entrant enters at all). The profit function of the incumbent is:

$$\pi^i = R^i(q^i, q^e) - C^i(q^i, K^i) \qquad (3.14)$$

R^i is the revenue raised by the incumbent. It is increasing and concave in q^i. Total and marginal revenue will decrease when the entrant increases q^e. C^i is increasing in q^i and convex. K^i is the strategic variable which the incumbent chooses in the first period and can be interpreted as capacity. For a given output q^i, there is an optimal level of K^i which minimises costs; C^i is convex in K^i as well. The marginal costs of output decrease when K^i rises:

$$C^i_{q^i K^i} < 0 \qquad (3.15)$$

This reflects the fact that investing in K^i in the first period lowers marginal costs in the second period because the costs of capacity K^i is sunk. The potential entrant has the profit function:

$$\pi^e = R^e(q^i, q^e) - C^e(q^e, M) \tag{3.16}$$

Its revenue function has the same properties as the revenue function of the incumbent. C^e is increasing in q^e and convex. $C^e_M > 0$ and $C^e_{q^eM} > 0$; an increase in M increases marginal costs. M reflects the introduction of the system of tradable emission permits when transaction costs are variable. The entrant has to buy permits and therefore has to pay transaction costs. This will increase its marginal costs because the transaction costs are variable. They will rise with the level of the transaction costs[12]. M is an exogenously determined variable which will be used to analyze the effect of a change in the marginal costs of the entrant on the equilibrium and the conditions for entry deterring.

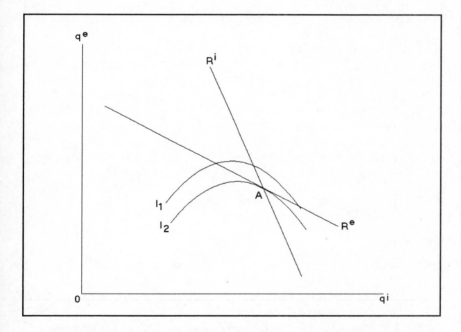

Figure 3.4 The Stackelberg equilibrium

The Stackelberg equilibrium of the two-stage game is illustrated in Figure 3.4. The x-axis gives the quantity of q^i produced by the incumbent, the y-axis the quantity of q^e produced by the entrant. R^e is the reaction curve of the entrant.

I_1 and I_2 are isoprofit curves for the incumbent. An isoprofit curve represents a given level of profit that can be obtained with different combinations of q^i and q^e (and setting K^i simultaneously at such a level that profits are maximized). The closer the isoprofit curve is to the q^i axis the higher is the incumbent's profit. In the first period, the incumbent maximizes his profits by choosing K^i and q^i, taking into account the reaction curve of the entrant. The highest attainable profit is presented by point A. At this point, the isoprofit curve I_2 is tangential to the entrant's reaction curve.

R^i is the reaction curve of the incumbent in the second stage of the game when K^i is fixed. Acting as a Cournot competitor the incumbent takes the quantity of the entrant q^e as given and adjusts q^i. The equilibrium in the second stage (and assuming entry) is at the intersection of the reaction curves of entrant and incumbent.

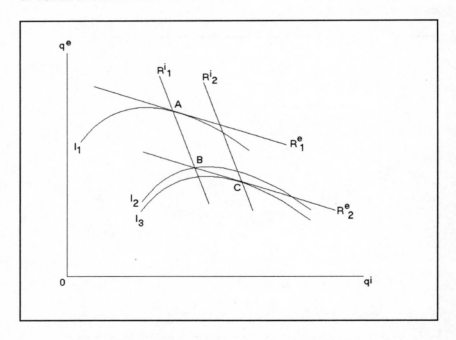

Figure 3.5   Change in the Stackelberg equilibrium due to higher marginal costs

We can proceed to analyse the consequences of introducing tradable emission permits with variable transaction costs on the permit market.

Variable transaction costs will increase the marginal costs of the entrant, represented by a positive change in M in equation (3.16), shifting his reaction curve downward. The impact of a change in M is illustrated in Figure 3.5. The initial equilibrium (before the introduction of tradable permits) is point A. At this point, the incumbent's initial profit is maximised: isoprofit curve I_1 is tangent to $R^e{}_1$. When K^i is fixed, the downward shift from $R^e{}_1$ to $R^e{}_2$ results in a new equilibrium (point B) which lies on an isoprofit curve which represents a higher profit. The incumbent produces more and the entrant produces less.

When a new level of K^i can be chosen the Nash equilibrium will shift to point C where the lowest possible isoprofit curve is tangential to $R^e{}_2$, isoprofit curve I_3. The optimal level of K^i is the level which yields reaction curve $R^i{}_2$ in the second period subgame. Consequently, the increase in the entrant's marginal costs caused by the variable transaction costs on the permit market will change the optimal level of the strategic investment chosen by the incumbent in the first period.

The reaction function of the entrant (in the second-period subgame) can be determined by maximizing π^e assuming that q^i (and M) is given. The first-order condition is:

$$R^e_{q^e} - C^e_{q^e} = 0 \qquad (3.17)$$

The second-order condition is:

$$R^e_{q^e q^e} - C^e_{q^e q^e} < 0 \qquad (3.18)$$

Total differentiation of (3.17) gives:

$$dq^e = \frac{-R^e_{q^e q^i}}{R^e_{q^e q^e} - C^e_{q^e q^e}} dq^i + \frac{C^e_{q^e M}}{R^e_{q^e q^e} - C^e_{q^e q^e}} dM \quad -1 < dq^e/dq^i < 0$$

$$(3.19)$$

In equation (3.19) $\partial R^e / \partial q^{e} \partial q^i < 0$ and $\partial C^e / \partial q^{e} \partial M > 0$. The first term in equation 3.19 is negative, therefore the reaction curve of the entrant, with slope dq^e/dq^i, is downward-sloping. It is assumed that the Nash equilibrium of the second-period subgame has an interior solution and that it is unique.[13] The second term on the right-hand side of equation (3.19) is also negative. An increase in the marginal costs of the entrant will shift its reaction curve downward, as was shown in Figure 3.5.

The reaction curve of the incumbent in the second period, *given the level of K^i* chosen in the first period, can be determined in the same way as the reaction function of the entrant. The first-order condition is:

$$R^i_{q^i} - C^i_{q^i} = 0 \qquad (3.20)$$

Totally differentiating (3.20) gives:

$$[R^i_{q^iq^i} - C^i_{q^iq^i}] \, dq^i = -R^i_{q^iq^e} \, dq^e + C^i_{q^iK^i} \, dK^i \qquad (3.21)$$

dq^i/dq^e is negative, therefore the reaction curve of the incumbent is also downward-sloping.

The incumbent can influence the second-period equilibrium determined by the intersection of the reaction curves by choosing the level of K^i in the first period (see Figures 3.4 and 3.5). The choice of K^i in the first period affects the reaction curve of the incumbent and thereby the equilibrium levels of q^i and q^e in the second period. The profit of the incumbent (equation (3.14)) in this two-stage game is:

$$\pi^i(q^{i*}(K^i),q^{e*}(K^i),K^i) = R^i(q^{i*}(K^i),q^{e*}(K^i)) - C^i(q^{i*}(K^i),K^i) \qquad (3.22)$$

in which q^{i*} and q^{e*} are the equilibrium levels of q^i and q^e in the second-period game. q^{i*} and q^{e*} are a function of K^i which is chosen in the first period. The optimal level of K^i which maximizes profit is found by differentiating (3.22) with respect to K^i and setting it equal to zero:

$$d\pi^i/dq^i \, dq^{i*}/dK^i + d\pi^i/dq^e \, dq^{e*}/dK^i + d\pi^i/dK^i = 0 \qquad (3.23)$$

This can be written as:

$$\frac{d\pi^i}{dK^i} = (R^i_{q^i} - C^i_{q^i}) \frac{dq^{i*}}{dK^i} + R^i_{q^e} \frac{dq^{e*}}{dK^i} - C^i_{K^i} = 0 \qquad (3.24)$$

The effect of a change in K^i on q^{i*} and q^{e*} (dq^{i*}/dK^i and dq^{e*}/dK^i) can be determined by differentiating the first-order conditions of the second-period equilibrium (equations (3.17) and (3.18)) with respect to K^i. Totally differentiating these first-order conditions with respect to K^i (and M) yields equations (3.19) and (3.21), in which dq^i and dq^e are written as functions of dK^i (and dM). In matrix format this yields:

$$
\begin{bmatrix}
R^i_{q^i q^i} - C^i_{q^i q^i} & R^i_{q^i q^e} \\
R^e_{q^i q^e} & R^e_{q^e q^e} - C^e_{q^e q^e}
\end{bmatrix}
\begin{bmatrix}
dq^{i*} \\
dq^{e*}
\end{bmatrix}
=
\begin{bmatrix}
C^i_{q^i k^i} \, dK^i \\
C^e_{q^e M} \, dM
\end{bmatrix}
\tag{3.25}
$$

Let Δ be the determinant of the coefficient matrix[14]. Δ must be positive for the equilibrium to be stable. Solving dq^{e*} from (3.25) and substituting it in (3.24) yields (in the Nash equilibrium of the second-period subgame, $\delta\pi^i/\delta q^i = 0$, therefore dq^i does not enter into the equation (the envelope theorem)):

$$
d\pi^i = -\left(\frac{R^i_{q^e} R^e_{q^i q^e} C^i_{q^i K^i}}{\Delta} + C^i_{K^i} \right) dK^i + \left(\frac{R^i_{q^e} (R^i_{q^i q^i} - C^i_{q^i q^i}) C^e_{q^e M}}{\Delta} \right) dM
$$

$$
\tag{3.26}
$$

The optimal level of K^i is at the point where the incumbent's profit in the Stackelberg game is maximized, point A in Figure 3.1. Profit is maximized when $d\pi^i/dK^i = 0$ in equation (3.26) (in equation (3.24) profit is maximized when $d\pi^i/dK^i = 0$; (3.24) has been rewritten as (3.26); therefore in (3.26) $d\pi^i/dK^i$ must be zero).

Subsequently we will analyse the consequences of an increase in the entrant's marginal costs caused by the transaction costs of tradable permits. In our model this is represented by an increase in M which shifts the reaction curve of the entrant downward (see Figure 3.5). First consider the consequences for the second-period Nash equilibrium. The consequences of a change in M on the levels of q^{i*} and q^{e*} in this second-period equilibrium are determined in the same manner as the effect of a change in K on the second-period equilibrium levels of q^{i*} and q^{e*}. Differentiating the the first-order conditions of the second-period equilibrium with respect to M has been done in equation 3.25. Writing out the effect of a change in M on q^{i*} and q^{e*} yields:

$$
dq^{i*} = - R^i_{q^i q^e} C^e_{q^e M} / \Delta \; dM > 0
\tag{3.27}
$$

The increase in the entrant's costs caused by the transaction costs (dM) increases the quantity produced by the incumbent and decreases the quantity

$$dq^{e\,*} \; = \; (R^{i}_{q^{i}q^{i}} - C^{i}_{q^{i}q^{i}}) \; C^{e}_{q^{e}} M \; / \; \Delta \; dM < 0 \qquad (3.28)$$

produced by the entrant. This is represented by the shift from A to B in Figure 3.5. As a result of these changes in dq^{i*} and dq^{e*} the profit of the incumbent increases because in equation (3.26) $d\pi^{i}/dM$ is positive: in the numerator R^{i}_{qe} is negative, $(\partial R^{i}/\partial^{2}q^{i} - \partial C^{i}/\partial^{2}q^{i})$ is negative and $\partial C^{e}/\partial q^{e}\partial M$ is positive, therefore the numerator is positive. The denominator Δ is positive as well.

The change in M will not only affect the second-period equilibrium but also the optimal choice of K^{i} in the first period. In Figure 3.5 this is shown by a shift in the incumbent's reaction curve which shifts the equilibrium from B to C. The optimal level of K^{i} is determined by maximizing the incumbent's profit, equation (3.24). Rewriting (3.24) yielded (3.26), therefore K^{i} is chosen such that $d\pi^{i}/dK^{i}$ in equation (3.26) is zero:

$$\frac{d\pi^{i}}{dK^{i}} \; = \; G \; = \; -(\; \frac{R^{i}_{q^{e}} \, R^{e}_{q^{i}q^{e}} \, C^{i}_{q^{i}K^{i}}}{\Delta} \; + \; C^{i}_{K^{i}} \;) \; = \; 0 \qquad (3.29)$$

The increase in M will affect condition (3.29): the second-period equilibrium has changed because of the change in M and the level of K which was chosen before M changed may no longer be optimal. The increase in M affects the optimality condition through the effect which it has on q^{i*} and q^{e*}: q^{i*} increases and q^{e*} decreases. The new second-period equilibrium levels of q^{i} and q^{e} influence the values of the terms in equation (3.29) and therefore $d\pi^{i}/dK^{i}$ may no longer be optimal, given the value of K^{i} chosen before the entrant's costs increased. We can determine the effect of the change in M on this optimality condition by differentiating (3.29) with respect to dM, holding K^{i} fixed:

$$dG/dM = dG/dq^{i*} \; dq^{i*}/dM + dG/dq^{e*} \; dq^{e*}/dM \qquad (3.30)$$

This yields (assuming that third-order derivatives are zero):

$$(R^{i}_{q^{i}q^{e}} R^{e}_{q^{i}q^{e}} C^{i}_{q^{i}K^{i}} \; / \; \Delta \; + \; C^{i}_{Kq^{i}}) \; dq^{i} \qquad (3.31)$$

All terms are negative except Δ, which is positive. Therefore the increase in q^{i} caused by the increase in M decreases the coefficient of $d\pi^{i}/dK^{i}$. Consequently $d\pi^{i}/dK^{i}$ becomes negative, given the level of K^{i} chosen when the entrant did not have transaction costs. In other words, the level of K^i is no longer optimal: the incumbent must change K^i to maximize profits. Increasing K^i increases C^i_K in (3.29), which counters the negative effect of the change in M. The incumbent will therefore increase the level of his strategic investment in K^i in the first period when tradable emission permits are introduced and the entrant has to bear transaction costs. The higher level of K^i increases the second-period level of q^i and decreases the second-period level of q^e as can be seen from equation (3.25):

$$dq^i = (R^e_{q^e q^e} - C^e_{q^e q^e}) \, C^i_{q^i K^i} / \Delta \, dK^i > 0 \qquad (3.32)$$

$$dq^e = - \, R^e_{q^e q^i} \, C^i_{q^i K^i} / \Delta \, dK^i < 0$$

This is shown in Figure 3.5 by the shift from B to C which results from the shift in the reaction curve caused by the higher level of K^i: q^i increases and q^e decreases. Profit is further increased because at the initial level of K^i profit was not maximized.

The conclusion is that a rise in (marginal) costs, which the entrant has to face because it has to bear the transaction costs arising from the imperfect permit market, has a direct and an indirect effect on the accommodating equilibrium. The direct effect is a downward shift in the entrant's reaction curve. The entrant enters at a smaller size and the incumbent increases both production and profits. (This is the same result as was derived in the more specific model with variable transaction costs on page 46.) The indirect effect is that the incumbent will increase his first-period strategic investment K^i, which further increases production and profit of the incumbent. The change in production of the incumbent and the entrant differs from the result which was derived for fixed transaction costs under accommodation (see the previous subsection). In that case, the quantities produced by the incumbent and the entrant did not change as long as the incumbent continued to accommodate the entrant after introduction of the permit scheme.

Transaction costs for the incumbent

A striking feature of tradable permits and entry barriers in the limit-pricing model is that it makes no difference in the entry accommodation case whether the incumbent firm has received all the permits it needs through grandfathering in the first period or through auction. When the incumbent has to buy permits in the first period it has to pay the permit price plus the transaction costs. Selling them in the second period will only yield the permit price; the transaction costs cannot be recouped, they are sunk. Consequently, the opportunity costs of using the permits in the second period are equal to their price only, not to the full price plus transaction costs paid for them in the first period. Let **G** represent the permits grandfathered in the first period, **E** the permits acquired in the first period and $E(q^i)$ the permits used (and therefore acquired) for emissions in the second period. P_P is the permit price and t is the variable transaction costs per unit of emissions bought. Writing out the cost function of the incumbent in the second period yields:[15]

$$C^i(q^i,K^i) + P_P(E(q^i) - \mathbf{G}) + P_P\,\mathbf{G} \qquad E(q^i)\mathord{<}\mathbf{E},\ \mathbf{E}\mathord{\leq}\mathbf{G} \qquad (3.34)$$

$$C^i(q^i,K^i) + P_P(E(q^i) - \mathbf{G}) + P_P\,\mathbf{G} + t(\mathbf{E} - \mathbf{G}) \qquad E(q^i)\mathord{<}\mathbf{E},\ \mathbf{E}\mathord{>}\mathbf{G}$$
$$(3.35)$$

$$C^i(q^i,K^i) + P_P(E(q^i) - \mathbf{G}) + P_P\,\mathbf{G} + t(E(q^i) - \mathbf{E}) + t(\mathbf{E} - \mathbf{G}) \qquad E(q^i)\mathord{\geq}\mathbf{E}$$
$$(3.36)$$

If the incumbent has received all the permits it uses in the second period through grandfathering in the first period, it has no transaction costs because it does not buy any permits: equation (3.34). If it buys more permits in the first period than it receives free, it pays transaction costs for the number of permits bought, $t(\mathbf{E} - \mathbf{G})$, equation (3.35). These costs cannot be recouped, therefore they are sunk. It can sell the permits acquired in the first period for their price P_P, therefore it has to take into account their opportunity costs. When the incumbent has to buy additional permits in the second period, transaction costs increase with the number of additional permits needed: equation (3.36).

Marginal costs in these three situations are:

$$C^i_{q^i} + PpE_{q^i} \qquad E(q^i)\mathord{<}\mathbf{E},\ \mathbf{E}\mathord{>}\boldsymbol{G} \qquad (3.37)$$

$$C^i_{q^i} + Pp\,E_{q^i} \qquad E(q^i)\mathord{<}\mathbf{E},\ \mathbf{E}\mathord{>}\boldsymbol{G} \qquad (3.38)$$

$$C^i_{q^i} + Pp\,E_{q^i} \qquad E(q^i)\mathord{=}\mathord{>}\mathbf{E} \qquad (3.39)$$

As long as the incumbent has acquired the permits needed in the first period, the variable transaction costs do not enter its marginal cost function in the second period, regardless of whether they were acquired through grandfathering or buying. Consequently, the Stackelberg equilibrium of the game presented above does not change whether or not the incumbent buys permits and incurs transaction costs in the first period. The conclusion that variable transaction costs on the permit market can raise the entry barrier in the Stackelberg game is therefore independent of the choice between grandfathering permits to the incumbent or auctioning to all firms, both entrants and incumbents.

However, it should be noted that the transaction costs made by the incumbent, $t(E(q^i) - G)$, do influence the profit made by the incumbent in the second period: both the accommodation profit and the profit made when entry is deterred will change. This will influence the choice between entry deterrence and entry accommodation. The reader is referred to the previous section on fixed transaction costs for a more detailed discussion.

Strategic investment in permits
We have discussed how variable transaction costs in the permit market can change the conditions under which incumbents can deter entry and how they change the conditions of entry accommodation when incumbents can commit themselves to output levels in the second period by investing in the first period. The strategic investment in the model discussed above was capacity, which cannot be sold without considerable losses and therefore creates sunk costs. An interesting feature of tradable emission permits with variable transaction costs is that investing in the permits themselves can act as a strategic investment because, as has been explained above, the transaction costs cannot be recouped in the second period and therefore are sunk.

The consequences for entry can be shown using a version of the Dixit model presented above. Let R^i again be the revenue of the incumbent. R is a function of q^i and q^e (R^i is increasing and concave in q^i and decreasing and concave in q^e). Production costs excluding permit costs are increasing in q^i and convex. For the moment it is assumed that acquiring permits is less expensive than abatement. Therefore, in addition to production costs, the incumbent has to buy permits if the number of permits grandfathered is not sufficient. Permit costs equal emissions (which are a function of the quantity produced) times their price P_p. The profit function of the incumbent in the second period is:

$$\pi^i = R^i(q^i, q^e) - C^i(q^i) - P_p \cdot E(q^i) - t(\mathbf{E} - \mathbf{G}) \qquad E(q^i) \leq \mathbf{E}$$

$$\tag{3.40}$$

$$\pi^i = R^i(q^i, q^e) - C^i(q^i) - P_p \cdot E(q^i) - t(E(q^i) - \mathbf{G}) \qquad E(q^i) > \mathbf{E}$$

$$\tag{3.41}$$

As long as the emissions resulting from the quantity produced in the second period are less than the number of permits acquired in the first period, $\mathbf{E}$, (either by grandfathering or buying), profit is determined by (3.40)). When the incumbent produces and emits more, it has to buy permits and its profits equal (3.41). Marginal costs are:

$$C_{q^i_i} + PpE_{q^i} \qquad E(q^i) \leq E \tag{3.42}$$

$$C^i_{q^i} + (Pp+t)E_{q^i} \qquad E(q^i) => E \tag{3.43}$$

The entrant's profit function is:

$$\pi^e = R^e(q^e, q^i) - C^e(q^e) - (P_p + t) E(q^e) \tag{3.44}$$

The second-period Nash–Cournot equilibrium will depend on the number of permits the incumbent has acquired in the first period. As long as the emissions resulting from the output produced by the incumbent are lower than the number of permits acquired, its marginal costs are given by (3.42). If it has to buy additional permits, its marginal costs will be higher, as shown by (3.43). This also has consequences for its reaction curves.

This is shown in Figure 3.6 (adapted from Dixit 1980). The reaction curve MM' is the reaction curve of the incumbent when it buys the permits it needs in the second period. Curve NN' is the reaction curve for the case where no additional permits have to be bought and therefore marginal costs are lower[16]. The reaction curve of the entrant is curve RR'. T is the Nash equilibrium when transaction costs matter for the incumbent; V when they do not. These two equilibria can be considered the extremes of the range of equilibria which the incumbent can achieve by choosing the number of permits it buys in the first period. For example, let the number of permits acquired by the incumbent in the first period be sufficient for the production of Q in Figure 3.6. For $q^i \leq Q$, the incumbent's reaction curve is curve NN'. When the incumbent produces more than Q, permits must be bought and transaction costs incurred. The reaction curve shifts to MM' for $q^i \geq Q$. The Nash equilibrium in this case is W, the point at which the entrant's reaction curve intersects the reaction curve of the incumbent (the dotted line). The incumbent can act as a Stackelberg leader and choose the optimal output level, provided that it falls within the range set by the Nash equilibria for the two extremes T and V.

Following the analysis presented above (see the previous section on fixed transaction costs, and Dixit 1980, pp. 100-1), several cases can be discerned:

1.   At T the profit of the entrant is negative. For $Q \geq Q_T$ the entrant can never

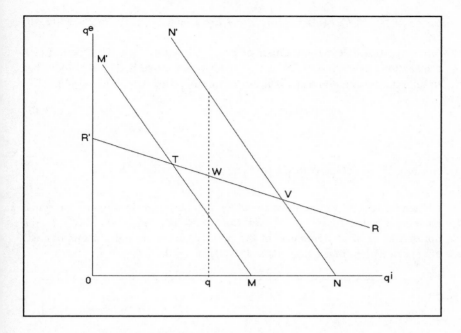

Figure 3.6 Strategic investment in tradable permits

make a positive profit and the incumbent is a monopolist.
2. At V the entrant's profit is positive. In this case the incumbent will accommodate the entrant and act as a Stackelberg leader, choosing the number of permits which correspond to the quantity and equilibrium needed to maximize profits, for example, Q and W in Figure 3.6.
3. At T the entrant makes a positive profit while at V profit is zero. This means that there is a point between T and V at which the entrant's profit is zero. Consequently the incumbent firm can deter entry by choosing the number of permits such that this equilibrium occurs. It will choose entry deterrence when this yields a higher profit than accommodation.

Abatement efficiency
A point of interest is whether strategic investment in tradable emission permits would affect abatement cost efficiency. In order to explore this, the model of the previous section is extended to include abatement. The abatement cost function is $A(E(q^i))$, with $A_E>0$. The total cost function of the incumbent in the second period is:[17]

$$C^i(q^i) + P_P\, E(q^i) + A(E(q^i)) + t\mathbf{E} \qquad E(q^i)\leq\mathbf{E} \qquad (3.45)$$

$$C^i(q^i) + P_p E(q^i) + A(E(q^i)) + t(E(q^i) - \mathbf{E}) + t\mathbf{E} \qquad E(q^i) > \mathbf{E} \quad (3.46)$$

For emissions below the number of permits bought in the first period (**E**), transaction costs are sunk. When emissions rise above **E** the incumbent has to take the transaction costs *if* it buys more permits. Marginal costs are:

$$C_{q^i_i} + PpE_{q^i} + A_E E_{q^i} = 0 \qquad E(q^i) \leq \mathbf{E} \qquad\qquad (3.47)$$

$$C^i_{q^i} + (Pp+t)E_{q^i} + A_E E_{q^i} = 0 \qquad E(q^i) > \mathbf{E} \qquad\qquad (3.48)$$

Abatement costs are minimized when the permit price equals marginal abatement costs, $P_p + A_E = 0$, for $E(q^i) \leq \mathbf{E}$. For emissions above **E**, the optimal level of abatement is at the point where marginal abatement costs equal price plus transaction costs, $P_p + A_E + t = 0$.

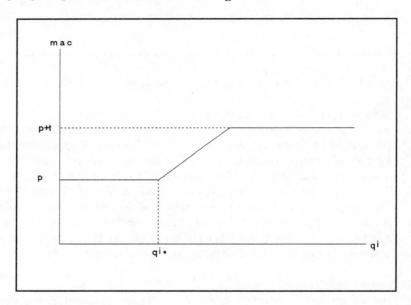

Figure 3.7 Marginal abatement costs

The higher the quantity produced in the second period, the higher are emissions. At a certain point, it will be optimal for the incumbent to use all the permits acquired in the first period (**E**). This point is denoted q^{i*}. If production increases further, the incumbent has the choice of either buying more permits and incurring transaction costs or abating more. Buying new permits is only attractive if marginal abatement costs equal the price of the permits plus the transaction costs (equation (3.48)). Marginal abatement costs will therefore rise when production increases beyond q^{i^*}, the point at which all previously acquired permits are used efficiently. This is illustrated in Figure 3.7. The x-axis shows the quantity of q produced, the y-axis shows marginal abatement costs. At q^{i^*}, abatement costs start rising, until they are equal to $P_p + t$. It should be noted that marginal abatement costs do not rise directly to $P_p + t$ at q^{i^*}. At q^{i^*}, marginal abatement costs equal P_p, the permit price. Increasing production beyond q^{i^*} increases emissions. The incumbent can either buy more permits, at costs $P_p + t$, or abate more. Increasing abatement will be cheaper (assuming that abatement costs are a continuous function of emissions $E(q^i)$) because the incumbent can abate at marginal costs lower than $P_p + t$. At some point marginal abatement costs will have risen to $P_p + t$: at that point it is more efficient for the incumbent to acquire more permits and pay the transaction costs instead of abating more.

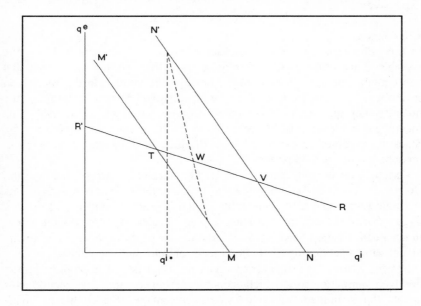

Figure 3.8 Strategic investment in permits with abatement costs

Given a certain number of permits bought in the first period, the reaction function of the incumbent will change given the increase in marginal abatement costs for $q^i > q^{i*}$. This is shown in Figure 3.8. Instead of jumping from reaction curve NN' to reaction curve MM' when q rises above q^{i*}, marginal production costs increase with q. The new reaction curve is shown by the dotted line which slopes towards the MM' line. Equilibrium is at W.

For the entrant, abatement does not really change the case. It will abate up to the point where marginal abatement costs equal the permit price plus transaction costs.Including abatement does not affect the conclusions concerning entry barriers and tradable permits in the limit-pricing model. The incumbent can still choose the optimal point in the Stackelberg game by investing in permits in the first period.

Abatement cost efficiency is not affected either. Total abatement costs will be minimized, even though marginal abatement costs of the incumbent can range between the permit price and the permit price cum transaction costs. For emissions up to the point where all permits acquired in the first period are used, the incumbent firm will equate marginal abatement costs with the permit price. Subsequently, it will increase abatement up to the point where buying more permits and paying in addition the variable transaction costs is less expensive.

Conclusions

In this subsection on variable transaction costs we have analysed how the variable transaction costs of buying pollution permits influence the consequences of entry barriers in the limit-pricing model. In this model, an incumbent firm can influence the size of potential entrants (in terms of the quantity they produce for the market) or even deter them completely. The incumbent achieves this by committing itself in the first period of the Stackelberg game, for example by installing capacity which cannot be fully recouped in the second period.

Variable transaction costs increase the marginal costs of the entrant. Consequently, under accommodation the incumbent firm will increase its strategic investment and the quantity which it produces and it will make a larger profit. The entrant will enter at a lower quantity. This conclusion is independent of the choice between grandfathering pollution permits to the incumbent or auctioning to all firms, both entrants and incumbents.

The entry barrier is raised for two reasons. The first is that buying permits involves transaction costs which cannot be recouped later. The second factor is that the incumbent has a first-mover advantage. It uses this to invest strategically and create sunk costs in the first period in order to commit itself to certain output levels in the second period. It can invest both in already available strategic investments, such as capacity, and in the permits themselves. The abatement cost efficiency of the permit scheme is not impaired when transaction costs increase entry barriers in the limit-pricing model.

3.5 CONCLUSIONS AND PRACTICAL CONSEQUENCES

In most of the programmes of tradable emission permits that have been implemented up till now, established firms have received their permits free while new firms have had to buy them. This difference in treatment between established firms and entrants has raised concern about the consequences for entry into industries. At the outset it should be noted that the naive notion that grandfathering creates a cost advantage for established firms compared with potential entrants is not necessarily true. Grandfathered permits have an opportunity cost when they are used. These opportunity costs are equal to the price at which they can be sold and therefore established firms do not have a cost advantage over entrants just because they received permits free.

This does not mean that the instrument of TDPs cannot raise entry barriers. Three types of entry barriers have been identified which in theory are affected by TDPs. First, in the limit-pricing model transaction costs on the permit market can have consequences for entry. Second, capital markets may not work perfectly, in which case grandfathering puts incumbent firms at an advantage. Third, firms can try to exclude entrants from the permit market by raising their costs and preventing entry. Imperfect capital markets and exclusion are studied in the next chapter.

In this chapter we have discussed how transaction costs on the permit market (borne by either the buyer or the seller of permits or by both) affect entry barriers in the limit-pricing model. The limit-pricing model is a two-period Stackelberg game in which the incumbent firm invests in the first period, taking into account how the potential entrant will react in the second period. In this way it influences the output of the entrant in the second period. It might also be profitable for the incumbent to deter entry completely.

In the first case considered it was assumed that transaction costs are fixed. Assuming that the incumbent firm receives through grandfathering all the permits it will use, entry can be deterred at lower output levels for the incumbent than would be possible in the absence of (fixed) transaction costs. Moreover, the transaction costs might make entry-deterrence attractive when entry was initially accommodated: entry deterrence takes place at a lower output level and therefore ensures a higher profit for the incumbent. In these cases total output will fall and welfare decline. If the most profitable option for the incumbent is to accommodate the entrant, transaction costs do not affect the output level of incumbent and entrant because the fixed transaction costs do not affect the equilibrium conditions for accommodation.

The analysis changes when the incumbent has to buy permits in addition to the number received free. Consequently, it will have to incur transaction costs as well. This does not influence the equilibrium under accommodation, but it might make accommodation more attractive than deterrence. This is the case when the number of permits grandfathered exceeds those needed when the incumbent firm accommodates but are less than its requirement when entry is deterred. Choosing to deter the entrant means that the incumbent has to pay transaction costs while with accommodation no permits have to be bought and therefore no transaction costs are incurred. Accommodation might therefore be more attractive in this special case.

In the section on variable transaction costs, the focus was on accommodation of the entrant. In contrast to the case with fixed transaction costs, the accommodation equilibrium will change with variable transaction costs. The incumbent produces more and makes a higher profit while the entrant produces less. The incumbent invests more in the strategic investment which commits it in the first period. Total output is reduced and welfare diminishes.

A perhaps surprising conclusion is that with variable transaction costs it makes no difference to the accommodation equilibrium whether the incumbent receives all the permits needed free or whether it has to buy additional permits and incur transaction costs as well. The reason for this is that it can buy permits in the first period. The transaction costs cannot be recouped in the second period: they are sunk. Therefore they do not enter the second-period equilibrium.

Instead of investing in already available strategic investments such as capacity, the incumbent can also invest in the permits themselves. Because the transaction costs are sunk, the incumbent is to some extent committed when it buys permits in the first period. In the limit-pricing model analysed here, the abatement cost efficiency of the permit scheme is not impaired when transaction costs increase entry barriers.

It should be stressed that the analysis presented here of the consequences of transaction costs in the permit market for entry barriers in the product market is only partial in nature. The strategic interactions between firms have been restricted to at most two periods. In reality, firms regularly make decisions which affect competitors and potential entrants. These long-term interactions should in principle be taken into account. Moreover, only one form of firm behaviour has been addressed, the limit-pricing model, although there is a wealth of competing theories and assumptions about firm behaviour.

Given the conclusions from the theoretical analysis of entry barriers and transaction costs on permit markets outlined above, it is still necessary to assess the practical implications for the system of tradable carbon permits described in Chapter 2. Although theoretically entry barriers can occur when the permit market does not function perfectly, the practical consequences appear to be small. The carbon permit market is large and has many potential actors; this increases the chance of a well-functioning market developing with low transaction costs. For example, in the market for sulphur allowances in the US the broker's costs are 5 per cent of the value of the permits traded (Klaassen and Nentjes 1995). Furthermore, the auction of some of the permits means that there is a primary market on which transaction costs are low because there are no search costs associated with buying permits in this way.

Another point is that the situations analysed in the previous section are theoretical cases. In general, game theory has not enjoyed overly much empirical support (see, for example, Tirole 1992, p. 3). Even though transaction costs might appear on the carbon permit market, it will be difficult to identify possible situations in the product markets concerned which bear similarity to the theoretical cases analysed. Therefore, the overall conclusion concerning transaction costs and entry barriers in the tradable carbon permit scheme is that in practice it is not a relevant issue.

NOTES

1. If they produce more than their quota allows, they have to repay part of the guaranteed price (the so-called super levy). This means that the surplus quantity produced has to be sold at lower (market) prices.
2. See also Gilbert (1989, p. 494).
3. The effect on the change in price depends on the relative elasticities. The more inelastic the abatement cost function is, the larger will be the effect upon the price for this firm. If abatement cost are inelastic a firm will accept higher transaction costs because abating more will be expensive. The firm which buys permits will have higher abatement costs. In general the higher abatement costs are, the less elastic is the abatement costs function. Consequently, the upward effect on the buyer's price will be larger than the downward effect on the seller's price (see Stavins 1994).
4. Transaction costs are presumably small at auction (the primary market).
5. This is the case when the number of grandfathered permits covers the need of the established firm, or when abatement is less expensive than buying additional permits.
6. In fact, the Stackelberg equilibrium does not differ in concept from the Nash equilibrium because both are non-cooperative equilibria. The only difference is that the Stackelberg game is a two-period game while the Nash equilibrium is the result of a one-period game.
7. It should be noted that if the transaction costs are high enough entry will be blockaded: this is the case if the entry-deterring level of q^i is equal to or lower than ½, the monopoly output level of q^i. In that case, the incumbent produces the monopoly quantity $q^i=$½ and entry is blockaded because at that level the entrant's profit is negative.
8. For the moment, abatement is not included in the analysis. In the next section, it will be included.
9. In the specific model presented here, entry deterrence remains attractive. However, this is a specific model; in a more general model this is not necessarily the case.
10. Transaction costs on the primary market (the auction) are presumably smaller (see note ?) than on the secondary market and therefore entry barriers will be affected to a lesser degree.

11. It should be noted that in Figure 3.3 the profit curves for accommodation, $\pi^i a$ and $\pi^i a'$, are not defined beyond the point at which $q^e < 0$. Beyond this point the incumbent enjoys a monopoly profit, curve π^i monopoly.

12. Apart from the rise in marginal costs due to the occurrence of transaction costs in the permit market, the marginal costs of both firms will also rise with the price of the permits and with pollution control costs. In order to focus on the strategic effect of the difference between the incumbent and the entrant with regard to transaction costs, the rise in the marginal costs due to the price of the permits will be ignored. When other instruments such as taxes are used, this rise in marginal costs will occur as well and the consequences for entry which result from this rise in marginal costs are therefore not unique to the system of tradable permits with transaction costs occurring in the permit market.

13. Uniqueness requires that the absolute value of the slope of the reaction curve is smaller than 1. Let r^j be the reaction function of firm j:

$$|r^j| = |\pi^j_{q^i q^j} \,/\, -\pi^j_{q^i q^i}| < 1 \Rightarrow |\pi^j_{q^i q^i}| > |\pi^j_{q^i q^j}|$$

$$\Rightarrow |R^j_{q^i q^i} - C^j_{q^i q^i}| > |R^j_{q^i q^j} - C^j_{q^i q^j}|$$

The absolute value of a change in marginal profit due to a change in its own quantity produced must exceed the change in its marginal profit when the quantity produced by the other firm changes, which is a plausible assumption.

14. $$(\Delta = (R^i_{q^i q^i} - C^i_{q^i q^i})(R^e_{q^e q^e} - C^e_{q^e q^e}) - R^e_{q^i q^e} R^i_{q^i q^e})$$

15. It is assumed here for the moment that abatement is less attractive than buying permits.

16. The reaction curve shifts leftward when marginal costs increase (for example, because of the transaction costs); see page 48. A simple model illustrates the leftward shift. Let the incumbent's profit be:

$$\pi^i = q^i(1 - q^i - q^e) - t\,q^i$$

Differentiating this profit function with respect to q^i yields the reaction function for the incumbent:

$$q^i = (1 - q^e - t)/2$$

Let t be initially zero (no transaction costs). For a given level of q^e, transaction costs will reduce the optimal quantity of q^i: a leftward shift of the reaction curve.

17. For the sake of clarity of the exposition, grandfathering is left out. Including it would not change the fundamental analysis and conclusions.

4. Entry Barriers and Tradable Permits: Imperfect Capital Markets and Exclusion

In the previous chapter three types of entry barriers were identified which might occur when a system of tradable permits is introduced. The consequences for entry of transaction costs on the permit market were discussed in the context of the limit-pricing model. In this chapter the two other types of entry barrier are investigated. In section 4.1 the consequences of imperfect capital markets and grandfathering for entry barriers are discussed. In section 4.2 exclusionary manipulation with tradable permits is examined. The practical consequences for the system of tradable carbon permits discussed in Chapter 2 are determined for both types of entry barrier.

4.1 TRADABLE PERMITS AND THE LONG PURSE THEORY

It was argued in the previous chapter that potential entrants are not necessarily put at a disadvantage by having to buy permits while established firms get them free. The incumbents have to take into account the opportunity costs of using their grandfathered permits and therefore they do not have a cost advantage over the entrants. However, in reality markets do not always work perfectly. In this section the focus is on the capital market. We shall consider whether the difference between incumbents and potential entrants with regard to grandfathering has consequences for the entry barriers when capital markets do not function perfectly. First, the long purse theory, which is based on imperfect capital markets, is discussed. Subsequently the theory is applied to tradable emission permits. Finally, we survey some empirical evidence on imperfect capital markets.

History of the Long Purse Theory

The analysis of the relationship between imperfect capital markets and entry

65

barriers is part of the literature on predatory pricing. Predatory pricing is a pricing strategy used by a firm (the predator) to force its rival (the prey) out of the market and/or to deter potential entrants. A general definition is:

> Predatory pricing behaviour involves a reduction of price in the short run so as to drive competing firms out of the market or to discourage entry of new firms in an effort to gain larger profits via higher prices in the long run than would have been earned if the price reduction had not occurred. (Tirole 1992, p. 373)

There are three types of predatory pricing: signalling predation; predation for reputation; and long purse predation (Ordover and Saloner 1989, p. 546). Signalling predation is used by predators when they possess information which the potential entrant does not have (asymmetric information), for example on the predator's costs or market demand. The price the predator sets provides the prey with information on the market conditions. Presumably, the predator wants to convey bad news to the potential entrant in order to discourage it from entering the industry. Setting a low price might indicate that demand is slack or that the predator has low costs and therefore that entering would not be profitable.

Firms predate for reputation when they not only want to drive out a firm which has just entered but also want to show by preying on the first entrant that they will fight all subsequent potential entrants. Fighting the first firm which enters has the added benefit (apart from driving it out) that other potential entrants will be deterred as well. This form of predation is also based on asymmetric information: the potential entrants do not know *a priori* whether the incumbent firm will want to fight or whether it will prefer to accommodate.

For our analysis in the following section the relevant variant of predatory pricing is the long purse theory; therefore we shall discuss its development in more detail. According to the long purse theory, predators which have larger financial resources than their prey will start a price war which in the end will financially exhaust their prey. Although the price war will initially diminish profits for the predator as well, predation will be attractive for the predator if the monopoly profits it expects to earn after the prey has left outweigh the price war losses. Because of its stronger financial position it can outlast the prey: when the prey goes bankrupt the incumbent is still solvent.

The long purse theory was initially quite popular. One of the earlier references is from Edwards (1955) who wrote:

> An enterprise that is big in this sense obtains from its bigness a special kind of power, based upon the fact that it can spend money in large amounts. If such a concern finds itself matching expenditures or losses, dollar for dollar, with a substantial larger firm, the length of its purse assures it of a victory.

Given that the (monopoly) profits the incumbent will enjoy after the prey has left the market outweigh the losses it has to sustain during the fight, predation will be an attractive strategy for the incumbent. It should be noted, however, that even if predation is profitable, it is not necessarily the most attractive strategy available to the predator (McGee 1958). For example, advertising or exclusionary manipulation are strategies that could have the same effect on the prey but which come at a lower cost.

Apart from McGee's observation, two other reservations have been voiced. One criticism, which was first made by Telser (1966) and subsequently by Benoit (1984), is that if long purse predation were to be really successful the potential entrant would not enter at all. Assuming complete information, the entrant can foresee that the incumbent will start a price war and that somewhere in the future the entrant will have to leave the market because it has run out of resources. Consequently it would prefer not to suffer the losses of the price war that is waged while it is in the market because it will not be able to recoup them. It can avoid these losses quite easily by staying out and using those initial resources on a more profitable enterprise. Given that long purse predation is an attractive strategy for the incumbent, the entrant will stay out and therefore long purse predation will not occur. The theory of the long purse is in this sense too successful because it predicts that long purse predation will never take place in practice. However, it demonstrates that 'having a long purse may provide a *credible threat* of post-entry predation and thus could deter entry' (Ordover and Saloner 1989, p. 548).

Benoit (1984) has shown that this criticism that long purse predation will never occur follows from the assumption that both firms have perfect information. This, however, is a strong assumption. Benoit assumed that, instead of possessing perfect information, the incumbent does not know whether the entrant is financially constrained or not. He showed that in that case it is possible for a firm to enter and subsequently to be driven out through long purse predation.

Another criticism of the long purse theory is that it is not clear why the potential entrant should be financially constrained. Evidently, if it had enough credit available it would stay in the market because eventually it would be able to make a profit (otherwise it would not enter at all). Therefore, it should be in the interest of the entrant's creditors to extend more credit to enable it to weather the price war. Presumably, there is no reason why firms should be financially constrained, and because the 'long purse story lacked theoretical foundations, it slowly fell from grace' (Tirole 1992, p. 377).

However, nowadays there is some justification for the theory. First of all there is evidence that in reality there may exist something like a financial constraint. This evidence stems from the study of the capital structure of enterprises. In order to explain how firms decide on the optimal levels of debt and equity, several theories have been formulated. One of these theories is the pecking order theory. Basically, this theory states that when firms need funds in order to finance new investments, they have a strong hierarchy of preferences for types of finance. They prefer to use internal finance as far as possible. If there are not enough internal funds available and they have to turn to external financing, they will first borrow, subsequently use convertible bonds or similar hybrid securities, and if none of these is possible they will issue equity (Myers 1984, p. 581). The aggregate figures seem to support this theory. Myers notes that in the decade of 1973–82, on average 62 per cent of the capital expenditures of nonfinancial corporations in the US were covered by internally generated cash. Of the external financing the largest part was debt; only 6 per cent of it was raised by issuing new stock. While this does not provide an explanation of the financial constraint in the long purse theory, it does indicate that financial constraints might exist.[1]

Other evidence for the existence of financial constraints is found in recent work on capital markets and asymmetric information. Gale and Hellwig (1985, p. 647) have studied the question: 'what is the firm's budget constraint?' More specifically, they wish to find out what the optimal debt contract is and whether credit rationing does appear. The model they study assumes that a firm has a project that yields a revenue which depends on the level of investment and the unknown state of the world. The firm does not have the necessary funds itself so it has to borrow money from an investor. At the time of investment, neither of them knows what the state of the world will be. When the investment matures, the returns will be known by the firm but the investor will not know them (this is asymmetric information). As long as the firm fulfils its contract and repays the debt, the investor has no reason to know how large the returns are. But if the firm does not repay its debt, the investor will have it declared bankrupt. In that case the worth of the firm is investigated and its scrap value is distributed among its creditors. The investor will have to bear the costs of bankruptcy. Gale and Hellwig conclude that the optimal contract for the investor who lends money is the standard debt contract. The firm pays a fixed interest on its debt; when it cannot pay the interest, the investor will investigate the state of the world; that is he will have the firm declared bankrupt. Another conclusion which Gale and Hellwig draw is that, under asymmetric information, credit is constrained compared with the first-best level of investment, that is the amount of money which would be supplied if there were no asymmetric information.

The last, and for our analysis the most important, point is that 'the lack of liquidity . . . lies at the root of the credit-rationing problem because, if the firm's net wealth were large enough to finance the first-best investment, the firm would obviously choose that level of investment' (Gale and Hellwig 1985, p. 648). If a firm's own capital suffices to finance an investment, it does not need to borrow and credit-rationing does not occur.

Fudenberg and Fudenberg (1985) have used the approach of Gale and Hellwig and they have shown how credit rationing might make it profitable for a predator to embark upon a price war against and drive its prey out of the market. In their two-period model, they assume that at the start of the second period the entrant firm has to invest a certain amount of capital if it wants to stay in the market. The sum which the entrant can borrow is limited by its own capital, as will be shown below. The own capital resources of the entrant are retained earnings from the first period. The incumbent can reduce these retained earnings by embarking on a price war which decreases the profits of both firms. The lower the retained earnings of the entrant, the larger is the additional capital which must be borrowed (at higher cost). Consequently, the chance that borrowing additional capital to invest is unattractive increases. Therefore it is more likely that the entrant will find it unprofitable to stay in the market.

This long purse theory is based on two assumptions: first, that there exists an asymmetry between the incumbent and the entrant because the latter must not invest if it wants to continue in the market while the former can stay in without investing;[2] second, external finance is limited (the financial constraint). We will look at the latter assumption and its consequences in more detail (the approach and notation is adopted from Tirole 1992, p. 378). In the following section the theory will be applied to investments in tradable permits.

Suppose a firm wishes to invest in a project which it needs to finance partly by borrowing. The gross profit (the total value of the firm after the project has finished) which the project will yield, π, falls within an interval $[\pi_L, \pi_H]$. The total investment is K, the amount of capital to be borrowed is D. As long as the profit made is larger than the debt and interest, the firm will not default on the loan and will repay the bank which has loaned the money. The firm earns a profit of $\pi - (1+r)D$. However, when the firm earns less than $(1+r)D$, it cannot repay the loan and will go bankrupt. Bankruptcy involves costs such as the cost of appointing receivers and probable losses when the firm's assets have to be sold. The firm retains nothing, the creditor receives $\pi - B$; B is the bankruptcy costs.

Let the random profit π be distributed with a density $f(\pi)$ on the interval $[\pi_L, \pi_H]$. The expected value of the profit if π is less then $(1+r)D$ is denoted π^d (defaulted). The probability that π is smaller than $(1+r)D$ is denoted $(1-F)$. The expected value of π if π is above $(1+r)D$ is denoted π^r (repaid), the probability that π is above $(1+r)D$ is F. The expected profit of the bank (the creditor), π_B, consists of the repayment of the loan and interest times the probability that the firms profit is above $(1+r)D$ and $\pi - B$ times the probability that its profit is below $(1+r)D$:

$$E(\pi_B) = (1+r)D \cdot F + (\pi^d - B)(1 - F) \tag{4.1}$$

If we assume that the capital market is competitive, the net profits of the bank (after deduction of its capital costs which are $r_0{}^3$) will be zero:

$$E(\pi_B) = (1+r_0)D \tag{4.2}$$

Equations (4.1) and (4.2) define an interest rate r which is larger than r_0 because the bank faces the risk of the firm defaulting on the debt.[4] We will assume that there exists a rate r at which the bank is willing to extend the loan. It is not necessarily profitable for the bank to extend a loan: the debt D might be too high with respect to the expected profits and the level of the bankruptcy costs. While a higher r might seem to compensate the bank for a higher default risk, it should be realized that a higher r also increases the probability of bankruptcy. The derivative of the bank's expected profit would in that case be a decrease in r.

The expected profit of the firm is equal to the profit it earns minus the repayment of the loan and interest times the probability of the profit being above $(1+r)D$ and the profit it gets when it has to default, which is zero. Its net expected profits $E(\pi_i)$ are equal to its gross profits minus the opportunity costs of the capital it has invested itself, $(1+r_0)(K - D)$:

$$E(\pi_i) = (\pi^r p - (1+r)D)F - (1+r_0)(K - D) \tag{4.3}$$

The firm's expected net profit, equation (4.3), can also be written as the total expected retained earnings from the project, denoted π^t, minus the opportunity costs of the firm's own capital, minus the expected bankruptcy costs (the bankruptcy costs times the probability that the firm goes bankrupt):[5]

$$E(\pi_i) = \pi^t - [B(1 - F)] - (1+r_0)(K) \tag{4.4}$$

When the firm has less own capital and therefore has to borrow more, its expected profits will decrease:

$$dE(\pi_i)/dD = - d[B \cdot (1 - F)]/dD < 0 \tag{4.5}$$

Equation (4.5) is negative because $(1 - F)$, the chance that the firm will go bankrupt, increases when the amount borrowed increases: the creditor will charge a higher rate of interest and the debt increases, therefore $(1+r)D$ increases and therefore the chance that the expected profits will at least equal $(1+r)D$ declines. An increase in the amount of capital the firm borrows increases the interest rate r the bank will charge and the probability that the firm will go bankrupt. Therefore, the chance that the project will yield a positive net profit for the firm decreases. In other words, the smaller the amount of own capital of the firm, the smaller is the probability that the project is worthwhile for the firm. Or, as has been noted above, the smaller the amount of own capital, the greater the probability that banks will not wish to extend a loan. Lack of (internal) funds can therefore restrict firms in the projects they undertake.

The foregoing analysis has consequences for entry barriers when there is a difference between incumbent firms and entrants in that entrants are more dependent on borrowed money than are incumbents. Consequently, the incumbent firm can engage the entrant in a price war and drive it out of the market; the entrant has smaller financial resources and therefore he cannot endure a price war as long as the incumbent can. Borrowing money does not help because the costs of lending money are higher for the entrant with its smaller resources than they would be for the incumbent.

In the following section this financial constraint theory will be adapted and applied to the problem of tradable emission permits. We shall show how the introduction of a system of tradable emission permits can create differences in access to internal and external (debt) finance, increasing the likelihood of predation and thereby raising entry barriers.

Predation and Grandfathering

We have shown that when firms are constrained in the amount of capital they can borrow their propensity to invest is smaller. Here, this theory is used in a simple game-theoretic model in order to illustrate how the introduction of tradable permits with grandfathering might make predatory pricing more attractive in order to drive entrants out (or to deter entry). The model used is an application to tradable permits of work done by Benoit (1984) and of the financial constraint theory of Fudenberg and Tirole (1985) described above (pp. 69–71).

Two different situations are discerned. As we described in Chapter 2, a tradable permit can be defined as one which gives a polluter the right to emit 1 ton of a certain pollutant. Each year, authorities can grandfather a number of permits to established firms. The entitlement to these future grandfathered permits can be termed a quota. Firms can sell (and buy) both quotas and permits. Buying a permit means that a firm acquires the right to emit 1 ton on one occasion. By buying a quota a firm buys the right to receive a number of free permits each year. Buying permits may therefore be looked upon as leasing a quota instead of buying it. In the first variant of the game considered below, the entrant firm leases quota in each period (it only buys the permits it needs for each period). In the second variant, the entrant buys a quota which provides it with all the permits it will need in the subsequent periods.

In addition to considering tradable permits, the potential for impeding entry under a system of TDPs with grandfathering will be compared with the effect that standards and emission charges have on entry barriers.

Leasing a quota

The game considered here is a repeated game. It consists of two firms, an incumbent (firm i) which initially has a monopoly, and a potential entrant (firm e). At the beginning of the first game, the entrant decides whether to enter or not. Subsequently, at each stage the incumbent first decides whether it will fight or accommodate the entrant. After this decision by the incumbent, the entrant decides whether to stay in or leave the industry. This game is a dynamic game with perfect and complete information.

A central assumption of the model is that at the beginning of each stage, including the first, both firms must invest (for example, in capital goods) in order to be able to produce and stay in the market. It is assumed that the investment can be undertaken after the firm has decided to stay (or leave). In order to be able to make these investments, the firm can either use retained earnings from the previous period of the game or borrow funds on the capital market. However, the capital market does not work perfectly; a firm is constrained in the amount it can borrow by its own wealth, as was described previously (pp. 69–71). Therefore, the lower the retained earnings of a firm in an earlier period, the higher is the proportion of capital for investment it must borrow in this period and the larger will be the probability that the investment (entry) will not be undertaken since expected net profits are negative or because creditors do not wish to extend a loan. Consequently, the firm is forced out of the market. At the end of each stage, firms which have borrowed money must repay their debt and the interest for that period out of their retained earnings (or go bankrupt).

Apart from investing in capital, firms also need a given quantity of emission permits in each period in order to be able to produce.[6] We will assume that the quantity of permits grandfathered has value G and that it covers exactly the permits needed for one period (this assumption can be made without loss of generality). Let K be the investment which both firms have to make at the beginning of each period, excluding the purchase costs of pollution permits. In addition they have to invest in the permits, therefore the total investment for both firms is $K + G$. It is assumed here that both firms, the incumbent and the entrant, are equal in all respects except with regard to emission permits. It is assumed that oif no permits were required both firms would start with the same amount of own capital, which by assumption is equal to K, the amount of investment needed to start in the market. The incumbent receives permits free (in all periods) and the entrant has to buy them. The free gift of the permits to the incumbent constitutes an increase in its own capital of G.[7]

As a result of these assumptions the entrant must borrow G at the start of the first period because it has to acquire permits worth G. The incumbent does not need to borrow any capital because it has been grandfathered the permits it needs. This means that the entrant will face higher costs than the incumbent because of the costs of borrowing money on the imperfectly working capital market. Its expenditure on permits plus interest costs exceeds the opportunity costs which the permits have for the incumbent.

The actions both players take determine the level of profits they will earn. Furthermore, it is assumed that the profits are also influenced by some random variable. One might, for example, think of this random variable as representing the level of economic growth, inflation or some other macro-economic variables which have an effect on demand in individual product markets. Consequently, the profits which firms can make, given the actions they take, are assumed to be random in an interval $[\pi_L, \pi_H]$ with density f. The different profits given in Table 4.1 should therefore be thought of as being the expected profits of the specific actions chosen, given the probability distribution f. For example, let the actions be to fight and to stay. The expected profit in the case of fight is π^F which is the expected profit based on a random profit in interval $[\pi^F_L, \pi^F_H]$ which has density f. The same reasoning applies to the other expected profits, π^A, $\pi^{F'}$ and π^M. It is assumed that all the various profits have the same density function f in their various intervals. In other words, the random variable which influences profits apart from the actions the players take is independent of the strategies chosen by the players.

Table 4.1 shows the pay-offs (in gross retained earnings) of the various actions both firms can take each period (the so-called extensive form of the game). The first profit between brackets is the profit which the incumbent will make, given the actions chosen by both firms, the second is the profit of the entrant.

Table 4.1 Pay-off matrix

		Incumbent	
		Fight	Accommodate
Entrant	Stay	(π^F, π^F)	(π^A, π^A)
	Leave	$(\pi^{F'}, 0)$	

When the incumbent chooses to fight and the entrant stays in the market, there will be a price war and both firms will earn π^F. We will assume that these (expected) earnings cover the investment in production capital (exclusive of the permits) that both firms must make in order to stay in the market in the next period: $\pi^F = K$. While these gross expected retained earnings are positive, the net expected profit in this price war is negative, both for the incumbent and for the entrant.[8]

When the entrant leaves, the expected profit of the incumbent is $\pi^{F'}$. In subsequent periods, when the entrant stays out of the market, the incumbent makes monopoly profits π^M. It is assumed that (for both firms):

$$\pi^M > \pi^A > \pi^{F'} > \pi^F \tag{4.6}$$

We will assume that when the incumbent firm has the choice between fighting and driving out the entrant in the first period and accommodating the entrant for ever, it will choose to fight. That is, the incumbent can make larger profits by fighting in one period and subsequently enjoying monopoly profits than by cooperating in this period and all following periods. Formally:

$$\pi^{F'} + \sum_{t=1}^{\infty} \frac{\pi^M}{(1+r_0)^t} > \sum_{t=0}^{\infty} \frac{\pi^A}{(1+r_0)^t} \tag{4.7}$$

The last assumption is that initially, at the start of the first period, the entrant would prefer to enter if it can be accommodated by the incumbent. The expected gross profits π^A are such that, given the amount of capital K and the amount of money it must borrow in order to buy permits with value G, its expected net profits are positive:

$$\pi^A - (1+r)G - (1+r_0)K > 0 \tag{4.8}$$

If this is not the case, the entrant would not find it attractive to enter and would stay out. Condition (4.8) states that the expected net benefits of entering are positive when the incumbent chooses to accommodate the entrant. The entrant's gross profits minus the repayment of its debt, which is equal to the value of the permits it has to buy, G, plus interest, are equal to or larger than the opportunity costs of its capital K.

Having described the game, we can proceed with the analysis of the equilibrium. Suppose the incumbent chooses to fight. The expected gross earnings are π^F for both firms. The expected net profit of the incumbent is:

$$\pi^F_i = \pi^F - (1+r_0)(K+G) \tag{4.9}$$

It was assumed that $\pi^F = K$, therefore the net expected profits of the incumbent are negative when both firms fight each other in the first period. They are negative because the firm does not earn enough to cover the opportunity costs of its investment $K + G$ (its total own capital: initial wealth plus the permits it received free). The expected net profit of the entrant after the first period is:

$$\pi^F_e = \pi^F - (1+r_0)(K+G) - B(1-F) \qquad (4.10)$$

(The reader is referred to pp. 69–71 for the derivation of the net profit of a firm which has to borrow on imperfect capital markets: equation (4.4).)

$(1 - F)$ is the chance that the gross expected profit π^F is smaller than $(1+r)G$, in which case the firm cannot repay its debt and goes bankrupt. B is the bankruptcy costs. The net expected profit of the entrant is lower than the net profit of the incumbent by $B(1 - F)$. The entrant has to borrow money on the (imperfect) capital market to buy permits and therefore incurs extra costs compared with those of the incumbent.

More important than net profits are the cash flows of the firms because these have consequences for the next stage. As has been described above, in order to be able to produce each firm has to invest before the start of each period (to be able to produce in that period). This investment consists of the capital investment, K, and the permits needed for production, G. The incumbent receives permits by grandfathering. Its retained earnings, which (in the case of fight) are equal to its gross profit π^F, are K. Therefore it can invest capital K in production without having to borrow money. It receives the permits needed in the next period free.

The entrant firm, however, is in a different situation. From its retained earnings, π^F, it has first to pay off its debt to the bank. This debt is $(1+r)G$, therefore it has left only $K - (1+r)G$. The capital needed for its investment in order to have production capacity for the next period consists of the investment capital K and the permits needed in the next period which have value G. Consequently, it must borrow again:

$$K + G - [K - (1+r)G] = (1+1+r)G \qquad (4.11)$$

The amount the entrant has to borrow rises with $(1+r)G$ as compared with the amount it borrowed at the start of the first period.

As the game continues, the entrant will have to borrow more and more as long as the incumbent plays 'Fight'.[9] Eventually, a point is reached at which either the project is no longer attractive any more to the entrant, because its net expected profits when accommodated fall below zero or because the bank no longer wishes to provide a loan (see p. 70). At this point (which we will call period N), the entrant will therefore play 'Leave' and exit the market.

The strategy of fighting is therefore an attractive strategy for the incumbent in period N because it will drive out the entrant and he can subsequently enjoy monopoly profits.

In period $N - 1$, fighting will also be attractive for the incumbent. If the entrant chooses to stay in the market, the next period game would be a stage game in which he would have to leave. However, choosing strategy 'Leave' in period $N - 1$ would save it the costs of fighting the price war in this period and therefore it would be optimal to leave already in $N - 1$. Proceeding by backward induction, as Benoit (1984) has shown, in each foregoing period it would be optimal for the entrant to leave, and therefore it would not be optimal to enter in the first period at all. In the subgame perfect Nash equilibrium of this entry–exit game with tradable emission permits the incumbent would choose 'Fight' in the first period and the entrant would not enter at all. The incumbent subsequently enjoys monopoly profits (which it preferred over accommodating the entrant: see the assumption in equation (4.7)).

In order to be able to draw conclusions about the consequences for entry into industries of introducing a system of grandfathered tradable emission permits, the situation described above must be compared with the situation in which no grandfathered tradable emission permits are introduced. In that case, neither firm needs to have emission permits, or both would have to buy all their permits (with auction); therefore, the necessary investment is confined to the capital investment K, respectively $K+G$ (with auctioning). In the first case (when neither firm has to buy permits) if the incumbent would choose to play 'Fight', both firms would have just enough retained earnings, $\pi^F = K$, to invest again. The entrant would never be restricted by the amount of capital it has to borrow and therefore would be able to endure the price war indefinitely in this situation. Because the incumbent cannot drive out the entrant, it will prefer to accommodate it: the pay-off from accommodating is higher than the pay-off from fighting indefinitely. The entrant will not be deterred when the incumbent chooses to fight: the threat to fight indefinitely is non-credible because accommodating is more attractive. The perfect equilibrium in this case is to accommodate entry for the incumbent and to enter for the entrant.

In the second case (when both firms have to buy permits), playing 'Fight' is not attractive for the incumbent either. Both firms would retain earnings $\pi^F = K$ minus their debt $(1+r)G$. Consequently, both firms would have to borrow more in order to invest for the next period. The incumbent does not have an advantage over the entrant and therefore cannot outlive a price war with it. Playing 'Accommodate' is therefore more attractive.

Consequently, it follows that the implementation of the TDP scheme with grandfathering and especially the different treatment of existing firms and newcomers raises entry barriers. Because of the imperfect capital market, the incumbent can force out the entrant by conducting a price war. This price war makes it progressively less easy for the entrant to raise the money needed to make the necessary investments to stay in the market. Finally, it is no longer attractive for it to stay in, and therefore it will leave. Looking forward, both firms can predict this outcome and therefore the entrant will decide not to enter at all.

Buying a quota

In the game discussed above, the entrant firm buys permits every period ('leases a quota'). Another possibility is that right at the start of the first period it buys a quota. Subsequently, it does not have to buy any more permits in the following periods. How would this affect the entry–exit game discussed above? First, the price of a quota must be determined. The price of a quota can be deduced from the price at which the rights are sold (or at which quota is leased). Because a quota is a right to receive a permit free every period, its current value is the sum of the discounted value it will have in the future:

$$value\ quota = \sum_{t=0}^{\infty} \frac{1}{(1+r_0)^t} G = \frac{1}{r_0} G \qquad (4.12)$$

where r_0 is the discount rate (the minimum lending rate) and G remains the value of the permits needed each period. If the entrant wants to buy a quota and enter the market at the beginning of the first period, it will have to invest the total sum of $K + 1/r_0 G$. Assuming that the initial capital of the entrant is K (as in the first variant of the game), this means that the firm will have to borrow more than in the variant presented above: $1/r_0 G$ instead of G. This will have consequences for its expected profits. As is stated in equation (4.8), it is a necessary condition that the expected profits of the entrant when it is accommodated (profits are π^A) are positive because otherwise it would not enter at all. This condition also holds when the entrant has bought a quota instead of the quantity of permits needed for one period. It will make the necessary investments as long as its net profit in the first and each subsequent period is positive. In this variant it must repay a larger loan at the end of the first period: not G but $1/r_0 G$.[10,11]

In addition, the interest on the loan will also be higher compared with the interest paid when a quota is leased. The amount borrowed is higher, therefore the risk of default is higher. Consequently, the bank will charge a higher interest rate (see p. 70 for proof of this proposition).

Because of the higher debt and next to that the higher interest rate, the expected profit of the entrant will be lower. The probability that entering is not profitable at all is therefore greater when the entrant buys a quota with borrowed money than when it leases a quota every period.

Assume for the moment that the net expected profit of the entrant firm is positive, therefore it prefers to enter the market if it is accommodated by the incumbent. What are the pay-offs if the incumbent chooses to fight? Again, both firms would make a gross expected profit of π^F if the incumbent chooses to stay in the industry. As has been described above, this leaves the incumbent with exactly enough capital to reinvest K and to continue in the industry.

The situation which the entrant faces is different from the variant in which it only leased a quota. Because it has acquired a quota, it does not need to buy any more permits: just like the incumbent, it 'receives' them free each in period. Consequently, it only needs to invest K instead of $K + G$ in all periods, starting at period 2. Its gross profits from the first period are $\pi^F = K$, its net retained earnings are $K - (1+r'/r_0)G$: the gross profits minus the amount borrowed plus interest on its debt (the interest is denoted r' to distinguish it from the interest which the entrant has to pay when it leases a quota). Therefore, it has to borrow $(1+r')/r_0 G$ in order to be able to stay in the market. If the incumbent continues to play 'fight' in all subsequent periods, the amount which the entrant needs to borrow will rise: at the beginning of period t, it has to borrow $(1+r')^t G/r_0$. Eventually, either it will be unable to borrow the capital it needs or reinvesting will no longer be attractive because net expected profit becomes negative.

Following the same argument as in the lease variant of the game discussed earlier, the perfect equilibrium is for the incumbent to play 'fight' if the entrant enters and for the entrant not to enter at all. In both variants, the fact that the entrant needs to borrow on an imperfect capital market makes it possible for the incumbent to drive the entrant out if he tries to enter the market at all. It should be noted that the entry barrier is no higher with buying than with leasing, even though the expected profit of the entrant is lower. In both cases, the entrant decides not to enter at all and the incumbent enjoys monopoly profits.

Three remarks can be made about this analysis. First, the debt contract specified above may not be the optimal debt contract. Second, the assumption about the amounts of capital owned by both firms at the start of the first period may be changed. Third, according to this game, entry does not occur and therefore long purse predation does not either. These three points are now dealt with in greater detail.

Debt contracts
The debt contract specified above assumed that the entrant had to repay its debt at the end of the first period. However, this is a strict condition. It is

more plausible to assume that the entrant will repay the loan over a longer period. An extreme form of such a debt contract is a credit facility, which allows a borrower to have an overdraft up to a certain limit. With such a debt contract, there is no need to repay the debt as long as the interest is paid in each period. If such a debt contract were available to the entrant, what would the consequences be for the outcome of the entry–exit game? At the start of the first period, it would borrow the amount needed to buy a quota: $1/r_0 G$. Assuming that the incumbent plays 'Fight' and that the entrant stays in the market, both firms will earn $\pi^F = K$. The entrant does not need to pay back his loan, nor does he have to buy permits in the second and subsequent periods. However, he does have to pay the interest, $r'/r_0 G$. Therefore, he has to borrow $r'/r_0 G$ if it wants to continue in the market. Assume that the extra borrowing falls within the entrant's credit facility limit and that it only has to pay the interest on this lending. After the second period, the interest which has to be paid is $r(1+r)/r_0 G$. If the incumbent continues to play 'Fight,' the interest which has to be paid by the entrant will continue to rise and in the end it must to exit the market. A lenient debt contract which takes the form of a credit facility where the sum borrowed need not be paid back does not change the outcome of the game. Fighting remains attractive for the incumbent and therefore the entrant will stay out.

Another point which concerns the form of the debt contract has been raised by Fudenberg and Tirole (1985, 1986). Suppose that the bank and the entrant sign a long-term contract under which the bank guarantees that the entrant will always be able to borrow money. In that case, there would be no incentive for the incumbent to prey upon the entrant because it cannot drive the entrant out. However, the problem with such a debt contract is that the promise of guaranteed finance is a non-credible promise. If the incumbent chooses to play 'Fight' in the first and all subsequent periods, the entrant would need to borrow more and more, as has been described above. When the point is reached where the expected net profit of the entrant is negative, it would be more profitable for the entrant and the bank to change the debt contract and to leave the market. As there is nothing to stop them from renegotiating the contract, the 'threat' of the long-term debt contract to stay in the market indefinitely is not credible, and therefore it still pays the incumbent to play 'Fight'.

Capital holdings
One of the assumptions made in the game described here is that both firms start with initial capital, K, which exactly covers their capital investment. If there were no emission reduction policy, and therefore no grandfathered tradable emission permit scheme was introduced, both firms would start equal and entry deterrence would not be possible (see p. 76). When a TDP scheme

with grandfathering is implemented, the entrant has to borrow in order to buy emission permits and therefore the incumbent can drive it out of the market.

However, the case is different if the entrant has enough capital itself to make the necessary investment in both capital and a quota of emission permits: $K + 1/r_0 G$ instead of K. In that case, it would not have to pay interest and therefore could endure a price war in which gross profits are K indefinitely. Essentially, the entrant's position in all subsequent games would be the same as the position of the incumbent. Playing 'Fight' would then be ineffective for the incumbent because the entrant would not need recourse to borrowing money.

While this argument might seem to weaken the case of entry deterrence as a result of the TDP scheme, it should be realized that in this situation an asymmetry is introduced between the incumbent and the entrant with regard to their initial capital resources. The entrant starts with $K + 1/r_0 G$ own capital while the incumbent starts only with K (in addition to which it receives TDPs worth $1/r_0 G$). Instead, it should be assumed that, if the entrant owns $K + 1/r_0 G$, the incumbent owns the same amount of money. With these assumptions, the entry–exit game studied here would still yield the conclusion that the incumbent would not be able to prevent entry. However, the game could be easily modified to allow the incumbent to impede entry effectively. If we assume that the price war results in a profit of π^f instead of π^F, with $\pi^f < \pi^F$, then both firms will have to borrow if they want to stay in the market. However, the entrant has smaller reserves than the incumbent and therefore it will be forced out, while the incumbent can still borrow.[12]

The consequences of incomplete information

The point has been raised that the deep pocket theory is too successful because under complete information the entrant would never enter (see p. 67). The same criticism applies to the game of perfect and complete information described above. Analogous to Benoit (1984), the game could be changed to allow for incomplete information. More specifically, it could be assumed that the incumbent is not sure whether the entrant firm already owns a quota (for example, because it had formerly been operating in an industry which also emitted the same type of pollution) or whether it does not have it yet. It could be shown that in that case a situation might arise in which an entrant with no permits could still enter and might or might not be driven out by the incumbent.[13]

Welfare consequences

The analysis of the welfare consequences of the conclusions of the game presented here is relatively simple. The incumbent will enjoy monopoly profits because the potential newcomer will stay out of the market. If the incumbent were unable to keep the entrant out, profits would lower. Their level depends on the form accommodation takes: the two firms might collude, in which case they would together produce the monopoly level,[14] or they might compete (either on quantity or on price). As compared with the latter case, welfare will be lower under the TCP scheme because the incumbent, being a monopolist, will produce the monopoly output. Consequently, there will be a deadweight loss as compared with the fully competitive case. When the two firms compete, they will produce at least the Cournot oligopoly quantity or even the full competitive quantity (Bertrand competition) with a corresponding smaller welfare loss.

Comparison with standards and taxes

The analysis presented so far has focused on the difference between implementing a TDP reduction policy with grandfathering and having no emission reduction policy at all. The conclusion was that such a type of policy would, under certain conditions, raise entry barriers. An important question is how entry barriers would be affected if other types of policy were implemented. Three other instruments will be analysed: standards, emission charges and auctioned tradable emission permits.

When standards are used, both the entrant and the incumbent have to meet them (assuming that the same standards apply both to established firms and to newcomers, which is not necessarily the case). Therefore there is no difference between the two firms. Fighting a price war does not limit the entrant in its ability to endure the price war and therefore it is not successful. The incumbent will therefore accommodate the entrant.

With emission charges, both firms will have to pay the charge on their remaining emissions. Because both firms are assumed to be equal in all respects, including their abatement cost functions, they have to pay the same amount of tax. If the tax level is equal to the price of the permits (which would be the case if the same emission reduction were achieved as with the permit scheme), the revenue they have to pay is equal to G, the value of the permits. If the incumbent chooses to play 'Fight', both firms would earn a gross profit of $\pi^F = K$. However, they would have to pay the tax, so their net retained earnings are $K - G$. Consequently, both firms have to borrow G if they want to continue in the market in the next period. If the incumbent again plays 'Fight' and the entrant stays, their net retained earnings are $K - (1+r)G$ and they will need to borrow $(1+r)G$. Eventually, playing 'Fight' will mean that neither firm can profitably reinvest at the start of the next period. In that case, the incumbent will prefer to play 'Accommodate'. Proceeding by backward induction, it follows that the optimal strategy for the incumbent is to accommodate the entrant right at the start of the first period. The entrant's optimal strategy is to enter. When emission reductions are pursued by means of emission charges, entry barriers are not raised.

This analysis and its conclusion also applies to the case in which all firms, both established and entrants, have to buy permits under a TDP scheme. The financial consequences for all firms of such a TDP scheme with auctioning of all permits are similar to a tax, therefore again entry barriers will not be raised either.

Conclusions

We have shown by means of a repeated game with complete and perfect information that the introduction of a system of TDPs can make entry unprofitable for new firms when, *ceteris paribus*, the incumbent firm receives permits free (through grandfathering) while the entrant has to buy them. The fundamental reason for this is that because of its larger financial resources the incumbent firm can start a price war which will eventually drive out the entrant (the deep purse theory). Because of the free gift of the permits, the incumbent can finance its losses internally at lower costs than the entrant, which has to borrow money on the capital market that is assumed to work imperfectly. A sufficient condition for the incumbent is that it can make higher profits by fighting in just one period and enjoying monopoly profits in the other periods than by accommodating the entrant.

Because the incumbent does not have to compete with others, the total output produced will be the monopoly output. As compared with a situation in which the incumbent competes with another firm, the quantity produced will be less (as long as the incumbent and the entrant do not collude when they are both active in the market) and welfare will be lower.

The conclusion that entry can be impeded when emissions are reduced by means of TDPs is specific to the instrument of grandfathered TDPs. The incumbent does not have a first-mover advantage when standards or taxes are used and therefore these instruments do not raise entry barriers.

What does this conclusion tell us about the practical consequences of introducing tradable emission permits in an economy? Obviously, the model presented here is quite theoretical in nature. It assumes that initially the incumbent has a monopoly and that both firms are equal in all respects except with regard to the way they are treated under the TCP scheme. Furthermore, a central assumption is that firms are limited in external financing by their initial capital endowment. These restrictions make it difficult to apply the conclusion directly to a more mundane setting. However, if there is a grain of empirical truth in the conclusions yielded by this game, grandfathered TDPs might reduce the competition of newcomers and therefore the dynamics in certain sectors of industry.

The logical next step is to take a closer look at the empirical evidence. Unfortunately, there is no empirical evidence on this model, and general, empirical evidence on game-theoretic models in industrial organization is scarce and difficult to get. However, there is a growing body of research which, although not based directly on the game-theoretic models, does investigate the empirical data on entry and exit. In the next section, this research is studied and applied to TDPs.

Empirical Evidence on Capital Requirements as an Entry Barrier

In the previous sections, the long purse theory has been analysed and applied to tradable emission permits. Now we shall discuss the empirical evidence for the theory that capital requirements can be an entry barrier. Given the findings of this analysis, we shall evaluate to what extent a system of tradable carbon permits with grandfathering might raise entry barriers.

Most recent empirical studies of the determinants of entry have used the model developed by Orr (1974) in his study of entry to the Canadian manufacturing industries. In this study, Orr has investigated various entry barriers in a cross-section of 71 Canadian three-digit industries[15] for five consecutive years (1963–67). In his model, he assumed that there is a certain price–cost margin below which no entry is induced. When the price–cost margin rises above this level, entrants will enter an industry. In the absence of entry barriers, this limiting price–cost margin is assumed to be equal across industries. However, entry barriers will differ between industries and therefore the limiting price–cost margin will differ as well. The model used to estimate the relative importance of the various entry barriers postulates that entry is a positive function of the difference between the actual profit rate which an industry enjoys and the long-run profit rate which can be predicted for an industry given the level of entry barriers. Moreover, entry will also be a positive function of the growth rate of the industry because a growing industry will induce additional entry. The model is (Orr 1974, p. 59):

$$E = f_1(\pi_p - \pi^*, \dot{z}) \tag{4.13}$$

$$\pi^* = f_2(\mathbf{X}) \tag{4.14}$$

where:

E = entry: number of entrants per year
π_p = past industry profit rate
π^* = long-run profit given the level of entry barriers in the industry
X = vector of entry barriers
$\dot{z}$ = past industry rate of growth output

The vector of entry barriers Orr used consisted of:

- the market share of the minimally effective size (MES) plant;
- capital requirements (CR);
- advertising intensity;
- research and development intensity;
- risk;
- concentration within the industry.

Here, our interest is in the second barrier, capital requirements. As is stated by von der Fehr (1991, p. 95):

> The hypothesis is that, with imperfect financial markets, average financial costs will increase with the amount needed to enter an industry. . . . If capital costs differ between entrants and incumbents, capital requirements act as a barrier to entry.

If the variable used for capital requirements is significant it indicates that CR acts as an entry barrier and that capital markets might work imperfectly and capital costs differ between entrants and incumbents. It might be seen as an empirical validation of the long purse theory. It should be noted that CR differs from the entry barrier which might be created by economies of scale. In the Orr model, the MES plant is used as a proxy for economies-of-scale type entry barriers.

The measure of CR used by Orr is the costs of fixed capital necessary for establishing a plant of minimally effective size. He calculated this by multiplying total industry fixed assets by the percentage of sales of a MES plant. The size of the smallest plant which still makes a profit was assumed to be an approximation of MES. In the final form of equation (4.15) which Orr has used for his estimations, he used the log value of both E and CR. Consequently, it was estimated whether there was a correlation between the variables in percentage terms, not in absolute values. In the wake of Orr, other empirical studies have been done to determine the significance of various forms of entry barriers. In Geroski and Schwalbach (1991) a number of recent empirical studies are collected, several of which use Orr-type models. Those studies which include CR in their entry barriers cover Portugal, Norway, Belgium and Korea. A study of the US which also includes CR uses a closely related model. Although the studies use the same type of model, their precise formulation, the definitions and measurements of the variables used and the time period covered differ. Table 4.2 presents the different approximations used for CR, the time period covered and the significance level of CR as a determinant of entry. With the exception of Belgium, in all the studies presented above CR, either as capital-to-output ratio or as the capital necessary for a MES plant, came out as a significant determinant of entry. The empirical evidence available therefore appears to confirm that capital requirements can act as an entry barrier.

Table 4.2: The significance of capital requirements (CR) as an entry barrier

Study	Time period	CR	Significance (%)
Canada (Orr 1974)	1963–67	Fixed capital for MES plant	1
Portugal (Mata 1991)	1979–82	Total capital for MES plant	1[a]
Norway (v/d Fehr 1991)	Not indicated	Fire insurance value MES plant	1
Belgium (Sleuwaegen and Dehandschutter 1991)	1980–84	Capital-to-output ratio	ns[b]
Korea (Jeong and Masson 1991)	1977–81	Capital for MES plant	5[c]
US (Dunne and Roberts 1991)	1963–82	Capital-to-output ratio	1

Notes

[a] In this study, a distinction was made between small and large entrants. For large-scale entrants, CR was not significant.

[b] Not significant. The model also included capital outlays on equipment and machinery as a percentage of total sales times MES. This variable was significant at the 1 per cent level.

[c] Significant at the 5 per cent level when tested for two different periods: 1977–8 and 1979–81. The first period was a period of economic expansion, the second one of contraction. When tested over the full period, CR was not significant.

What are the consequences for tradable emission permits? It should be noted that in the studies mentioned above the capital requirements were determined on the basis of a measure of fixed capital. Variable costs are not included in the capital requirements necessary for entering a market. The idea behind this is that the costs which an entrant has to incur when it wishes to enter a market, the entry costs, are its fixed costs for the first period. The division between fixed and variable costs depends on the time period considered; in the long run, there are no fixed costs because in the long run no costs have to be borne, regardless of whether a firm produces or not. In contrast, in the short run some costs are unavoidable. How should the costs of tradable emission permits be considered in this respect? When tradable emission permits (as defined in Chapter 2) can be bought at any time and in any quantity, their costs are variable costs; firms need only buy their permits when they need them. However, when there is no day-market in permits, they will have to buy them in advance and consequently they need to invest in permits when they enter the market. To what extent firms will want to invest in permits before they enter a market will depend on the organization of the permit market. The more frequently markets take place, the more frequently firms can acquire permits. Consequently the number of permits that firms need when they start production will be less when markets take place more frequently.[16] Presumably, trade in permits will take place both at regularly organized markets and through brokers. In the US acid rain tradable permit scheme, there is a yearly auction of permits and there is a secondary market which functions to a large extent through brokers (Klaassen and Nentjes 1995).

Another factor which might influence the number of permits which a firm needs initially is the life span of its investments. For example, a power-generating company building a new plant might want to assure itself of a supply of permits to cover its CO_2 emissions in the period during which its plant is economically viable. Power-generating equipment can last for up to 20 or 30 years; such a firm might therefore want to acquire permits to cover emissions for 30 years.

We will take a permit supply which covers emissions for one year as the lower limit to the number of permits which firms will buy when they enter the market.

The extent to which entry barriers might be raised will depend on the increase in capital requirements when entrants have to buy permits. Presumably, there will be differences between different sectors of industry. Table 4.3 provides an overview of different sectors in the Dutch economy. Unfortunately, the data required were only available at the two-digit level. Consequently, the data can only very roughly indicate in which sector a tradable emission permit scheme might increase capital requirements for new firms. A considerable disadvantage of these aggregated data is that it is not possible to focus on specific markets. Moreover, the average capital requirements are only a very rough indication because within a sector plant sizes will differ considerably, depending on the specific market concerned.

Column 2 of Table 4.3 gives the CO_2 emissions of each sector in 1990; column 3 gives the number of firms per sector; and column 4 gives the value

Table 4.3 Increase in CR with TCPs, Dutch economy

1	2	3	4	5	6	7
Sector	CO_2 emissions 1990 (1,000 ton)	Number of firms 1990	Capital goods stock (CGS) 1 Jan. 1991 (mln f)	Average CGS (mln f)	1 year expenditure with permit price of 20 ECU[a]/ton CO_2 (mln f)	%
Mineral extraction	1,406	-	45,631	-	58	0.13
Petroleum industry	9,219	24	22,641	943	382	1.69
Food and beverages	4,010	875	58,006	66	166	0.29
Textiles	273	217	6,710	31	11	0.17
Paper	1,551	146	12,382	85	64	0.52
Chemicals	13,385	263	70,066	266	554	0.79
Building materials	2,006	299	15,149	51	83	0.55
Base metal	4,001	52	24,395	469	166	0.68
Other metal	1,219	2,500	76,534	31	50	0.07
Other industry	513	1,778	44,661	25	21	0.05
Total	37,583	6,154			1,556	0.41

Note: [a] 20 ECU/ton CO_2 is the tax which according to Barrett (1991, p. 14) would be needed to stabilize CO_2 emissions in the EU in 2010 at the 1989 level (1 ECU = $f2.07$).

Sources: CBS (1990,1991,1992)

of the capital stock at 1 January 1991 in 1991 prices. Dividing column 4 by column 3 yields the average capital stock per firm (column 5). The petroleum industry has the highest average CR, followed by base metal and chemicals. In order to assess the impact of a TCP scheme on the CR, a permit price is required. It is assumed here that this is 20 ECU. This is the price calculated by Barrett (1991) which is needed to stabilize CO_2 emissions in the EU in 2010 at the 1988 level. This price is used to calculate the expenditure that each sector would have to make on permits for one year's CO_2 emissions (column 6).[17] Dividing this expenditure by the total CR gives the percentage increase in capital requirements for each sector. This is the average increase in capital which new firms have to face when they enter the market. On average, the CR increase is small, only 0.41 per cent. The sectors with the highest percentage increase are, in descending order, the petroleum industry

(1.69 per cent), chemicals (0.79 per cent) and base metal (0.68 per cent), all three sectors with a high energy use. These are also the sectors with high average capital requirements. The sectors where the CR increase is largest, and therefore where a system with grandfathered tradable permits might erect an entry barrier, are those where presumably the entry barrier caused by CR is already high.

The overview presented here of the empirical consequences of CR for entry indicate that in practice CR does limit entry; this can be viewed as a confirmation of the long purse theory. Introducing a system of TCP will increase the CR for new firms (as long as the permits are grandfathered to established firms) and therefore can reduce entry. However, the extent to which entry will be reduced appears to be small. In our calculations it was assumed that firms acquire permits to cover the emissions of one year. Entry will be further impeded if firms start with more permits. The sectors most affected are the energy-intensive industries because their CO_2 emissions are relatively large and therefore the CR of acquiring sufficient permits is large as well. The average CR in these sectors is high to start with; therefore it might be expected that the entry barrier due to the CR would already be high before the introduction of the permit scheme.

4.2 TDPs AND EXCLUSION

Absolute cost advantages are one type of entry barrier described by Bain (1965). There are numerous ways in which established firms can raise the costs of (potential) rivals. Indeed, firms have been rather inventive in finding ways to increase their rivals' costs. Cost-raising strategies include:

> exclusive dealing arrangements, inducing input suppliers to discriminate against rivals, lobbying legislatures or regulatory agencies to create regulations that disadvantage rivals, commencing R&D and advertising wars, and adopting incompatible technologies. (Salop and Scheffman 1987)

A famous example of the first type is the Alcoa case. Alcoa, the major aluminium producer in the US post-World War II is reported to have concluded agreements with power companies not to provide electricity to its potential rivals (Krattenmaker and Salop 1986a, p. 227). As electricity is an important input for aluminium production, rivals were put at a considerable disadvantage and therefore competition was reduced. Another example, from the European Community, is the case of the Commission of the European Community against Instituto Chemioterapico Italiano (ICI; Case 6-7/93 1974). ICI is a firm which is owned by the US firm Commercial Solvents

Corporation (CSC). CSC is a major world producer of aminobutanol, a semi-manufacture for some types of medicines. ICI is both a producer of these medicines itself and a resaler of the semi-manufacture to other firms in the Common Market. In 1970, CSC and ICI decided to stop the resale of aminobutanol to other firms. One of those firms was Zoja, also a producer of medicines based on aminobutanol. It discovered that, because the sale of aminobutanol by ICI was stopped, acquiring the semi-manufacture on the world market was impossible because the only producer appeared to be CSC, which refused to sell. In this way, CSC and ICI excluded other producers of the medicines from obtaining a necessary input. Consequently, when Zoja brought the case to the court, ICI and CSC were obliged to resume supplying Zoja with aminobutanol (Decision of the Court, 6 March 1974).

In both cases, the established firm in some way controlled an important input and used its power to foreclose the product market. Competition was completely excluded, which is an extreme position. Instead of effectively deterring entry, incumbents can use their market power on an input market to reduce competition from (potential) rivals.

Tradable emission permits are also an input. Therefore, firms which have power in the market for emission permits can in theory use it to reduce competition. If an established firm could reduce the supply of permits sufficiently to drive up their price, rival firms' costs would be increased. They would either have to abate more or buy the permits at their higher price. This would reduce competition from rival firms and potential entrants. However, driving up the permit price also increases costs for the incumbent firm.

Cost-raising strategies have been studied extensively by Salop in conjunction with Scheffman and Krattenmaker (Salop and Scheffman 1983, 1987; Krattenmaker and Salop 1986a and 1986b). Subsequently, Misiolek and Elder (1989) have used the Salop–Scheffman model and applied it to tradable emission permits. Here, the Salop–Scheffman–Misiolek–Elder (SSME) model is reproduced to determine under what conditions TDP lends itself to exclusion. Subsequently, we analyse whether the TCP system described in Chapter 2 is susceptible to exclusionary manipulation.

The Model

In the standard SSME model, there is an established firm which can be either a price-taker or a dominant firm which has control over the price of its products.[18] Furthermore, there is a competitive fringe. Here, it will be assumed that there is an incumbent firm which faces potential competition from a rival entrant. Initially, when there is no potential rival, the incumbent maximizes:

$$\pi^i = p\,q^i - C^i(q^i, L) \text{ subject to } q^i = D(p) \tag{4.15}$$

$$q_P^i < 0, \; C_{q^i}^i > 0, \; C_L^i \text{ is convex}$$

where:

p = product price
q^i = quantity produced by the incumbent
C^i = incumbent's costs (including abatement and permit costs)
$D(p)$ = market demand for the product
L = tradable emission permits acquired by the incumbent

From the market equilibrium condition the inverse demand function $p(q^i)$ can be derived. The first-order conditions are:

$$\pi_P^i = q^i + pq_P^i - C_{q^i}^i q_P^i = 0 \tag{4.16}$$

$$\pi_L^i = C_L^i = 0 \tag{4.17}$$

Equation (4.16) gives the usual monopoly profit-maximization condition: marginal revenue equals marginal costs. Equation (4.17) determines the optimal amount of permits: given the amount of q^i produced, the number of permits L is chosen such that the sum of the abatement costs plus permit costs are minimized. The monopoly quantity produced in this non-strategic equilibrium is denoted q^{i*}, the number of permits used is denoted $\bar{L}$.

When there is a potential entrant, the market conditions for the incumbent change. Instead of total market demand, he now faces a residual demand curve. The maximization problem becomes:

$$\max_{(p, q^i, L)} \pi^i = pq^i - C^i(q^i, L) \text{ s.t. } q^i = D(p) - q^e(p, P_p) \quad P_p > 0$$
$$P_p = P_p(L)$$

$$\tag{4.18}$$

where:
q^e = quantity produced by the entrant
P_p = permit price

The permit price P_p depends on the quantity of the permits acquired by the incumbent, reflecting the market power it is assumed to have on the permit market. The entrant is a price-taker on the market both for outputs and inputs, including permits. The quantity which the entrant produces is determined by maximizing its profit function:

$$\max_{(q^e)} \pi^e = pq^e - C^e(q^e, P_p) \quad s.t. \quad \pi^e > 0 \quad C_{q^e}^e, C_{P_p}^e > 0 \quad (4.19)$$

An increase in the product price will increase the quantity produced by the entrant, an increase in the price of the permits P_p will increase its marginal costs and therefore it will reduce its production: $q_p^e > 0$, $q_{P_p}^e < 0$.

Optimizing (4.19) yields the following first-order conditions (for an interior solution):

$$\pi_p^i = q^i + pq_p^i - C_{q^i}^i q_p^i = 0 \quad \Rightarrow p - C_{q^i}^i = -q^i/q_p^i \quad (4.20)$$

$$\pi_L^i = pq_{P_p}^i P_{PL} - C_{q^i}^i q_{P_p}^i P_{PL} - C_L^i = 0 \quad \Rightarrow p - C_{q^i}^i = C_L^i/(P_{PL} q_{P_p}^i) \quad (4.21)$$

Using $q_p^i = D_p - q_p^e$ and $q_L^i = - q_{P_p}^e P_{PL}$, equations (4.20) and (4.21) can be rewritten as:

$$\frac{q_L^i}{D_p - q_p^e} = \frac{C_L^i}{q^i} \quad (4.22)$$

The evaluation of equation (4.22) is straightforward (see Salop and Scheffman 1987, p. 22; Misiolek and Elder 1989, p. 161). The left-hand side of the equation is equal to $\partial p/\partial L \big|_{qi}$, that is the rise in the product price which results from the reduction in output of the entrant as a result of price-rise of the permits following an increase in L, holding q^i constant.[19] Or, as Salop and Scheffman (1987 p.22) stated, this derivative represents 'the vertical shift in the residual demand curve' of the incumbent. The right-hand side of equation (4.22) equals the change in its average costs, with output q^i remaining fixed, resulting from an increase in L.

Instead of an interior solution, there is the possibility of a corner solution. A necessary condition for the entrant is that his profit is positive (equation (4.19)). At a certain level of L, below the strategic equilibrium level of L determined by equations (4.20) and (4.21), the costs of the entrant might increase to such a level that profit falls below zero. Consequently, the entrant will not enter. The incumbent will buy permits up to the point where the entrant's profits are nil. Using Bain's terminology, this could be called *effectively deterred entry*. Another possibility is that at the non-strategic equilibrium $(q^{i^*},\bar{L})$, the price of the permits P_P is such that the entrant cannot make a positive profit and therefore will not enter at all. In that case, entry is *blockaded*.

From an analytical point of view, the most interesting case is when entry is *accommodated*. It can now be determined whether it will be profitable for the incumbent to raise the entrant's costs through raising the price of the permits. This is the case when:

$$\partial p/\partial L > \partial(C^i/q^i)/\partial L \qquad (4.23)$$

evaluated at $(q^{i^*},\bar{L})$, with q^{i^*} and $\bar{L}$ defined as the quantity produced and the number of permits used in the non-strategic equilibrium (where the incumbent is a monopolist and the entrant does not produce). The increase in permit purchases by the incumbent will raise the price of the permits. The change in the product price resulting from the reduction of the entrant's supply which follows this price increase must at least equal the increase in the incumbent's average costs in the non-strategic equilibrium $(q^{i^*},\bar{L})$. If this condition is not fulfilled, increasing the entrant's costs through manipulation of the permit market is not attractive for the incumbent. The probability that increasing the entrant's cost is profitable is larger when (see Salop and Scheffman 1987, p. 23; Misiolek and Elder 1989, p. 161):

1. the effect on the permit price of increased purchases of permits by the incumbent is larger;
2. the effect on the entrant's supply of a rise in the permit price is larger;
3. market demand for the incumbent's product is less elastic;
4. the supply of the entrant is less elastic with respect to changes in the product price.

Given these conditions, systems of tradable emission permits can be evaluated with respect to their susceptibility to exclusionary manipulation (EM). First of all, it is important that the incumbent firm has sufficient market power and therefore considerable influence on the permit price. If the costs (of extra permits) it incurs to raise the price are too large, its average costs will rise too much and exclusion will not be profitable.

Moreover, the increase in the permit price must sufficiently raise the entrant's costs. If permit outlays per unit of product are relatively small, the increase in the entrant's marginal costs is relatively small also and therefore its supply to the product market will only be marginally affected. This implies that EM is more profitable for the incumbent if the entrant's production is pollution intensive.

Last, the demand for the product should be inelastic. The rise in price of the product due to the reduction in the entrant's supply will then be large, which means that the incumbent will be able to make a large profit.

Given these considerations, how susceptible is the system of TCPs described in chapter 2 to EM? The foremost requirement is that a firm that wishes to reduce competition from potential rivals should be able to influence the price of the permits without having to incur costs which are too large. In the case of TCPs, however, this requirement is rather stringent because carbon permits are used in almost all branches of industry and the carbon permit market is not divided up into regional markets. As Misiolek and Elder (1989, p. 160) rightly note, EM is more likely to occur when permit markets are relatively small and tied to one branch of industry. If the permit market is not divided up into regional markets and all branches of industry require permits, it will be much more costly for a specific firm to raise the permit price sufficiently to influence its rivals. This is illustrated in Table 4.4, which shows emissions per sector, the number of firms, and the average market share on the permit market if the TCP system described in Chapter 2 were introduced in the Netherlands. The highest average market shares are in the refinery industry and the fertilizer industry. However, the highest average share is only 1.2 per cent. Given these shares, influencing the permit price would indeed be a costly enterprise, even for firms from these industries. As regards other industries, market shares on the permit market are negligible.

The total value of the permits on this market, calculated on the basis of a price per ton of CO_2 of 20 ECU, is about 6 billion guilders (this is the price which is calculated by Barret 1991, p. 14, as being the CO_2 price necessary to stabilize CO_2 emissions in the EU in 2010). Table 4.4 covers only the Netherlands. In effect, it is more realistic to assume that a TCP system would operate EU-wide (see Chapter 2). Consequently, the permit market would be still larger and therefore power on this market is even less likely to occur. With 2,676 million tons of CO_2 emissions in the EU in 1988, the market value of the permits in an EU-wide system would be 111 billion guilders in 2010 if emissions were stabilized at the 1988 level.

Given the size of the market, it will be difficult for any one firm to influence the permit price. However, it might be different if the permit market functioned imperfectly. If, as in the early examples of implemented tradable emission permit schemes (see Hahn 1989), there is only a small supply of permits, influencing their price is less difficult because the actual market is small. In the TCP system, this problem is less likely to occur because some of the permits are auctioned by the authorities. This means that there is a large primary market. EM would in that case require that firms could control the price on the primary market, the auction. With about half of the permits available annually put up for auction, any effort to influence the price of the permits would still be costly, even though the secondary market might be

Table 4.4 CO_2 emissions, Dutch economy, 1989

Sector	CO_2 emissions (million tons)	Number of firms	TCP market share per firm (%)
Food and beverages	3.9	7258	0.0004
Textiles	0.3	1515	0.0001
Paper	1.5	362	0.0029
Fertilizer	6.6	12	0.3881
Other chemicals	3.8	838	0.0032
Building materials	2.2	684	0.0023
Base metal	8.8	119	0.0522
Other metal	1.8	14563	0.0001
Other industries	0.5	21358	< 0.0001
Refineries	12.1	7	1.2199
Power companies	36.8	88	0.2951
Transport	26.4		
Households	19.3		
Horticulture	6.4		
Others	11.3		
Total	141.7		

Source: Koutstaal (1992, p. 74).

small.

The foremost requirement for influencing prices, which possesses some degree of market power, appears not to be fulfilled in the TCP scheme. However, if a firm could control prices, its chances of EM being profitable would also depend on the product market. Sectors in which demand for the product is inelastic are more vulnerable, as has been argued above (p. 92). Another factor is the emission intensity of a sector. If emissions are large per unit of product, permit prices have a large effect on the average and marginal production costs. This, however, is a two-edged sword, because while it increases the effect on the entrant's supply and therefore the profitability of EM for the established firm, it also increases the average costs of the incumbent.

Conclusions

Exclusionary manipulation is a strategy by which firms try to deny (potential) rivals the use of important inputs to their production processes. This can take the form either of excluding rivals completely or of driving up the price of the strategic inputs. Consequently, these firms must either use more expensive or less suitable substitutes or use the more expensive input. EM can be an effective way to limit competition, especially when a firm can exert control over a strategic input at reasonable costs. EM does not exist only as a theory: it also occurs in practice. In this section, we have studied whether it might be possible to use tradable permits to exclude rivals. Following the analysis of Misiolek and Elder (1989), several conditions have been derived which can be used to establish the susceptibility of systems of tradable emission permits to EM. Important factors are that the increase in the rival's costs due to EM is large and that the costs of controlling the supply of the permits (the costs of driving up the permit price) is small.

Surveying the evidence, it can be concluded that the system of TCPs sketched in this study is not very susceptible to EM. The market for TCPs, especially in an EU-wide system, appears to be too large for one firm to exercise any market power. Moreover, the auctioning of some of the permits alleviates the danger of the market being too thin, which would make it easier for a firm to influence the price.

4.3 CONCLUDING REMARKS

In this chapter the analysis of tradable permits and entry barriers is continued from the previous chapter. Two types of entry barrier which might be afffected by tradable permits have been studied in addition to transaction costs which were studied in Chapter 3. First is imperfect capital markets: grandfathering puts incumbent firms at an advantage. Second, firms can try to exclude entrants from the permit market; this will raise their costs and reduce entry.

Where capital markets are imperfect, firms with greater financial resources can outcompete those with less. The incumbent firm initiates a price war, which the entrant will lose because of its smaller financial resources and consequently higher costs of capital. This form of predatory pricing is known as the long purse theory. We have applied this theory to the instrument of TDPs, assuming that the incumbent and the entrant are equal in all respects except as regards the allocation of permits: the incumbent receives them free while the entrant has to buy permits. Grandfathering permits is in effect the same as making a capital gift. Therefore, the incumbent will have larger financial resources than the entrant. Consequently, the incumbent can drive potential entrants out of the market in a price war and therefore entrants will not enter the market. Grandfathering effectively reduces entry.

Subsequently, we investigated how serious this threat is in practice. There is some evidence from empirical studies that capital requirements do create entry barriers: there is a negative correlation between capital requirements and entry rates across industries.

Introducing the system of tradable carbon permits described in Chapter 2 means that new firms will have to buy carbon permits, thereby increasing their capital requirements. Given the negative correlation between capital requirements and entry rates, this might raise entry barriers. However, the increase in capital requirements appears to be small in the system of tradable carbon permits. Assuming a permit price of 20 ECU (necessary for the stabilization of EU emissions in 2010 at the 1988 level), any increase in capital requirements is small in the Dutch economy. The energy-intensive industries are the worst-affected sectors (the largest increase is in the petroleum industries, 1.7 per cent). In these sectors, the entry barrier is already high as far as the capital requirement for the average firm is concerned.

The last and most extreme form of entry barrier studied here occurs when a firm or group of firms controls a vital input and excludes other firms from the use of this input. This forces these latter firms to use less optimal and more expensive substitutes, reducing their competitive ability, or even excluding them from the market. An essential condition for exclusion is that a firm has market power on the input market. Without the power to influence the price of the input, a firm cannot drive up the costs of its rivals.

In the tradable carbon system described in Chapter 2, the market for permits will be large, especially if the system were introduced across the whole of the European Union. It would be very costly or even practically impossible to influence the permit price on this market. Exclusionary manipulation would not be a problem on this market.

To sum up our results, grandfathering permits to established firms and auctioning them to entrants does not necessarily raise entry barriers because of the opportunity costs of the permits. However, in the case of imperfect capital markets, grandfathering will raise entry barriers. As far as the system of tradable carbon permits studied here is concerned, grandfathering and imperfect capital markets will raise entry barriers only to a small extent. The worst-affected sectors are the energy intensive sectors.

NOTES

1. Whether the pecking order supports the financial constraint of the long purse theory or not depends on its rationale. One of the reasons why firms might prefer internal financing is that external financing is more expensive because of administration and underwriting costs. However, these costs do not seem to be large enough to warrant the preference for internal funding (Myers 1984, p. 582). Another explanation relies on asymmetric information. Myers and Majluf assume (a) that managers have more information about the benefits of an investment project than potential investors and (b) that it is their objective to increase the intrinsic value of the shares of the 'old' shareholders. They conclude that, given these assumptions, profitable projects which would be undertaken when firms can use internal funding might not be undertaken when they have to be financed by external funds because of the asymmetric information between the managers and the investors. Also, debt is preferred over new issue of equity. According to this explanation of the pecking order theory, there is not necessarily a financial constraint for the firm. Firms *prefer* internal funds but they would use external ones if they had to.

2. It should be realised that this assumption makes the model less general: if the incumbent has to reinvest as well, the price war will not be attractive. Presumably, this asymmetric investment requirement is part of the first-mover advantage of the incumbent.

3. r_0 is the capital cost for the bank. Or, in other words, it is the interest rate charged in the absence of risk.

4. Combining equations (4.1) and (4.2) yields: $(1+r)D + (\pi^d - B)(1 - F) = (1+r_0)D$. Rewriting yields: $r = r_0 + (\pi^d - B)(1 - F)/D$. An increase in the chance that the firm will default (represented by a decrease in F) increases the margin between r and r_0, between the interest which the firm has to pay and the no-risk market interest.

5. This is achieved by including into equation (4.3) the zero-profit condition for the bank: $(1+r)D - (\pi^d - B)(1 - F) - (1+r_0)D = 0$. The total expected retained earnings from the project are: $\pi^t = \pi^r F + \pi^d (1 - F)$.

6. In reality, firms will normally have the choice between buying permits or reducing their emissions. It is assumed that the amount of permits needed represents the least-cost solution for both firms, given the (exogenously determined) price of the permits. The entrant does not need to buy permits, but as this is the least-cost solution, it is the most attractive option.

7. It should be noted that it does not necessarily matter how large the initial amount of money is. The crucial element is that both firms start equally, the only difference between them is the difference in treatment under the tradable permit scheme. The assumtion that both firms start with K own capital is attractive from the point of view of comparison with a situation in which no permits are needed.

8. This is not necessarily the only way in which the effects of a price war can be modelled. For example, one could imagine a price war reducing profits even further such that both firms would have to borrow. This does not basically alter the game; the crucial point is that the entrant has fewer resources because it has not received permits free. Consequently its capital costs are higher.

9. The amount to be borrowed in period t is $\Sigma (1+r)^t G$. As t rises, the amount to be borrowed rises as well.

10. The requirement for the whole loan to be repaid at the end of the first period is a strict condition. Another possibility is that the incumbent and the bank sign a debt contract which allows the incumbent firm to spread its repayments. This would be more in line with the fact that the expected profits he makes on his investment in the quota of emission permits are also spread out over a long time. Other forms of debt contracts will be discussed below.

11. The entrant could sell its quota in order to pay off its debt (assuming there is a well-functioning market for emission permits and quota). However, this would mean that in the next period it would have to buy another quota if it wanted to stay in the market. Selling and buying a quota at the same time, however, does not make much sense.

12. See also Benoit (1984).

13. It would be going too far in the context of this study to elaborate on this game with incomplete information. Moreover, the basic analyses of such a game can be found in Benoit (1984).

14. Note that, in the game described here, collusion is less attractive for the incumbent than fighting a price war because it can drive the entrant out. When it cannot forestall the entrant, collusion might be preferable to competing, especially if the discount rate is not too low (Folk theorem, see Tirole 1992, p. 246).

15. Industries are classified according to such systems as the International Standard Industry Code. In these classification systems the number of digits stands for the level of disaggregation: the larger the number of digits, the higher the level of disaggregation.

16. Instead of buying permits (leasing a quota), a new firm can also choose to buy a quota, assuring itself of a supply of permits. In that case, it buys permits for an indefinite period. Its initial capital requirements will then increase with the quota price. However, when capital markets are not perfect and the costs of a quota would therefore increase the entry barrier, entrants have the option of buying permits for a more limited period instead.

17. Instead of emitting CO_2 and consequently needing permits to cover their emissions, another option for firms is to abate more. This would, however, also require expenditure, the abatement costs. These costs will consist partly of investment in more energy-efficient equipment, an investment which firms will have to make when they enter the market. Consequently, these costs will also increase their CR. The extent to which firms prefer to abate more rather than buy permits will depend on their abatement cost function. For simplicity, it is assumed here that firms will buy permits.

18. It should be noted that it is not necessarily the case that the established firm has market power in the product market. The essential fact is that it uses its market power on the input market to influence the product market. See Salop and Scheffman (1984) for an analysis of the model in which the established firm is a price-taker.

19. $\partial p / \partial L \big|_{qi}$ is determined by totally differentiating $D(p) - q^e(p, P_P(L)) = q^i$ with $\partial q^i = 0$.

5. Coordination of Environmental Policy in a Second-best World

5.1 INTRODUCTION

We have focused attention on a system of tradable carbon permits operating within one country. However, the enhanced greenhouse effect is an environmental problem which occurs worldwide. Tradable permits and other economic instruments such as taxes can also play a role at an international level. The main advantage of these instruments is that, for a given emission reduction, total abatement costs are minimized because all sources of carbon dioxide limit their emissions up to the point where their marginal abatement costs are equal. In the case of a tax, emitters reduce their emissions up to the point where their marginal abatement costs are equal to the tax. With a system of tradable permits such as has been described in Chapter 2, marginal abatement costs are equal to the price of the permits. To minimize worldwide costs of CO_2 abatement, marginal costs would have to be minimized not only by sources within countries but also across countries. When the marginal abatement costs are higher in one country than in another, it would be efficient to reduce emissions in the country with low marginal costs further and to increase the emissions in the country with high marginal costs. Introducing a tax on carbon dioxide which is equal in all countries would in theory equalize marginal costs in all countries and result in the lowest aggregate reduction costs, as has been shown by Hoel (1991).

This straightforward result and the clear implication for policy which follows from the standard analysis does not necessarily hold in a more realistic world. One of the complications which has to be faced is that the use of fossil fuels, the main source of anthropogenic CO_2 emissions, is already taxed for various reasons in most countries of the OECD at different tax rates. The question arises how a carbon tax should be combined with these existing taxes on fossil fuels. This question is not only of academic interest, but also has practical policy implications. Countries with high current implicit taxes on fossil fuels will argue that they have already limited their emissions and should therefore be exempted from a tax which is equal to the carbon tax introduced in countries with current low taxes. Hoeller and Coppel (1992) have investigated the differences in taxes (and subsidies) on fossil fuels in OECD countries. They show that introducing a uniform carbon tax on top of the existing implicit taxes on fossil fuels leads to higher total abatement costs than would equalizing the existing taxes and introducing a uniform tax. Their analysis, however, is only partial: they only look at abatement costs in different countries and do not take into account the welfare consequences of the revenue raised by the existing taxes and the carbon tax. As has been shown by Hoel (1993), in a general equilibrium model in which there is no deadweight loss from taxation, carbon taxes should also be uniform across countries in order to maximize collective welfare.

In this chapter, the issue of how to combine carbon taxes with existing taxes on fossil fuels is addressed in the setting of a second-best world, using a simple general equilibrium model (described in section 5.2). A second-best problem can best be described as an allocation problem with a constraint on the policies feasible which makes it impossible to reach the first-best optimum (Bohm 1988, p. 282). In the context of the optimal taxation problem explored here, the constraint on government policies is that lump-sum taxes are not possible, nor can proportional excise taxes be used because not all goods and endowments can be taxed. Therefore, revenue has to be raised by means of a distorting taxation, such as taxation on fossil fuels.

The problem is set in an international context since we are interested in solutions which are optimal in the sense that they maximize welfare (net benefits) for participating countries, collectively and individually. Account should be taken of the way in which countries behave with respect to each other's policies. There is a wide range of strategies available to countries: from free-rider behaviour and non-cooperation to optimal cooperation with side payments. To simplify the analysis we restrict our model to a world comprising two countries which are involved in global pollution; that is, the damage caused in a country by the pollutant is independent of the country in which it was emitted.

This contribution differs from the earlier literature on the subject by extending the second-best equilibrium analysis of pollution to an international context. Second-best general equilibrium models including pollution for national economies have been developed by Sandmo (1975), Auerbach (1987), Pezzey (1992) and Bovenberg and van der Ploeg (1992).

The object of this chapter is to determine the welfare-maximizing tax structure when two countries cooperate in abating pollution and use a tax on a polluting good (the carbon tax) as the instrument or, alternatively, a system of national or international tradable permits. Moreover, it is examined whether side payments are necessary to induce countries to cooperate and how they cooperate. The two countries are assumed to be equal except with respect to the government budget and the damage suffered from pollution. Our interest is in how these two variables affect the changes in tax structure and side payment when countries cooperate.

The structure of this chapter is as follows. In the next section, the model used is introduced for one country. In sections 5.3 and 5.4, the model is extended to two countries and the non-cooperative and cooperative equilibria (with and without side payments) are determined. Moreover, the optimal tax structures in both countries are established and we determine how different levels of government budget and pollution damage influence the equilibria.

This chapter serves as a basis for the analysis in the next chapter in which the role of tradable permits in cooperation in a second-best world is examined.

5.2 GENERAL EQUILIBRIUM MODEL OF A TAX ON AN EXTERNALITY IN A SECOND-BEST WORLD

In this section, the model used in the remainder of this book is presented. It is comparable to that used by Sandmo (1975), Auerbach (1987), Pezzey (1992) and Bovenberg and van der Ploeg (1992). The economy consists of one representative consumer, with the following utility function:

$$U = u(x,y,l) \quad \text{subject to} \quad (1+tx)\, x + (1+ty)\, y \le M - l \qquad (5.1)$$

$u_x,\ u_y,\ u_l > 0$
$u_{xx},\ u_{yy},\ u_{ll} < 0$

Where:
x = dirty good
y = clean good
ty = tax on good y
tx = tax on good x
l = leisure
M = given time endowment

The consumer can consume two products, x and y, which are produced by sacrificing leisure. His or her budget constraint is determined by the production function $(1+tx)\, x + (1+ty)\, y = M - l$ which has constant returns to scale. Prices of the two products x and y and of labour (the wage rate) are normalized at unity without loss of generality (Bovenberg and van der Ploeg 1992). The consumer maximizes utility under the constraint of the production function without taking account of the externalities, that is, the pollution generated by the consumption of the dirty good x. Maximizing this utility function under the constraint of the production function gives demand functions for good x, good y and leisure l which are functions of tx and ty. Although labour $(M - l)$ is not taxed, the amount of leisure 'consumed' by the consumer will react to changes in the tax rates on good x and good y. When the taxes on x and y increase, the consumer's real income will fall and consequently he or she will work less and take more leisure. From the demand functions, the indirect utility function for the consumer can be derived: $V = V(tx,ty)$.

The government must raise a given revenue requirement, R, by means of the taxes on good x and good y. A lump-sum tax is not available, leisure l (or labour $M - l$) is the untaxed good. This defines a so-called second-best world; second-best because distorting consumption taxes have to be used instead of non-distorting taxes such as lump-sum taxes or proportional excise taxes on all goods and leisure/labour.

Furthermore, the government must limit the environmental damage which results from the consumption of the dirty good x. Direct abatement is not possible in this model, so all abatement has to come from a reduction in the consumption of x. This is the prevailing situation as regards the emission of CO_2, which can only be reduced by limiting the consumption of fossil fuels. The problem for the government is to choose the tax structure which will maximize consumer welfare, taking into account both the distortions of taxation and environmental damage. First, the (standard) optimal tax rules for the second-best world will be established ignoring pollution caused by the consumption of x. Subsequently, the optimal tax rates are determined when the environmental damage caused by the consumption of x is taken into account.

The optimal tax rates (ignoring pollution) are determined by maximizing the following function:

$$V(tx,ty) \quad \text{subject to} \quad tx\, x + ty\, y \geq R \tag{5.2}$$

Consumer utility is maximized (by maximizing the indirect utility function V) subject to the revenue constraint of the government, which states that the amount of revenue raised by the taxes on x and y is at least R (which is exogenously determined).

The first order-conditions are:

$$L_{tx} = V_{tx} + \mu[x + tx\, x_{tx} + ty\, y_{tx}] = 0 \tag{5.3}$$

$$L_{ty} = V_{ty} + \mu[y + ty\, y_{ty} + tx\, x_{ty}] = 0 \tag{5.4}$$

$$L_{\mu} = tx\, x + ty\, y - R = 0 \tag{5.5}$$

Equations (5.3) and (5.4) present the standard formulas for optimal tax rates in situations where no lump-sum taxation is possible.[1] μ, the Lagrange multiplier, can be interpreted as the shadow costs in terms of utility of raising an additional dollar of revenue R by the government.

Next, the optimal tax rates in the presence of pollution emanating from the consumption of x are determined by maximizing the following function:

$$V(tx,ty) + D(x) \text{ subject to } tx\, x + ty\, y \geq R \qquad (5.6)$$

in which $D(x)$ is the damage from pollution which is a result of the consumption of good x. Damage is negative benefit, so $D(x)$ is negative. Furthermore, damage increases when x increases, therefore $D_x < 0$. It is assumed that $D_{xx} < 0$, so *marginal* damage rises when x increases.

The first order-conditions are:

$$L_{tx} = V_{tx} + D_x\, x_{tx} + \mu[x + tx\, x_{tx} + ty\, y_{tx}] = 0 \qquad (5.7)$$

$$L_{ty} = V_{ty} + \mu[y + ty\, y_{ty} + tx\, x_{ty}] + D_x\, x_{ty} = 0 \qquad (5.8)$$

Equations (5.7) and (5.8) can be rewritten as:

$$V_{tx} + \mu[x + (tx + 1/\mu\, D_x)\, x_{tx} + ty\, y_{tx}] = 0 \qquad (5.7a)$$

$$V_{ty} + \mu[y + ty\, y_{ty} + (tx + 1/\mu\, D_x)\, x_{ty}] = 0 \qquad (5.8a)$$

Marginal environmental damage D_x can be internalized in the decisions of the representative consumer by adding an appropriate pollution tax to the existing revenue-raising tax on good x. Let tx^R be the optimal tax when pollution was ignored (the Ramsey tax) and tx^{RP} the tax when pollution is taken into account (the Ramsey–Pigou tax): tax tx in equations (5.7) and (5.8) and in (5.7a) and (5.8a). Comparing equations (5.3) and (5.4) with (5.7a) and (5.8a), it follows that tx^{RP} can be written (Auerbach 1987, p. 113) as:

$$tx^{RP} = tx^R - 1/\mu\, D_x \qquad (5.9)$$

Equation (5.9) states that the optimal tax on good x in the presence of pollution is composed of two elements: (a) a tax on x which is calculated by the standard optimal tax formulas as given in equations (5.3) and (5.4) (tax tx^R, the Ramsey part of the tax on x); (b) a tax which corrects for the damage resulting from the pollution caused by the consumption of x (the Pigouvian part of the tax on x, termed subsequently tx^P) which is equal to the marginal damage $\partial D/\partial x$ divided by the marginal disutility of government revenue μ.

When μ, the shadow costs in terms of utility of raising an additional dollar of government revenue, rises (for example, because the government raises its revenue requirement), this Pigouvian part of the tax declines. As Bovenberg and van der Ploeg (1992, p. 9) state: 'The government can afford less tax differentiation aimed at environmental protection as the revenue raising objective of the tax system becomes relatively more important'. This also implies that in this second-best world, where tax revenue is exogenously given and independent of environmental damage, relative environmental protection will be weaker the higher is the revenue requirement of the government. The consequences for the absolute level of pollution are not clear. With a rise in R, tx^R will increase while tx^P will fall. Under certain conditions (see appendix to this chapter) total tax tx will increase when R is raised. Assuming that x is a normal good, consumption will fall and environmental quality will improve.

From equations (5.7a) and (5.8a), it follows that the optimal tax rules for the tax on good y, the non-polluting good, are not affected by the internalization of environmental damage in the tax system. Note, however, that the level of ty will change: the environmental tax will bring in revenue, which reduces the absolute level of the Ramsey taxes on both x and y.

In the following sections, this model will be extended and used to analyse the consequences for the optimal taxes for two countries.

5.3 NON-COOPERATION AND COOPERATION IN A SECOND-BEST WORLD

When pollution is transboundary, as is the case with carbon dioxide, the problem is to coordinate environmental policy between independent states. In contrast with environmental problems which are confined within the boundaries of one country, the difficulty is that there is no single authority to carry out a cost-benefit analysis and implement an international abatement scheme. It is realistic to assume that countries will base their own policies upon the behaviour of other countries with respect to the transboundary pollution. For example, the European Community has formulated a CO_2 policy which includes a tax on energy and carbon, but it is only to be implemented if Japan and the US also reduce their emissions. Therefore, it is necessary to determine how countries would react to reduction strategies in other countries. We examine, first, the non-cooperative Nash equilibrium, and then the cooperative equilibrium. Finally, the cooperative equilibrium is extended by allowing the countries to use side payments.

Non-cooperative Nash equilibrium

At the outset, the model presented in the previous section must be amended to account for the transboundary character of pollution. It is assumed that there are two countries; in both x and y are consumed and both governments have to fulfil their (given) revenue requirement by taxing the two consumption goods x and y. It is assumed that the environmental damage which results from the consumption of x occurs everywhere, regardless of the location in which it is consumed. Therefore, the damage function for both countries, $D1$ and $D2$, are not only a function of the consumption of x in the own country, but also of the consumption of x in the other country:

$$D1 = D1((x_1+x_2)) \tag{5.10}$$

$$D2 = D2(x_1+x_2) \tag{5.11}$$

The social welfare function, equation (5.6), then becomes (for country 1):

$$V_1(tx1,tx2) + D(x_1 + x_2) \text{ subject to } tx1\ x_1 + ty1\ y_1 \geq R_1 \tag{5.12}$$

In order to determine the optimal taxes and pollution that both countries end up with when they do not coordinate their policies (the non-cooperative Nash equilibrium) it is assumed that both countries take the pollution in the other country as given. Taking x_2 as given, country 1 will maximize its social welfare function (5.12) (and vice versa for country 2), yielding the following first-order conditions:

$$L_{tx1} = V_{tx1} + D1_{x1}\ x_{tx1} + \mu_1[x_1 + tx1\ x_{tx1} + ty1\ y_{tx1}] = 0 \tag{5.13}$$

$$L_{ty1} = V_{ty1} + D1_{x1}\ x_{ty1} + \mu_1[y_1 + ty1\ y_{ty1} + tx1\ x_{ty1}] = 0 \tag{5.14}$$

Comparing these first-order conditions with those in the single country-case, the only difference is the occurrence of x_2 in the derivative of the damage function. Damage is not only caused by the pollution resulting from consumption of x in the own country but also by the given level of pollution imported from the other country.

In order to determine the way country 1 will react to a change in emissions in country 2, we take the total differential of the first-order conditions (including $tx1x1 + ty1y1 = R1$) with $tx2$ as a parameter change. Solving the system gives:

$$d t_{x}1 / d t_{x}2 = (y1 + y_{ty1} t_{y}1)\, D1_{x1x2}\, x2_{tx2} \qquad (5.15)$$

$$[(y1 + y_{ty1} t_{y}1)\, x1_{tx1} - (x1 + x_{tx1} t_{x}1)\, x1_{ty1}] / |\mathbf{H}|$$

$\mathbf{H}$ is the Hessian matrix.

The right hand side of equation (5.15) is negative (see appendix to this chapter). Therefore, when tax $t_{x}2$ rises, tax $t_{x}1$ decreases. When country 2 raises its tax on good x and therefore reduces consumption of x and emissions, the marginal damage resulting from the consumption of x will diminish (in absolute terms), not only in country 2 but also in country 1. Consequently, country 1 can increase pollution and therefore consumption of x and it will be able to lower the Pigouvian part of its tax on x. In Figure 5.1 curve R_1 represents this reaction of country 1, and R_2 for country 2 if country 1 changes its tax on x. (It is assumed that an interior solution exists, for proof of the existence of the equilibrium see the appendix to this chapter.) The non-cooperative Nash equilibrium is point N in Figure 5.1.

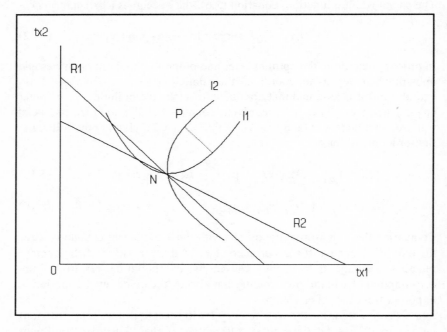

Figure 5.1 Cooperative and non-cooperative equilibrium

Cooperative equilibrium

Here it is assumed that countries negotiate in order to agree on abatement policies. Cooperation geared to a Pareto-optimal solution can be represented by the following function (see also Hoel 1991, p. 58):

$$V_1(tx1,ty1) + D_1(x_1+x_2) \text{ subject to } tx1 \ x_1 + ty1 \ y_1 \geq R_1 \qquad (5.16)$$
$$tx2 \ x_2 + ty2 \ y_2 \geq R_2$$
$$V2 + D2 \geq W_2^*$$

where W_2^* is the welfare level of country 2 in the non-cooperative equilibrium. In other words, welfare in country 1 is optimized by setting taxes in both countries subject to the government revenue constraint and subject to welfare in the other country staying at least equal. The Lagrange function to be maximized is:

$$L = V_1(tx1,ty1) + D_1(x_1+x_2) + \mu_1[x_1 tx1 + y_1 ty1 - R_1] + \qquad (5.17)$$

$$\gamma[V_2(tx2,ty2) + D_2(x_1+x_2) - W_2^*] + \mu_2[x_2 tx2 + y_2 ty2 - R_2]$$

γ is the Lagrange multiplier of the welfare constraint for country 2. The first-order conditions are:

$$L_{tx1} = V1_{tx1} + D1_{tx1} + \mu_1(x_1 + tx1 \ x_{tx1} + ty1 \ y_{tx1}) + \gamma \ D2_{tx1} = 0 \qquad (5.18)$$

$$L_{ty1} = V1_{ty1} + D1_{ty1} + \mu_1(y_1 + ty1 \ y_{ty1} + tx1 \ x_{ty1}) + \gamma \ D2_{ty1} = 0 \qquad (5.19)$$

$$L_{tx2} = \gamma(V2_{tx2} + D2_{tx2}) + \mu_2(x_2 + tx2 \ x_{tx2} + ty2 \ y_{tx2}) + D1_{tx2} = 0 \qquad (5.20)$$

$$L_{ty2} = \gamma(V2_{ty2} + D2_{ty2}) + \mu_2(y_2 + ty2 \ y_{ty2} + tx2 \ x_{ty2}) + D1_{ty2} = 0 \qquad (5.21)$$

$$L_{\mu1} = x_1 \ tx1 + y_1 \ ty1 - R_1 = 0 \qquad (5.22)$$

$$L_{\mu2} = x_2 \ tx2 + y_2 \ ty2 - R_2 = 0 \qquad (5.23)$$

$$L_\gamma = V_2 + D_2 - W_2^* = 0 \qquad (5.24)$$

The maximization procedure is depicted in Figure 5.1 as a movement, starting at N, along the constant welfare curve I_2 (where $W_2 = W_2^*$), searching for the point where W_1 is at its maximum. That is shifting I_1 upwards until it is tangential to I_2. This is point P. Given the form of the iso-welfare curves in Figure 5.1, welfare in country 1 has been increased, while at the same time holding welfare in country 2 constant, by raising simultaneously both $tx1$ and $tx2$ as compared with the non-cooperative equilibrium. Therefore, pollution will be lower in the cooperative equilibrium than in the non-cooperative equilibrium.

The difference with the non-cooperative solutions (equation (5.13) and (5.14)) is that the government of country 1 in choosing its tax level for $tx1$ and $ty1$ has to take into account its valuation of the marginal damage in country 2 ($\gamma D2_{tx1}$) caused by consumption of x_1 (see (5.19) and (5.20)).[2] In the same way damage in country 1 caused by consumption of x_2 in country 2 is taken into account in setting $tx2$ and $ty2$. The Pareto-optimal solution (in point P in Figure 5.1) can be viewed as an agreement between the two governments to increase taxes on x reciprocally in order to reduce pollution further than in the non-cooperative case.

In the cooperative equilibrium, the Pigouvian taxes will increase, as can be seen by splitting the tax on good x into a Ramsey part and a Pigouvian part (see equation (5.9)). Now, $tx1$ and $tx2$ can be written as:

$$tx1 = tx1^R - 1/\mu_1 \ (D1_{x1} + \gamma D2_{x1}) \qquad (5.25)$$

$$tx2 = tx2^{R'} - 1/\mu_2 \ (D1_{x2} + \gamma D2_{x2}) \qquad (5.26)$$

The Pigouvian taxes include marginal damage caused in the other country in addition to the marginal damage of consuming x in the own country. The Pigouvian taxes will probably rise and pollution will fall when countries cooperate. However, μ_1 and μ_2 will change as well: it is therefore not a simple result that Pigouvian taxes are higher when countries cooperate compared with non-cooperation. The Pigouvian taxes in both countries will not be equal (except when $\mu_1 = \mu_2$, which is not necessarily the case).

It should be noted that the cooperative game examined here can produce more than one equilibrium. Solving optimization problem (5.17) yields the highest attainable welfare level for country 1, given the welfare constraint W_2^* for country 2. Varying this constraint W_2^* generates a range of welfare levels for country 1. In Figure 5.1, the contract curve, lying between the original iso-utility curves I_1 and I_2, represents these combinations. All the combinations of welfare levels which leave both countries better off after cooperation than with non-cooperation are solutions to the cooperative game.

Joint Optimum and the Use of Side Payments

The range of Pareto-optimal solutions with tax rates as the only instruments that are coordinated does not necessarily yield the highest attainable benefits from cooperation. In a first-best approach, the possibility of using side payments makes it possible to increase welfare in both countries by redistributing the abatement effort relative to the initial cooperative solutions and compensating the country which would be worse off in terms of welfare (see Nentjes 1994). The country which lowers its tax on x and increases consumption of x (and therefore its pollution) compared with the initial cooperative solution will have to compensate the other which increases its pollution tax and decreases its consumption of x. Without side payments this country would be worse off than when it did not cooperate.

However, side payments raise problems of their own. They must be raised by way of the (distorting) taxes on x and y. Therefore, regard must be taken of the welfare effects of raising (and receiving) side payments by means of these taxes. The optimization problem becomes:

$$\max \; V_1 + D_1 \quad \text{subject to } x_1 t x 1 + y_1 t y 1 - (R_1 + S) \geq 0 \qquad (5.27)$$
$$V_2 + D_2 - W_2^* \geq 0$$
$$x_2 t x 2 + y_2 t y 2 - (R_2 - S) \geq 0$$

W_2^* is the welfare level in country 2 in the non-cooperative Nash equilibrium. S is the side payment made by one country to the other country. S can be positive or negative: if S is positive, country 1 will pay country 2. From the budget constraint for country 1, we can see that in that case the revenue requirement for country 1 increases with the side payment, while the revenue requirement for country 2 decreases by the same amount. An increase (decrease) in the revenue requirement has several effects. On the one hand, taxes on both goods will increase (decrease) because more (respectively less) revenue is to be raised. On the other hand the Pigouvian tax will decline (increase) because it becomes more (less) costly to levy an environmental tax. The net effect on aggregate pollution can be positive or negative (see p. 124).

In equation (5.27), the effects of side payments on tax levels and the excess burden of taxation are taken into account explicitly. Comparing equation (5.27) with (5.17), the difference between the maximization problem in the cooperative equilibrium with side payments and the cooperative equilibrium without them is the additional instrument of side payments, which makes it possible to acquire higher welfare levels through cooperation.

The first-order conditions of maximizing (5.27) are mainly equal to the first-order conditions of the cooperative solution without side payments (equations (5.18)–(5.24)). Only equations (5.22) and (5.23) change:

$$L_{\mu 1} = x_1 t x 1 + y_1 t y 1 - (R1 + S) = 0 \qquad (5.22a)$$

$$L_{\mu 2} = x_2 t x 2 + y_2 t y 2 - (R2 - S) = 0 \qquad (5.23a)$$

Furthermore, the first-order derivative of variable S, the side payment, is added:

$$L_S = -\mu_1 + \mu_2 = 0 \qquad (5.28)$$

Again, we can split the taxes on good x into two parts, yielding the same formulas as in the cooperative optimum without side payments (see equations (5.25) and (5.26)). However, the difference is that $\mu_1 = \mu_2$ (equation (5.28)), therefore the Pigouvian part of the tax is now equal in both countries. Both countries will levy the same Pigouvian or 'carbon' tax. It should be noted that the other part of the total tax on x will still differ between the two countries. *Aggregate tax levels on the polluting good* x *will still differ between the two countries.* This is the main difference with the outcome in a first-best world (without tax revenue constraints) mentioned above (p. 99), where it was argued that in such a first-best world tax rates are equalized between countries.

Another point worth repeating is that even though $\mu_1 = \mu_2$, the shadow costs of taxation in both countries will still differ. As has been noted above, μ_2 does not represent the shadow cost of taxation for country 2 in equation (5.26). Instead, it represents the effect which a marginal change in the revenue requirement for country 2, R_2, has on the welfare of country 1. The constraint is not a constraint on the welfare of country 2 in this equation but a constraint on the welfare of country 1. When the revenue requirement in country 2 is lower, that country can gear its tax structure more to reducing consumption of x, which increases welfare in country 1, given its welfare constraint W_2^*, than when R_2 is higher.

Who pays whom is determined by the Lagrange multipliers μ_1 and μ_2. When μ_1 is lower than μ_2 in the initial bargaining solution without transfers, country 1 pays country 2, which in return raises its tax on good x. However, when μ_1 is initially higher than μ_2, country 1 receives the side payment. All other things being equal, a decrease in R_1 increases the attractiveness of making a side payment for country 1 (because μ_1 declines). The higher the revenue requirement is, the higher will be the welfare loss (deadweight loss) of raising the revenue for the side payment). A higher R_2 increases μ_2, increasing the attractiveness of a positive side payment (country 1 pays country 2) as well. It should, however, be noted that changes in the revenue requirement also affect the non-cooperative Nash equilibrium and therefore W_2^*, the welfare constraint on country 2 in equation (5.27). Consequently, comparing cooperative equilibria in situations with different initial revenue requirements is highly problematical and does not yield clear results.

As has been mentioned above (p. 108), the cooperative game discussed above produces more than one equilibrium. The literature on cooperative games does provide a number of solutions to these cooperative games which do yield unique outcomes[3] in which both countries improve their welfare levels as compared with a non-cooperative solution. Examples of these are the Nash bargaining solution and the Raiffa–Kalai–Smorodinsky solution (Friedman 1986, ch. 5). The Nash bargaining solution (used also in the context of coordinating environmental policy between two countries by Hoel 1991) takes as a starting point for negotiations the welfare levels in the non-cooperative Nash equilibrium. In the Nash bargaining solution $(U_1 - T_1)(U_2 - T_2)$ is maximized subject to the revenue constraints where T_1 and T_2 are the welfare levels in the Nash equilibrium for country 1 and country 2. This approach has not been used in this general section because the second-best Nash bargaining model does not yield interpretable results.

In order to overcome these problems, in the next section the Nash bargaining solution will be considered for a more specific functional form of the welfare function. We shall analyse how differing revenue requirements influence which country will make the side payment; how the tax structure in both countries is affected by cooperation with and without side payments; and what the consequences are of cooperation for the level of pollution.

5.4 SIMULATIONS

Introduction

As we stated in the introduction to this chapter, the aim of this research is to determine the equilibrium when two countries cooperate in reducing environmental pollution by means of coordinating taxation in a second-best world where polluting and non-polluting commodities are taxed. The general model considered does not yield clear answers to the questions posed in the introduction. In particular, it does not answer how the tax structure will change when countries cooperate, how pollution is affected and in what way side payments can be used to increase welfare. In this section, the equilibrium will be simulated using a more specific model. The form chosen for the simulations is the following welfare function:

$$U_i(x_i, y_i, l_i) + D_i(x_i + x_j) = x_i^\alpha y_i^\beta l_i^\tau - a(x_i + x_j)^2 \qquad (5.29)$$

The first term of (5.29) is a Cobb–Douglas utility function. Utility is derived from two goods, x and y, and from the time not worked, leisure l. It is assumed that $\alpha = \beta = \tau = 1/3$. The representative individual maximizes this first term subject to his or her budget constraint:

$$(1+tx)x + (1+ty)y = (M - l) \tag{5.30}$$

M is the maximum amount of time available to the consumer (his or her endowment). The wage level is set at unity. A Cobb–Douglas function is chosen because it has the characteristic that it yields demand functions for both goods x and y which are independent of the price of the other product (cf. Sandmo 1975). This assumption does not basically change the evaluation as we are interested in the interaction between the two countries, given the need for them to raise revenue by means of distorting taxation, and not in the cross effects of price changes *per se*.

The second term in (5.29) represents environmental damage. The marginal damage coefficient, a, is positive. First- and second-order derivatives are negative. The individual consumer's maximization yields demand functions for x and y (l is fixed):

$$x = M/(3*(1+tx)), \quad y = M/(3*(1+ty))$$

Using these demand functions, the authorities maximize welfare function (5.29) subject to their revenue constraint:

$$x \; tx + y \; ty = R \tag{5.31}$$

The time endowment M is set at 1,000. R is a fraction of M. Both countries are assumed to have the same welfare functions and private budget constraints. The revenue requirements ($R1$ and $R2$) and the marginal damage coefficients (a and b) are allowed to vary. This makes it possible to determine how the revenue requirements and marginal damage coefficients influence the side payment, the tax structure and the level of pollution.

The specific cooperative solution with tax coordination as the instrument examined is the Nash bargaining solution, which is found by maximizing the following function:

$$(U_1(x_1,y_1,l_1)+D_1(x_1,x_2)-T_1)*(U_2(x_2,y_2,l_2)+D_2(x_1,x_2)-T_2) \tag{5.32}$$

$$= [x_i^\alpha y_i^\beta l_i^\tau - a(x_i+x_j)^2 - T_1] \, [x_j^\alpha y_j^\beta l_j^\tau - b(x_j+x_i)^2 - T^2]$$

subject to $x_1 tx1 + y_1 ty1 \geq R_1$

$\qquad\qquad x_2 tx2 + y_2 ty2 \geq R_2$

T_1 and T_2 are the welfare levels for country 1 and country 2 in the non-cooperative Nash equilibrium. Maximizing (5.32) is equal to finding the hyperbole which has as asymptotes the utility levels T_1 and T_2, and has a point of tangency with the frontier of the set of possible solutions to the cooperative game. This is shown in Figure (5.2). The y-axis shows the utility level for country 2, the x-axis the utility level for country 1. Line AA′ represents the possible welfare levels attainable when both countries cooperate by coordinating their taxes when no side payments are used. The non-cooperative welfare levels (the Nash solution, point N in Figure 5.1) are the origin of Figure 5.2. Therefore, the x-axis and the y-axis are the asymptotes for the hyperboles which are the iso-utility curves of function (5.32). P_1 is the Nash bargaining solution for this case.

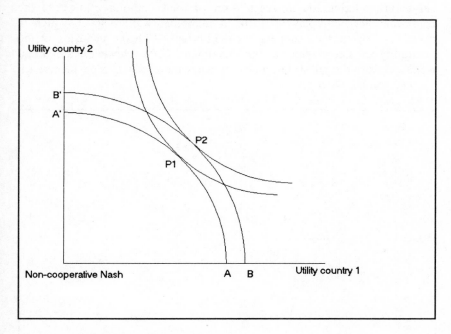

Figure 5.2 Nash bargaining solution

When the possibility of side payments is included, the maximization problem (5.32) changes. In addition to setting the four taxes on both goods x and y in both countries, the cooperating countries can also set the optimal side payment. The side payment enters equation (5.32) by way of the revenue constraints. R_1 becomes R_1+S, R_2 becomes $R_2 - S$. S can be both negative of positive. When S is positive, country 1 pays country 2.

When side payments are possible in addition to tax coordination, the attainable utility levels will increase. This is shown in Figure 5.2 by shifting line AA′, the cooperative possibilities curve when no side payments are used, outwards to line BB'. When the set of cooperative solutions increases, the Nash bargaining solution will also change, from point P_1 to point P_2 in Figure 5.2.[4]

A striking feature of the Nash bargaining solution with side payments is that the welfare level of one of the countries in the cooperative equilibrium with side payments can be smaller than its welfare level in the cooperative equilibrium without side payments. It may seem strange that the inclusion of an additional instrument (side payments) would result in a lower welfare level for one of the countries. However, it is necessary to realize that the Nash bargaining solution maximizes a form of joint optimum subject to the constraint that both players realize a minimum welfare level, which is determined by the non-cooperative equilibrium. With the inclusion of the possibility of side payments, this maximum shifts. However, the initial welfare constraints will still be met: both with and without side payments each country will be better off.

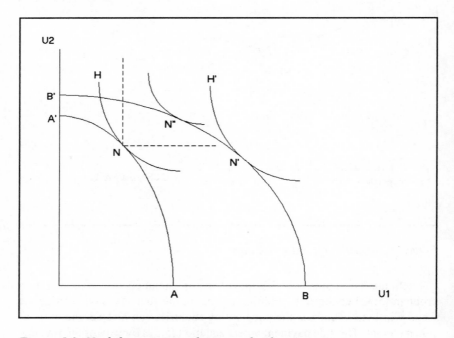

Figure 5.3 Nash bargaining solution and side payments

Figure 5.3 provides an illustration of this point. Curve AA' shows the possible welfare combinations which leave both countries better off as compared with the non-cooperative equilibrium (the origin) with no side payments. The Nash bargaining solution is point N, the point of tangency of curve AA' and the highest attainable hyperbole, H. Curve BB' gives the welfare combinations including side payments, H' the highest hyperbole and N' the new Nash bargaining equilibrium. The value of the Nash bargaining solution including side payments is necessarily equal to or higher than the Nash bargaining solution without side payments. Country 1's welfare level rises compared with the Nash bargaining solution without side payments, country 2's welfare declines.

However, it is not realistic that one country would accept lower welfare levels when side payments are allowed compared with the equilibrium without side payments. A more relevant approach, therefore, is to take the welfare levels of the Nash bargaining solution without side payments as the threat-points for determining the new Nash bargaining solution with side payments.[5] This is illustrated in Figure 5.3. Point N represents the new threat points. Consequently, the Nash bargaining solution with side payments is determined by the intersection between the welfare possibilities curve BB' and the highest attainable hyperbole which has as its focus N instead of the origin. The Nash bargaining solution with side payments which has these new threat-points as asymptotes is shown by N''. Necessarily, neither of the two countries will be worse off when side payments are included compared with the N–B solution without side payments.

This two-stage negotiation process, in which countries cooperate in a first stage without side payments and side payments are introduced in the second stage, is taken as the starting point for the simulations. We shall determine how different revenue requirements and different marginal damage coefficients affect the Nash bargaining equilibrium including side payments. The optimal side payment will be calculated and the change in tax structure and consumption of good x in both countries will be established when side payments are used in a second round as compared with the equilibrium without side payments. Initially, the first-best case will be analysed, and this will serve as a benchmark for the subsequent second-best analysis.

First-best Analysis

In a first-best world, governments can levy revenue by means of non-distortionary taxation (proportional excise taxes on all goods) or lump-sum taxes. These types of taxes are non-distortionary because revenue is raised by means of taxes on all goods and endowments or by a direct tax on income. Consequently, they do not distort the price ratios between goods as would be the case in the second-best model in which taxes are levied on goods x and y and not on leisure. Such taxes distort the price ratios between the two goods and leisure, and consequently they have an additional negative impact on welfare. In the model discussed in the previous section, proportional excise taxes entail that leisure is also taxed in addition to x and y. Consequently the government budget constraint is:

$$x \cdot tx + y \cdot ty + l \cdot tl = R \qquad (5.33)$$

Alternatively, a lump-sum tax can be used instead of proportional excise taxes. In that case, the budget constraint for the consumer is:

$$x(1+tx) + y + l = M - R - x \cdot tx \qquad (5.34)$$

in which tx follows from maximizing $V(tx) + D(x(tx))$. The required government revenue is raised by means of the lump-sum tax R which occurs in the consumer's budget constraint. The tax on good x is a Pigouvian tax which is levied solely to reduce consumption of x because of the marginal damage caused by the pollution resulting from its use. The revenue raised by the tax, $x \cdot tx$, is returned to the consumer by means of a lump-sum transfer (see equation (5.34)). The demand curve for x is different from the second-best model because the revenue raised by the tax on x is returned as a lump-sum transfer. The demand curve for x is:

$$x = (M - R)/(2tx+3) \qquad (5.35)$$

The demand curves for y and l (which are equal in the first-best case) now are (with $ty = tl = 0$):

$$y = l = \tfrac{1}{2}(M - R - x) \qquad (5.36)$$

When a country makes a side payment in this first-best case, it is taken directly from the consumer's budget through a lump-sum tax. When a side payment is received, it is given to the consumer by means of a lump-sum transfer.

The results of a number of simulations are presented in Figures 5.4–5.6 and Tables 5.1–5.3. The x-axes show either the marginal damage coefficient or the revenue requirement for country 1. The y-axes show the changes for x_1, x_2 and x_1+x_2 (dpol. in the figures), which is equal to pollution in both countries, as compared with the equilibrium without side payments. Furthermore, the optimal side payments are shown.

In Figure 5.4, the revenue requirement for country 1 is varied from 150 to 450 while R_2 is set at 300. Marginal damage coefficients for both countries are set at 0.1. When both countries cooperate without side payments instead of non-cooperation, taxes on good x increase in both countries and pollution declines. Allowing side payments reduces pollution further. The side payment is negative as long as R_1 is smaller than R_2, therefore country 2 pays country 1 as long as government spending in country 1 is lower than in country 2.

The reason for this can be found in Table 5.1 which shows the consumption levels and tax rates for goods x and y in both countries in the Nash equilibrium and the cooperative equilibria. In the Nash equilibrium, the taxes on x are equal in both countries.[6] In the cooperative equilibrium without side payments, the Pigouvian tax in the country with the lower revenue requirement is lower than in the other country. In the first-best model examined here, taxes on good x will be equal in the cooperative equilibrium,[7] therefore the country with the lower tax on x in the equilibrium without side payments (the country with the lower revenue requirement) will raise its tax on good x while the other country reduces tx. The result is that taxes on x will be equal in the cooperative equilibrium with side payments (see Table 5.1).

It should be noted that the size and sign of the side payment depends on the cooperative equilibrium without side payments. Here, the Nash bargaining equilibrium is chosen. However, there are other equilibria which will also leave both countries better off compared with the non-cooperative Nash equilibrium. With another equilibrium as the starting point, the size and possibly the sign of the side payment will change.

In the simulation presented in Figure 5.5, revenue requirements are both set at 300 while the marginal damage coefficient of country 1, a, varies from 0.9 to 1.1. The marginal damage coefficient in country 2, b, is set at 1. The country with the lower marginal damage coefficient levies lower taxes on good x in both the non-cooperative and the cooperative equilibrium. Consequently this country receives the side payment, increases its tax on the polluting good and consumes less of it, while the other country decreases the tax on x and consumes more of the dirty good. Using side payments reduces pollution further compared with the cooperative equilibrium without side payments.

In Figure 5.6, both the marginal damage coefficients and the revenue requirements differ. In country 2, government spending is set at 250. Country 1 has a marginal damage coefficient of 0.95, country 2 of 1. The revenue requirement of country 1 is allowed to vary from 220 to 420. Over the whole range of revenue requirements for country 1, country 2 makes a side payment to country 1. The advantage of the lower marginal damage coefficient for country 1 outweighs the higher revenue requirement of country 1, although the side payment from country 2 to country 1 becomes smaller the larger R_1 is (which confirms our earlier findings that an increase in R reduces the probability that the country will be on the receiving side of the transfer). Country 2 pays the transfer, reduces tx (and consumption of y). Therefore it can increase its consumption of good x and hence its pollution; country 1 receives the transfer, increases tx and reduces pollution.

A striking point is that as R_1 rises above 300, total pollution actually *increases*. Allowing for side payments can apparently mean that in the Nash bargaining solution pollution is higher than in the equilibrium without side payments. This can be explained by looking more closely at what happens in both countries. Reducing pollution more in country 1 and less in country 2 is attractive because marginal damage in country 1 is lower: therefore the welfare costs of reducing pollution are lower in country 1. Consequently, country 2 pays country 1 and consumes more of good x. However, this has the additional effect that the country with the higher revenue requirement (country 1) and therefore lower income increases its income. The positive income effect on the consumption of x will partially offset the reduction in x brought about by the price effect of a higher tax on it. In total, consumption of x by the consumers of the two countries will rise and therefore pollution will increase. In country 1 welfare increases because it receives the side payment. In country 2 welfare increases because it focuses less on emission reduction. This compensates for the increase in pollution.

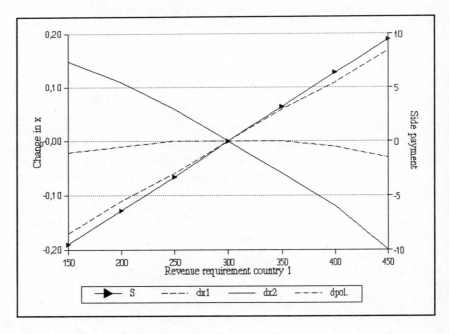

Figure 5.4 Cooperation with side payments in a first-best world:
$R_1 = 300, MD_1 = MD_2 = 0.1$

Table 5.1 Coordination with side payments in a first-best world
$R_2 = 300$, $MD_1 = MD_2 = 0.1$

Country 1

	Non-cooperative Nash equilibrium			Cooperative equilibrium without side payments			Cooperative equilibrium with side payments			
R_1	x_1	y_1	tx_1	x_1	y_1	tx_1	x_1	y_1	tx_1	S
150	10.45	419.77	39.16	7.19	421.41	57.63	7.02	426.24	59.74	−9.5
200	10.03	394.99	38.38	6.83	396.59	57.10	6.71	399.84	58.57	−6.4
250	9.59	370.20	37.60	6.45	371.77	56.60	6.40	373.45	57.38	−3.3
300	9.14	345.43	36.80	6.07	346.96	56.13	6.07	346.96	56.13	0.0
350	8.67	320.77	35.99	5.68	322.16	55.73	5.74	320.53	54.88	3.2
400	8.18	295.91	35.17	5.27	297.36	55.41	5.38	294.11	53.62	6.4
450	7.67	271.16	34.34	4.85	272.57	55.19	5.02	267.74	52.36	9.5

Country 2

R_1	x_2	y_2	tx_2	x_2	y_2	tx_2	x_2	y_2	tx_2	S
150	8.61	345.70	39.16	5.49	347.25	62.22	5.64	342.43	59.68	9.5
200	8.78	345.61	38.39	5.67	347.16	60.18	5.78	343.91	58.50	6.4
250	8.95	345.52	37.60	5.87	347.07	58.16	5.92	345.39	57.31	3.3
300	9.14	345.43	36.80	6.07	346.96	56.14	6.07	346.96	56.14	0.0
350	9.34	345.33	35.99	6.29	346.85	54.13	6.23	348.48	54.93	−3.2
400	9.54	345.23	35.17	6.52	346.74	52.15	6.40	350.00	53.69	−6.4
450	9.77	345.12	34.34	6.77	346.61	50.17	6.58	351.46	52.43	−9.5

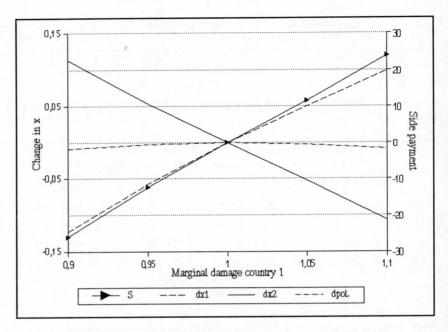

Figure 5.5 Coordination with side payments in a first-best world: $R_1 = R_2$
= 300, $MD_2 = 1$

Table 5.2 Coordination in a first-best world with side payments
$R_1 = R_2 = 300, MD_2 = 1.0$

	Non-cooperative Nash equilibrium			Cooperative equilibrium without side payments			Cooperative equilibrium with side payments			
					Country 1					
MD_1	x_1	y_1	tx_1	x_1	y_1	tx_1	x_1	y_1	tx_1	Side
0.90	2.60	498.25	190.86	1.77	498.67	281.24	1.64	511.73	310.31	-26.0
0.95	2.46	498.30	201.64	1.65	498.70	301.46	1.59	504.88	316.17	-12.0
1.00	2.33	498.33	212.69	1.54	498.73	322.54	1.54	498.73	322.54	0.0
1.05	2.22	498.37	223.89	1.44	498.75	344.52	1.49	492.88	329.02	12.0
1.10	2.11	498.40	235.32	1.35	498.77	367.42	1.45	486.72	334.02	24.0

					Country 2					
MD_1	x_2	y_2	tx_2	x_2	y_2	tx_2	x_2	y_2	tx_2	Side
0.90	2.22	498.39	223.30	1.42	498.79	349.84	1.54	485.73	315.29	26.0
0.95	2.28	498.36	217.68	1.48	498.76	335.25	1.54	492.58	319.42	12.0
1.00	2.33	498.33	212.69	1.54	498.73	322.58	1.54	498.73	322.54	0.0
1.05	2.38	498.31	208.20	1.60	498.70	311.45	1.54	504.58	325.84	-12.0
1.10	2.43	498.29	204.14	1.65	498.68	301.65	1.54	510.73	330.56	-24.0

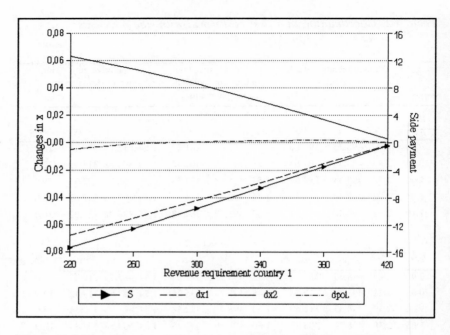

Figure 5.6 Coordination with side payments in a first-best world:
$R_2 = 250$, $MD_1 = 0.95$, $MD_2 = 1$

Table 5.3 Coordination in a first-best world with side payments
$R_2 = 250$ $MD_1 = 0.95$ $MD_2 = 1.0$

	Non-cooperative Nash equilibrium			Cooperative equilibrium without side payments			Cooperative equilibrium with side payments			
					Country 1					
R_1	x_1	y_1	tx_1	x_1	y_1	tx_1	x_1	y_1	tx_1	Side
220	2.60	388.70	148.67	1.75	389.12	220.85	1.69	396.86	234.38	-15.4
260	2.51	368.75	146.20	1.68	369.16	219.30	1.62	375.49	230.68	-12.6
300	2.41	348.80	143.73	1.60	349.20	217.92	1.55	354.02	226.95	-9.6
340	2.31	328.84	141.23	1.51	329.24	216.67	1.48	332.56	223.16	-6.6
380	2.21	308.89	138.71	1.43	309.29	215.57	1.41	311.04	219.11	-3.5
420	2.11	288.95	136.14	1.34	289.33	214.71	1.34	289.58	215.21	-0.5
					Country 2					
$R1$	x_2	y_2	tx_2	x_2	y_2	tx_2	x_2	y_2	tx_2	Side
220	2.32	373.84	160.49	1.49	374.25	249.54	1.56	366.52	234.40	15.4
260	2.35	373.82	157.87	1.54	374.23	242.64	1.59	367.91	230.40	12.6
300	2.39	373.80	155.21	1.58	374.21	235.89	1.62	369.39	226.69	9.6
340	2.44	373.78	152.50	1.63	374.19	229.17	1.66	370.87	222.97	6.6
380	2.48	373.76	149.77	1.67	374.16	222.50	1.69	372.40	219.25	3.5
420	2.53	373.74	147.01	1.73	374.14	215.87	1.73	373.89	215.41	0.5

Second-best Analysis

In the second-best simulations, the model described in the introduction to this section is used; consumers maximize utility function (5.29) (which includes two goods, x and y, and leisure, l) under the constraint of (5.30). This implies distortionary taxation: revenue is raised only through taxing x and y while leisure remains untaxed, therefore prices are distorted and taxation causes a welfare loss in addition to the welfare loss of the income transfer. The first second-best simulation analyses the role of the revenue requirement. In Figure 5.7, R_2 is set at 300 while R_1 is allowed to vary from 100 to 500. Marginal damage coefficients are set at 0.1. As can be seen in Table 5.4, in the non-cooperative equilibrium and the cooperative equilibrium without side payments the price ratio between good x and good y in the low revenue country, px/py (the price is equal to the tax plus the unity price of 1) is larger than the price ratio in the high revenue country. Therefore the low revenue country will pay the other country (the side payment is positive as long as R_1 is smaller than R_2) and reduce its tax on x while the other country increases its tax on x and decreases consumption of x. This is in contrast with the first-best case analysed above (see Figure 5.4).

In this simulation pollution rises, which is in contrast with the first-best case (see p. 116). The side payment has the additional effect of lowering aggregate deadweight loss of taxation because the country with the lower revenue requirement will raise more revenue while the other country will raise less. This results in an overall higher consumption of x and therefore a higher level of pollution as compared with the Nash bargaining solution without side payments.

In Figure 5.8, the difference between first-best and second-best is illustrated. Both countries have equal marginal damage coefficients (set at 0.1), country 1's revenue requirement is 200, which is lower than that of country 2's (R_2 = 300). The x-axis shows on the left the first-best case and on the right the second-best case (the whole revenue requirement has to be levied through distortionary taxation).[8] On the left-hand side (first-best), country 1, which has the lower revenue requirement, is paid by country 2. As we move to the right, towards second-best, the side payment increases. On the right, country 2, the country with the higher revenue requirement, receives the side payment from country 1. Moreover, pollution increases when no lump-sum taxes are used, on the right-hand side of the figure, while it decreases on the left-hand side, where lump-sum taxes are used.

In Figure 5.9, revenue requirements are held equal at 300 while the marginal damage coefficient in country 1 is varied from 0.7 to 1.2. In country 2, the marginal damage coefficient is 1. The side payment is negative. The country with the higher marginal damage (country 2) pays the other country.

Pollution declines. The results are the same as in the first-best case; this is not surprising. The country which has high marginal damage will initially reduce emissions further than the other country, accepting higher abatement costs. When side payments are possible, it will do less while it pays the other country to do more.

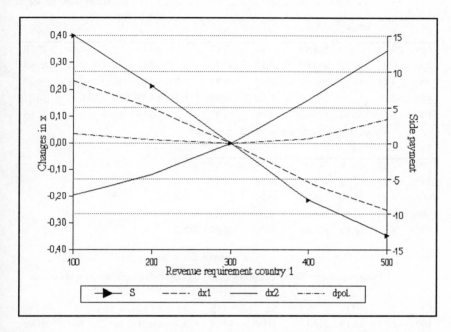

Figure 5.7 Coordination with side payments in a second-best world:
$R_2 = 300, MD_1 = MD_2 = 0.1$

Table 5.4 Coordination in a second-best world with side payments
$R_2 = 300$ $MD_1 = MD_2 = 0.1$

Country 1

	Non-cooperative Nash equilibrium					Cooperative equilibrium without side payments				
R_1	x_1	tx_1	y_1	ty_1	px/py_1	x_1	tx_1	y_1	ty_1	px/py_1
100	10.69	30.19	555.98	-0.40	52.02	7.38	44.16	559.29	-0.40	75.78
200	9.98	32.40	456.69	-0.27	45.76	6.78	48.17	459.89	-0.28	67.83
300	9.14	35.47	357.53	-0.07	39.11	6.07	53.89	360.59	-0.08	59.37
400	8.10	40.16	258.57	0.29	31.93	5.21	63.01	261.46	0.27	50.21
500	6.70	48.74	159.97	1.08	23.87	4.07	80.89	162.60	1.05	39.95

Cooperative equilibrium with side payments

R_1	x_1	tx_1	y_1	ty_1	px/py_1	Side
100	7.61	42.79	544.05	-0.39	71.47	15.0
200	6.91	47.24	451.76	-0.26	65.38	8.0
300	6.07	53.89	360.59	-0.08	59.37	0.0
400	5.06	64.86	269.61	0.24	53.26	-8.0
500	3.82	86.32	175.85	0.90	46.07	-13.0

Country 2

	Non-cooperative Nash equilibrium					Cooperative equilibrium without side payments				
$R1$	x_2	tx_2	y_2	ty_2	px/py_2	x_2	tx_2	y_2	ty_2	px/py_2
100	8.52	38.13	358.15	-0.07	42.04	5.39	60.81	361.27	-0.08	66.99
200	8.80	36.89	357.87	-0.07	40.68	5.70	57.52	360.97	-0.08	63.37
300	9.14	35.47	357.53	-0.07	39.11	6.07	53.89	360.59	-0.08	59.38
400	9.58	33.78	357.08	-0.07	37.26	6.57	49.75	360.10	-0.07	54.83
500	10.21	31.65	356.46	-0.06	34.91	7.28	44.79	359.39	-0.07	49.37

Cooperative equilibrium with side payments

R_2	x_2	tx_2	y_2	ty_2	px/py_2	Side
100	5.20	63.14	376.47	-0.11	72.44	-15.0
200	5.58	58.75	369.09	-0.10	66.16	-8.0
300	6.07	53.89	360.59	-0.08	59.38	0.0
400	6.73	48.52	351.94	-0.05	52.28	8.0
500	7.62	42.72	346.04	-0.04	45.39	13.0

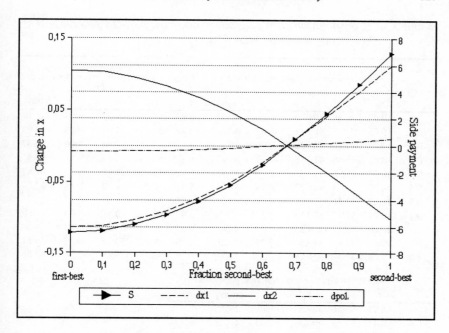

Figure 5.8   Coordination with side payments in a second-best world, from first- to second-best: $R_1 = 200$, $R_2 = 300$, $MD_1 = MD_2 = 0.1$

Economic Policy and Climate Change

Table 5.5a Coordination with side payments, from first- to second-best
$R_1 = 200$ $R_2=300$ $MD_1 = MD_2 = 0.1$

	Country 1									
	Non-cooperative Nash equilibrium					Cooperative equilibrium without side payments				
	x_1	tx_1	y_1	ty_1	px/py_1	x_1	tx_1	y_1	ty_1	px/py_1
0.0	10.03	38.38	394.99	0.00	39.38	6.83	57.10	396.59	0.00	58.10
0.1	10.03	37.77	401.15	-0.03	40.00	6.83	56.17	402.91	-0.03	59.03
0.2	10.03	37.16	407.32	-0.06	40.62	6.82	55.26	409.24	-0.06	59.97
0.3	10.02	36.56	413.48	-0.09	41.25	6.82	54.35	415.57	-0.09	60.91
0.4	10.02	35.96	419.65	-0.12	41.88	6.82	53.45	421.89	-0.12	61.87
0.5	10.02	35.35	425.82	-0.14	42.51	6.81	52.56	428.22	-0.15	62.84
0.6	10.01	34.76	431.99	-0.17	43.15	6.81	51.66	434.55	-0.17	63.81
0.7	10.01	34.17	438.16	-0.20	43.79	6.80	50.78	440.88	-0.20	64.80
0.8	10.00	33.57	444.34	-0.22	44.44	6.80	49.91	447.22	-0.23	65.80
0.9	9.99	32.99	450.51	-0.25	45.10	6.79	49.03	453.55	-0.25	66.81
1.0	9.98	32.40	456.69	-0.27	45.76	6.78	48.17	459.89	-0.28	67.83

Cooperative equilibrium with side payments

	x_1	tx_1	y_1	ty_1	px/py_1	Side
0.0	6.71	58.56	399.84	0.00	59.56	-6.4
0.1	6.71	57.55	406.44	-0.03	60.53	-6.3
0.2	6.72	56.46	412.78	-0.06	61.40	-5.8
0.3	6.73	55.36	418.94	-0.09	62.23	-5.1
0.4	6.75	54.22	424.81	-0.12	62.96	-4.1
0.5	6.76	53.06	430.43	-0.15	63.63	-2.9
0.6	6.79	51.88	435.69	-0.18	64.20	-1.4
0.7	6.81	50.70	440.45	-0.20	64.65	0.5
0.8	6.84	49.57	445.02	-0.22	65.09	2.4
0.9	6.86	48.45	449.11	-0.24	65.42	4.6
1.0	6.89	47.37	452.87	-0.26	65.71	6.9

Table 5.5b Coordination with side payments, from first- to second-best
$$R_1 = 200 \quad R_2 = 300 \quad MD_1 = MD_2 = 0.1$$

					Country 2				
	Non-cooperative Nash equilibrium					Cooperative equilibrium without sidepayments			
	x_2	tx_2	y_2	ty_2	px/py_2	x_2	tx_2	y_2	ty_2	px/py_2
0.0	8.78	38.39	345.61	0.00	39.39	5.67	60.18	347.16	0.00	61.18
0.1	8.78	38.25	346.84	-0.01	39.53	5.67	59.94	348.55	-0.01	61.42
0.2	8.78	38.10	348.07	-0.01	39.66	5.68	59.68	349.93	-0.02	61.66
0.3	8.78	37.96	349.29	-0.02	39.80	5.68	59.43	351.31	-0.02	61.89
0.4	8.78	37.81	350.52	-0.03	39.93	5.68	59.17	352.69	-0.03	62.12
0.5	8.78	37.66	351.75	-0.03	40.06	5.68	58.91	354.07	-0.04	62.34
0.6	8.78	37.51	352.97	-0.04	40.19	5.68	58.64	355.45	-0.05	62.56
0.7	8.79	37.36	354.20	-0.05	40.31	5.68	58.37	356.83	-0.05	62.77
0.8	8.79	37.20	355.42	-0.06	40.43	5.69	58.09	358.21	-0.06	62.97
0.9	8.79	37.04	356.65	-0.06	40.56	5.69	57.81	359.59	-0.07	63.18
1.0	8.80	36.89	357.87	-0.07	40.68	5.70	57.52	360.97	-0.08	63.37

	Cooperative equilibrium with side payments					
	x_2	tx_2	y_2	ty_2	px/py_2	Side
0.0	5.78	58.51	343.91	0.00	59.51	6.4
0.1	5.78	58.35	345.02	-0.01	59.72	6.3
0.2	5.77	58.28	346.39	-0.01	60.03	5.8
0.3	5.76	58.25	347.94	-0.02	60.42	5.1
0.4	5.74	58.25	349.78	-0.03	60.89	4.1
0.5	5.73	58.29	351.86	-0.04	61.45	2.9
0.6	5.70	58.35	354.32	-0.04	62.11	1.4
0.7	5.68	58.46	357.27	-0.06	62.93	-0.5
0.8	5.65	58.51	360.41	-0.07	63.77	-2.4
0.9	5.62	58.57	364.03	-0.08	64.74	-4.6
1.0	5.59	58.58	367.97	-0.09	65.77	-6.9

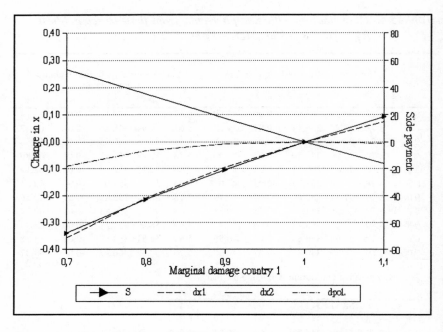

Figure 5.9 Coordination with side payments in a second-best world:
        $R_1 = R_2 = 300, MD_2 = 1$

Table 5.6 Coordination in a second-best world with side payments
$R_1 = R_2 = 300, MD_2 = 1.0$

Country 1

	Non-cooperative Nash equilibrium				Cooperative equilibrium without side payments				
MD_1	x_1	tx_1	y_1	ty_1	px/py_1	x_1	tx_1	y_1	ty_1	px/py_1
0.7	3.31	99.80	363.36	-0.08	109.88	2.38	139.03	364.29	-0.08	153.04
0.8	2.92	113.31	363.75	-0.08	124.74	2.04	162.35	364.63	-0.09	178.69
0.9	2.60	127.35	364.07	-0.08	140.19	1.77	187.72	364.90	-0.09	206.59
1.0	2.33	141.94	364.33	-0.09	156.23	1.54	215.31	365.13	-0.09	236.94
1.1	2.11	157.05	364.56	-0.09	172.86	1.35	245.31	365.31	-0.09	269.94

Cooperative equilibrium with side payments

MD_1	x_1	tx_1	y_1	ty_1	px/py_1	Side
0.7	2.02	163.82	364.64	-0.09	180.30	-68.0
0.8	1.83	181.09	364.84	-0.09	199.30	-43.0
0.9	1.67	198.56	365.00	-0.09	218.52	-21.0
1.0	1.54	215.31	365.13	-0.09	236.94	0.0
1.1	1.43	232.38	365.24	-0.09	255.72	19.0

Country 2

	Non-cooperative Nash equilibrium				Cooperative equilibrium without side payments				
MD_1	x_2	tx_2	y_2	ty_2	px/py_2	x_2	tx_2	y_2	ty_2	px/py_2
0.7	1.95	169.85	364.72	-0.09	186.94	1.14	292.50	365.53	-0.09	321.86
0.8	2.10	158.03	364.57	-0.09	173.94	1.29	258.04	365.38	-0.09	283.94
0.9	2.22	149.02	364.44	-0.09	164.02	1.42	233.54	365.25	-0.09	257.00
1.0	2.33	141.94	364.33	-0.09	156.23	1.54	215.32	365.13	-0.09	236.96
1.1	2.43	136.23	364.24	-0.08	149.95	1.65	201.34	365.02	-0.09	221.57

Cooperative equilibrium with side payments

MD_1	x_2	tx_2	y_2	ty_2	px/py_2	Side
0.7	1.40	236.57	365.26	-0.09	260.33	68.0
0.8	1.46	226.84	365.20	-0.09	249.63	43.0
0.9	1.51	219.93	365.16	-0.09	242.02	21.0
1.0	1.54	215.32	365.13	-0.09	236.96	0.0
1.1	1.57	211.72	365.10	-0.09	232.99	-19.0

Summary

Simulations have been used to determine the changes in tax structures and pollution when countries cooperate in pollution control. Two types of cooperation have been examined: with and without side payments. The cooperative solution analysed here is the Nash bargaining equilibrium. Therefore, the results derived only show the role of side payments and the changes in tax structures for this specific cooperative solution. The most striking conclusion is that it is not necessarily the case that including side payments in cooperative agreements will lead to lower pollution levels compared with cooperative agreements without side payments. Simulations show that in both first-best and second-best models the use of side payments can lead to higher pollution levels, although both countries will (necessarily) increase their welfare. This can occur in the first-best models in situations where the revenue requirement in one country is higher while marginal damage is lower than in the other country. In the second-best models, pollution increases when marginal damage coefficients are equal and the revenue requirements differ.

Furthermore, the simulations show that by introducing side payments starting from an initial Nash bargaining equilibrium in terms of cooperatively set tax rates, in the first-best case, *ceteris paribus*, the country with the higher revenue requirement will make the side payment. This country will reduce its tax on good x and consume more of it (and raise its tax on y substantially), while the other country will raise its tax on good x. These conclusions are reversed in the second-best case. The country with the lower revenue requirement will pay the other country. When the two countries are equal except as regards the marginal damage done by the pollution, the country with the lower marginal damage will receive the side payment. This holds in both the first-best and the second-best case.

5.5 CONCLUSIONS

In this chapter, we have investigated how countries can cooperate in reducing transboundary pollution such as the enhanced greenhouse effect, which is caused to a large extent by CO_2 emissions. In order to take into account the complicating problem that countries already tax fossil fuels, the main source of CO_2 emissions, a two-country second-best model was used. The essence of this second-best model is that the authorities have to use distortionary taxation to raise the revenue they need because it is assumed that no first-best non-distortionary taxation can be used. Therefore, the polluting good is already taxed, such as the existing taxes on fossil fuels, and an initial second-best solution is assumed to exist before the pollution problem is discovered and a pollution tax is introduced as an instrument to reduce environmental damage. The revenue requirement of each country is assumed to be an exogenous variable (which is not necessarily equal in both countries). The pollution which results from the consumption of the dirty good occurs in both countries, regardless of the country from which it emanates, and reduces welfare. The damage caused in the two countries can differ between them.

The tax on the polluting good may be split up into a Pigouvian tax, which is levied to reduce pollution, and a Ramsey part, which is intended to raise revenue. The main conclusion from the earlier part of the chapter is that countries can increase their welfare when they cooperate to reduce emissions instead of acting on their own. With cooperation they will increase the Pigouvian part of the tax which they levy on the dirty good. However, these Pigouvian taxes differ between the two countries when their revenue requirements differ.

Cooperation can be extended if countries use side payments when they cooperate. In that case, one country pays the other country, reduces its Pigouvian tax and consumes more of the dirty good (and therefore pollutes more), while the second country raises its Pigouvian tax and consumes less of the dirty good. With side payments, the Pigouvian taxes in both countries will be equal, even if the revenue requirements and the damage functions differ. The Ramsey taxes, however, will still differ (with different revenue requirements) therefore the aggregate taxes on the polluting good differ as well between the two countries (this in contrast to cooperation in a first-best world).

Unfortunately, the general model does not tell us how the tax structure in both countries will change when they cooperate (with and without side payments). Therefore, a more specific functional form has been used (a Cobb–Douglas utility function) to run several simulations with different damage functions and revenue requirements. The cooperative equilibrium analysed is the Nash bargaining solution; the results are therefore specific for this cooperative equilibrium. Simulations have been done with both non-distortionary taxation (first-best) and distortionary taxation (the second-best case). An interesting conclusion is that including side payments in agreements on emission abatement can actually increase pollution compared with agreements which do not include side payments. This can occur both in a first-best and in a second-best world.

The simulations show that in the first-best case, *ceteris paribus*, the country with the higher revenue requirement (and the higher tax on x) makes the side payment. This country reduces its tax on the polluting good and consumes more of it, while the other country raises its tax on the dirty good. These conclusions are reversed in the second-best case. The country with the lower revenue requirement pays the other country and pollution will increase.

When the two countries are equal except as regards the marginal damage done by pollution, the country with the lower marginal damage will receive the side payment. This holds in both the first-best and the second-best case.

NOTES

1. The optimal tax problem was originally discussed by Ramsey. See Auerbach 1987.
2. It should be noted that μ_2 does not represent the shadow cost of taxation for country 2 in equation 5.9. Instead, it represents the effect a marginal change in the revenue requirement for country 2, R_2, has on the welfare of country 1. The constraint is not on the welfare of country 2 in this equation but on the welfare of country 1.
3. The fact that there are several possible approaches is in itself a weakness: there is no reason to prefer one of the approaches above the other.
4. When both countries are equal in all respects, the optimal side payment is zero in the Nash bargaining solution and the equilibrium does not change.
5. In negotiations which include side payments right from the start, this problem would not arise. The step from non-cooperative equilibrium to cooperative equilibrium will necessarily increase welfare levels in both countries. Only when side payments are allowed after the implementation of the Nash bargaining solution without side payments will the problem arise that one country can end up worse off. It is assumed here that negotiations will follow this two-step aproach.
6. This is the case because the marginal damage coefficient is set equal in both countries. Consequently, marginal damage is equal, given the levels of x consumed in both countries in the Nash equilibrium. In a first-best world, the Pigouvian tax is equal to marginal damage, therefore taxes are the same in both countries.
7. In the first-best model examined here, revenue is raised through a lump-sum tax, therefore the only taxes levied on good x are the Pigouvian taxes. It has been shown above that the Pigouvian taxes are equal in both countries in the equilibrium with side payments.
8. In this simulation, the revenue raised by the tax on x exceeds the revenue requirements in both countries. The percentage values shown on the x-axis are the percentage of the tax revenue (minus revenue requirement and side payment) returned to the consumers through a non-distortionary lump-sum tax. The part of the excess tax revenue which is not restored through the lump-sum tax is returned through a (distortionary) subsidy on good y (a negative tax t_y).

APPENDIX: NON-COOPERATIVE NASH EQUILIBRIUM

Sign of the Reaction Curve in the Non-cooperative Nash Equilibrium

The reaction curve of the non-cooperative Nash equilibrium is given by equation (5.7):

$$d_{tx1}/d_{tx2} = (y1+y_{ty1}ty1)\, D1_{x1x2}\, x2_{tx2}\, [(y1+y_{ty1}ty1)\, x1_{tx1} - (x1+x_{tx1}tx1)\, x1_{ty1}\,] \tag{A5.1}$$

$(y1+y_{ty1}ty1)$ and $(x1+x_{tx1}tx1)$ are the changes in revenue of a marginal change in tax $tx1$ or $ty1$, $\partial R/\partial t$. The Lagrange multiplier μ is the change in welfare due to a slight change in the constraint R. A lower revenue requirement means a higher welfare level, therefore $\mu = \partial V/\partial - R > 0$. μ can be written as:

$$\mu = \partial V/\partial t\, /\, -\partial R/\partial t \geq 0 \tag{A5.2}$$

$V_t \leq 0$, therefore $\partial R/\partial t \geq 0$.

If revenue would rise with a fall in one of the taxes, this tax would not be optimal: lowering the tax would raise the welfare level while at the same time the revenue constraint would be fullfilled as well. Therefore, tax revenue will rise in equilibrium when one of the taxes is raised.

D_{x1x2} is equal to D_{x1x1} which was assumed to be negative. x_{tx} and y_{ty} are negative in both countries, $x1_{ty1}$ is assumed to be positive (a rise in the price of one good raises demand for the other good). As a result, d_{tx1}/d_{tx2} is negative.

Existence of the Non-cooperative Nash Equilibrium

The existence of the non-cooperative Nash equilibrium is proved by showing that the equilibrium is asymptotically stable (see Fudenberg and Tyrole 1993, p. 24). A sufficient condition for this is that:

$$U1_{tx1tx2}\, U2_{tx1tx2} < U1_{tx1tx1}\, U2_{tx2tx2} \tag{A5.3}$$

$$\Rightarrow D1_{x1x2}\, x1_{tx1}\, x2_{tx2}\, D2_{x1x2}\, x1_{tx1}\, x2_{tx2} < U1_{tx1tx1}\, U2_{tx2tx2} \tag{A5.4}$$

The second derivatives of the welfare functions on the right hand side of equation (A5.4) also contain the second derivative of the damage functions. These cancel out the terms on the left hand side. Consequently, (A5.4) can be written as:

$$[V1_{tx1tx1} + D1_{x1}\, x1_{tx1tx1} + \mu_1(2x_{tx1} + x_{tx1tx1}\, tx1 + y_{tx1tx1}\, ty1)]\; *$$

$$[V2_{tx2tx2} + D2_{x2}\, x2_{tx2tx2} + \mu_2(2x_{tx2} + x_{tx2tx2}\, tx2 + y_{tx2tx2}\, ty2)] > 0 \quad (A5.5)$$

Both terms are negative when the utility functions are concave and the constraints are convex. Consequently, inequality (A5.5) holds and therefore the Nash equilibrium is asymptotically stable.

6. Tradable Permits and Coordination of Environmental Policy in a Second-best World

6.1 INTRODUCTION

In the previous chapter a two-country model was used to analyse coordination of environmental policy in a second-best world. In this model a damage function was included to reflect the damage done by polluting emissions such as CO_2. However, one of the problems with the greenhouse effect is the uncertainty about a future temperature rise and the even greater uncertainty about damage caused by the rising temperature. Therefore in practice countries formulate their greenhouse policies not on the basis of damage functions; instead they set emission reduction targets. We can introduce these given emission targets into the model in place of the damage function (section 6.2). Subsequently, we can again analyse how the optimal tax structure changes when the two countries cooperate. Using simulations, we study how different government budgets and different initial emission quotas influence the tax structures in both countries in the cooperative equilibrium (sections 6.3 and 6.4).

Our main interest in the study of cooperation in a second-best world here and in the previous chapter is to examine the role which economic instruments and especially tradable permits can play in attaining the optimal cooperative equilibria. This is the subject of section 6.5. We consider how to design international agreements on CO_2 abatement to take into account the complexities of international cooperation when taxes or TCPs must both reduce emissions and raise revenue. Another point of interest is one of the recurrent themes of this study: grandfathering versus the auctioning of permits. At first sight it might be expected that auctioning is to be preferred because the authorities also have to raise revenue: grandfathering permits means that revenue has to be raised in another way. We examine whether and under what conditions this intuition holds. The chapter ends with an overview of the main conclusions (section 6.6).

6.2 THE MODEL

The two countries are assumed to be equal except with respect to their (initial) emission limit and the government budget. Our interest is in how these two variables affect the tax structure and the sidepayment when countries cooperate. For one country, the maximization problem then becomes:

$$\max V + \mu(x \, t_x + y \, t_y - R) - \eta(x - q) \tag{6.1}$$

q is the limit to the emissions, and thus the limit to the consumption of good x (as emissions are directly related to the consumption of x).

The first-order conditions are:

$$V_{t_x} + \mu(x + x_{t_x}(t_x - \eta/\mu) + y_{t_x}t_y) = 0 \tag{6.2}$$

$$V_{t_y} + \mu(y + x_{t_y}(t_x - \eta/\mu) + y_{t_y}t_x) = 0 \tag{6.3}$$

$$x \, t_x + y \, t_y - R = 0 \tag{6.4}$$

$$x - q = 0 \tag{6.5}$$

Tax t_x can be split in the Ramsey tax t_x^R which is the tax levied when there is no emission ceiling, and a Pigouvian tax t_x^P:

$$t_x = t_x^R + \eta/\mu \tag{6.6}$$

where $\eta/\mu = t_x^P$. η is the shadow price of the emission reduction, that is of reducing the consumption of x by one unit. In a second-best world, the Pigouvian tax is equal to the shadow price of the emission limit divided by the shadow price of taxation.

The next step is to extend the model and include a second country. An important difference with the analysis in the previous chapter which included damage functions is that the first-order conditions for the non-cooperative Nash equilibrium and the cooperative equilibrium without side payments are the same. The countries do not affect each other's welfare level because there are no damage functions and therefore they have no incentive to cooperate by changing the tax structure. The exogenously determined emission ceilings of the two countries, q_1 and q_2, can be interpreted either as the result of uncoordinated policies: each country sets its own emission quota independently, or as the result of a coordinated policy. As it does not matter how the emission quotas are arrived at for the following analysis, no specific assumption will be made.

Although there is no difference between the non-cooperative Nash equilibrium and the cooperative equilibrium without side payments, there is still scope for improving welfare in both countries by allowing the use of side payments. Such a form of cooperation is nowadays termed joint implementation: one country abates less and makes payments to the other country which in turn will reduce its emissions further. Total emissions necessarily remain the same. The consequences for the optimal tax structures in both countries can be determined by establishing the cooperative equilibrium with side payments:

$$\max V_1 + \mu_1(x_1 tx1 + y_1 ty1 - (R_1+S)) + \mu_2(x_2 tx2 + y_2 ty2 - (R_2-S))$$

$$+ \gamma(V_2 - W_2^*) - \eta(x_1 + x_2 - (q_1+q_2)) \tag{6.7}$$

The first-order conditions are:

$$L_{tx1} = V_{tx1} + \mu_1(x_1 + tx1\, x_{tx1} + ty1\, y_{tx1}) - \eta x_{tx1} = 0 \tag{6.8}$$

$$L_{ty1} = V_{ty1} + \mu_1(y_1 + ty1\, y_{ty1} + tx1\, x_{ty1}) - \eta x_{ty1} = 0 \tag{6.9}$$

$$L_{tx2} = \gamma V_{tx2} + \mu_2(x_2 + tx2\, x_{tx2} + ty2\, y_{tx2}) - \eta x_{tx2} = 0 \tag{6.10}$$

$$L_{ty2} = \gamma V_{ty2} + \mu_2(y_2 + ty2\, y_{ty2} + tx2\, x_{ty2}) - \eta x_{ty2} = 0 \tag{6.11}$$

$$L_{\mu1} = x_1\, tx1 + y_1\, ty1 - R_1 = 0 \tag{6.12}$$

$$L_{\mu2} = x_2\, tx2 + y_2\, ty2 - R_2 = 0 \tag{6.13}$$

$$L_\gamma = V_2 - W_2^* = 0 \tag{6.14}$$

$$L_\eta = x_1 + x_2 - (q_1+q_2) = 0 \tag{6.15}$$

$$L_S = -\mu_1 + \mu_2 = 0 \tag{6.16}$$

When $S > 0$, country 1 pays country 2 (a positive S increases R_2 and decreases R_1 (equation (6.7)): a transfer from country 1 to country 2). With a negative S it is the other way around. S is positive if initially $\mu_1 < \mu_2$, because a positive S increases μ_1 and decreases μ_2 (equation (6.7)) and because $\mu_1 = \mu_2$; the first-order derivative of 6.7 with respect to S, equation (6.16). Splitting the tax on good x in a Ramsey and a Pigouvian part, the

Pigouvian taxes can be written as:

$$tx_i{}^P = \eta/\mu_i \quad i=1,2 \tag{6.17}$$

As $\mu_1 = \mu_2$ (equation (6.16)), the Pigouvian taxes will be equal in both countries. However, the Ramsey taxes will still differ. Therefore total tax on the dirty good will not be the same in both countries. This conclusion is similar to the result in the second-best model with damage functions (section 5.3). It is in contrast with the result in a first-best world, as we indicated in the introduction to this chapter.

How will the side payment affect taxes in both countries? When country 1 pays country 2, tax tx_2 will necessarily increase. A decrease in the revenue constraint on country 2, R_2, must raise welfare in country 1. This is only possible when tx_2 increases and therefore x_2 decreases because it allows country 1 to increase consumption of x relative to its initial consumption level of x, given the fixed emission limit. In country 1, tx_1 will fall and consumption of x_1 will rise.

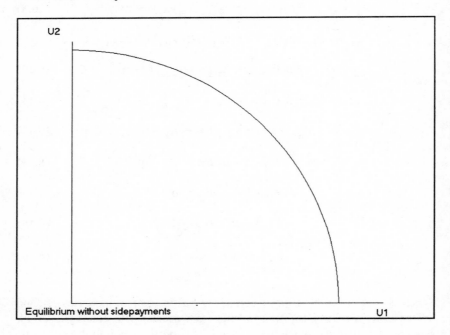

Figure 6.1 Non-cooperative and cooperative equilibria

Optimization problem (6.7) yields an equilibrium point in which country 2 has welfare level W_2^* (the constraint on its welfare) and country 1 the highest achievable welfare. Choosing another welfare constraint for country 2 will yield another welfare level for country 1. There is a range of equilibria which will leave both countries better off compared with the situation in which no side payments are used. This is illustrated in Figure 6.1.

One specific solution is the Nash bargaining solution, which maximizes:

$$(U_1 - T_1)(U_2 - T_2) \text{ subject to } x_1 tx1 + y_1 ty1 \geq (R_1 + S) \qquad (6.18)$$
$$x_2 tx2 + y_2 ty2 \geq (R_2 - S)$$
$$x_1 + x_2 \leq q_1 + q_2$$

The threat points T_1 and T_2 are the welfare levels in the equilibrium without side payments. Assuming that the Nash bargaining solution represents the outcome of negotiations on the use of side payments and the allocation of its benefits, we can analyse who pays whom for different revenue requirements and different initial quotas. However, formal analysis does not yield interpretable results. In the next section, simulations will be carried out using a specific welfare function in order to determine the Nash bargaining equilibrium for cooperation with side payments.

6.3 SIMULATIONS OF THE NASH-BARGAINING EQUILIBRIUM

In the simulations, the Cobb–Douglas function from section 5.4 is used to determine the cooperative Nash bargaining solution with side payments (see for more details section 5.4):

$$\max (U_1 - T_1)(U_2 - T_2) \text{ subject to } x_1 tx1 + y_1 ty1 \geq R_1 + S \qquad (6.19)$$
$$x_2 tx2 + y_2 ty2 \geq R_2 - S$$
$$x_1 + x_2 \leq q_1 + q_2$$

$$U_i = x^\alpha y^\beta l^\gamma \qquad \alpha = \beta = \gamma = 1/3 \qquad (6.20)$$

T_i is each country's welfare level when both countries achieve their emission targets without joint implementation.

First, the effect of different revenue requirements on the side payment is analysed in a first-best setting. Instead of distortionary taxation, a lump-sum tax is used to raise revenue. The result of this simulation is shown in Figure 6.2. The initial emission ceilings or quotas for both countries are set at 10, the revenue requirement in country 2 is 25, the revenue requirement for country 1 varies from 20 to 30. As we can see in Table 6.1, the country with the lower revenue requirement levies a higher tax on good x in the initial situation than the other country: given the higher income left for the consumer, the tax on x has to be higher to meet the quota. When side payments are introduced it is therefore more efficient for the country with the higher tax on x to reduce that tax and to pay the other country to reduce further its consumption of x. Moreover, the country with the lower revenue requirement can better afford to pay the other country than vice versa because the marginal utility of income is lower because its income is higher.

The second simulation is similar to the first except that revenue has to be raised by distortionary taxation. The result is shown in Figure 6.3 and Table 6.2. The price ratios between good x and good y (the full price is the tax plus the unity price of 1) show that good x is taxed relatively more in the low revenue country. Consequently the country with the lower revenue requirement pays the other country as in the case of non-distortionary taxation.

The country's lower revenue requirement makes it less costly in welfare terms to make a payment to the other country than would be the case the other way round. This argument holds more weight in a second-best world than in a first-best world because the side payment has to be raised by distortionary taxation. Indeed, a side payment made by the country with the low R to the country with the high R has the additional benefit of reducing the overall deadweight loss of taxation. This is shown in Figure 6.4 and Table 6.3, the result of a simulation in which country 1 has a revenue requirement of 20 and country 2 of 25. The emission quotas for both countries are set initially at 10. The x-axis shows the percentage of the revenue which is raised (returned) by lump-sum taxes. On the left-hand side of the graph, revenue is raised (returned) by a non-distortionary lump-sum tax; on the right-hand side distortionary taxation is used. The more distortionary the taxation is, the larger is the side payment, reflecting the additional benefit of side payments in a second-best world. This is shown in Table 6.3 in the columns headed ΔU_1 and ΔU_2. In these columns the increase in welfare in both countries when side payments are allowed is given. In both countries the welfare increase rises as the side payment increases. Moreover, the higher the side payment is, the larger is the shift in emission reduction from the low revenue country to the high revenue country.

Not only the revenue requirements can differ, but also the emission limits set by both countries. Figure 6.5 shows the result of a simulation in which country 1 has a lower quota than country 2 ($q_1 = 8$, $q_2 = 10$). The revenue requirements are equal at 30. Both first-best and second-best are considered, the percentage of the revenue which is raised by non-distortionary taxation is shown on the x-axis. In both a first-best and a second-best world, the country with the lower emission ceiling and therefore lowest initial consumption of

x will pay the other country. As this country faces higher abatement costs in terms of forgone utility of consuming x, it will be advantageous to pay the other country to take on a larger part of the aggregate emission reduction. The burden shift and the side payment are smaller the more distortionary is the taxation. In a second-best world, the side payment has to be raised by distortionary taxation, increasing the welfare costs for the paying country. Because both countries have the same revenue requirement, this is not compensated by a reduction in overall deadweight loss of taxation, as is the case when revenue requirements differ.

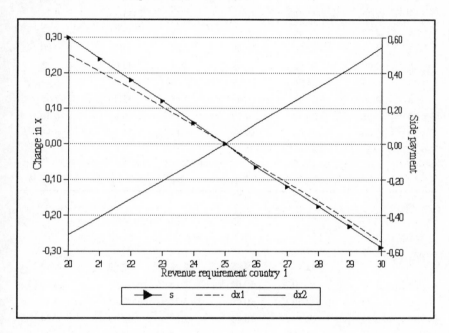

Figure 6.2 Coordination with side payments: emission limits in a first-best world; $R_2 = 25$, $q_1 = q_2 = 10$

Table 6.1 Coordination with side payments and emission limits in a first-best world; $\underline{R}_2 = 25$, $\underline{q}_1 = \underline{q}_2 = 10$

	Initial situation		Cooperative equilibrium with side payments			
			Country 1			
R_1	tx_1	y_1	x_1	tx_1	y_1	Side
20	2.50	35.00	10.25	2.37	34.57	0.60
21	2.45	34.50	10.20	2.35	34.16	0.48
22	2.40	34.00	10.16	2.32	33.74	0.36
23	2.35	33.50	10.10	2.30	33.33	0.24
24	2.30	33.00	10.05	2.27	32.91	0.12
25	2.25	32.50	10.00	2.25	32.50	0.00
26	2.20	32.00	9.94	2.23	32.09	-0.13
27	2.15	31.50	9.89	2.20	31.67	-0.24
28	2.10	31.00	9.84	2.18	31.26	-0.35
29	2.05	30.50	9.79	2.15	30.84	-0.46
30	2.00	30.00	9.73	2.13	30.43	-0.58
			Country 2			
R_1	tx_2	y_2	x_2	tx_2	y_2	Side
20	2.25	32.50	9.75	2.38	32.93	-0.60
21	2.25	32.50	9.80	2.35	32.84	-0.48
22	2.25	32.50	9.85	2.33	32.76	-0.36
23	2.25	32.50	9.90	2.30	32.67	-0.24
24	2.25	32.50	9.95	2.28	32.59	-0.12
25	2.25	32.50	10.00	2.25	32.50	0.00
26	2.25	32.50	10.06	2.22	32.41	0.13
27	2.25	32.50	10.11	2.20	32.33	0.24
28	2.25	32.50	10.16	2.17	32.24	0.35
29	2.25	32.50	10.21	2.15	32.16	0.46
30	2.25	32.50	10.27	2.12	32.07	0.58

Note: In the initial situation, x_1 and x_2 equal q_1 and q_2.

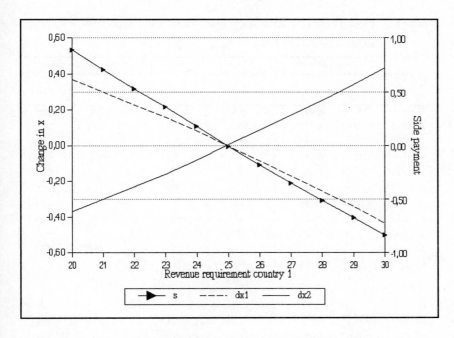

Figure 6.3 Coordination with side payments: emission limits in a second-best world; $R_2 = 25$, $MD_1 = MD_2 = 10$

Table 6.2 Coordination with side payments and emission limits in a second-best world; $R_2 = 25$, $q_1 = q_2 = 10$

		Initial situation			Cooperative equilibrium with side payments					
					Country 1					
R_1	$tx1$	y_1	$ty1$	px/py	x_1	$tx1$	y_1	$ty1$	px/py	Side
20	2.33	36.67	-0.09	3.67	10.37	2.21	36.30	-0.08	3.50	0.89
21	2.33	35.67	-0.07	3.57	10.30	2.24	35.37	-0.06	3.43	0.71
22	2.33	34.67	-0.04	3.47	10.23	2.26	34.44	-0.03	3.37	0.53
23	2.33	33.67	-0.01	3.37	10.16	2.28	33.51	-0.01	3.30	0.36
24	2.33	32.67	0.02	3.27	10.08	2.31	32.59	0.02	·3.23	0.18
25	2.33	31.67	0.05	3.17	10.00	2.34	31.67	0.05	3.17	-0.01
26	2.33	30.67	0.09	3.07	9.92	2.36	30.75	0.08	3.10	-0.18
27	2.33	29.67	0.12	2.97	9.83	2.39	29.84	0.12	3.03	-0.35
28	2.33	28.67	0.16	2.87	9.75	2.42	28.92	0.15	2.97	-0.51
29	2.33	27.67	0.20	2.77	9.66	2.45	28.01	0.19	2.90	-0.67
30	2.33	26.67	0.25	2.67	9.57	2.48	27.10	0.23	2.83	-0.83
					Country 2					
R_1	$tx2$	y_2	$ty2$	px/py	x_2	$tx2$	y_2	$ty2$	px/py	side
20	2.33	31.67	0.05	3.17	9.63	2.46	32.04	0.04	3.33	-0.89
21	2.33	31.67	0.05	3.17	9.70	2.44	31.97	0.04	3.30	-0.71
22	2.33	31.67	0.05	3.17	9.77	2.41	31.90	0.05	3.26	-0.53
23	2.33	31.67	0.05	3.17	9.84	2.39	31.83	0.05	3.23	-0.36
24	2.33	31.67	0.05	3.17	9.92	2.36	31.75	·0.05	3.20	-0.18
25	2.33	31.67	0.05	3.17	10.01	2.33	31.66	0.05	3.16	0.01
26	2.33	31.67	0.05	3.17	10.09	2.31	31.58	0.06	3.13	0.18
27	2.33	31.67	0.05	3.17	10.17	2.28	31.50	0.06	3.10	0.35
28	2.33	31.67	0.05	3.17	10.25	2.25	31.41	0.06	3.06	0.51
29	2.33	31.67	0.05	3.17	10.34	2.22	31.33	0.06	3.03	0.67
30	2.33	31.67	0.05	3.17	10.43	2.19	31.23	0.07	2.99	0.83

Note: In the intial situation, x_1 and x_2 equal q_1 and q_2.

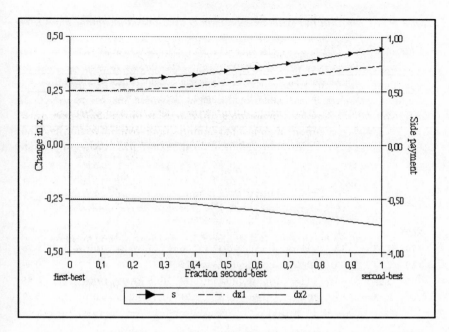

Figure 6.4 Coordination with side payments: emission limits, from first- to second-best; $R_1 = R_2 = 25$, $q_1 = q_2 = 10$

Table 6.3 Coordination with side payments and emission limits, from first-to second-best; $R_1 = 20$, $R_2 = 25$, $q_1 = q_2 = 10$

	Initial situation				Cooperative equilibrium with side payments						
					Country 1						
frc[a]	$tx1$	y_1	$ty1$	px/py	x_1	$tx1$	y_1	$ty1$	ΔU_1	px/py	Side
0.00	2.50	35.00	0.00	3.50	10.25	2.37	34.57	0.00	0.003	3.37	0.60
0.10	2.48	35.17	-0.01	3.52	10.25	2.36	34.70	-0.01	0.004	3.39	0.60
0.20	2.47	35.33	-0.02	3.54	10.26	2.35	34.81	-0.01	0.004	3.38	0.61
0.30	2.45	35.50	-0.03	3.56	10.27	2.33	34.92	-0.02	0.004	3.40	0.63
0.40	2.43	35.67	-0.04	3.57	10.27	2.32	35.02	-0.03	0.004	3.42	0.65
0.50	2.42	35.83	-0.05	3.60	10.29	2.30	35.10	-0.03	0.005	3.40	0.69
0.60	2.40	36.00	-0.06	3.62	10.30	2.28	35.18	-0.04	0.006	3.42	0.72
0.70	2.38	36.17	-0.06	3.60	10.32	2.26	35.25	-0.04	0.006	3.40	0.76
0.80	2.37	36.33	-0.07	3.62	10.33	2.25	35.31	-0.05	0.007	3.42	0.80
0.90	2.35	36.50	-0.08	3.64	10.35	2.23	35.36	-0.05	0.009	3.40	0.85
1.00	2.33	36.67	-0.09	3.66	10.37	2.21	35.41	-0.06	0.010	3.41	0.89

					Country 2						
frc[a]	$tx2$	y_2	$ty2$	px/py	x_2	$tx2$	y_2	$ty2$	ΔU_2	px/py	Side
0.00	2.25	32.50	0.00	3.25	9.75	2.38	32.93	0.00	0.003	3.38	0.60
0.10	2.26	32.42	0.01	3.23	9.75	2.38	32.89	0.00	0.004	3.38	0.60
0.20	2.27	32.33	0.01	3.24	9.74	2.39	32.85	0.00	0.004	3.39	0.61
0.30	2.28	32.25	0.02	3.22	9.74	2.40	32.83	0.01	0.004	3.37	0.63
0.40	2.28	32.17	0.02	3.22	9.73	2.40	32.81	0.01	0.004	3.37	0.65
0.50	2.29	32.08	0.03	3.19	9.71	2.42	32.82	0.01	0.005	3.39	0.69
0.60	2.30	32.00	0.03	3.20	9.70	2.42	32.82	0.01	0.006	3.39	0.72
0.70	2.31	31.92	0.04	3.18	9.68	2.43	32.83	0.01	0.007	3.40	0.76
0.80	2.32	31.83	0.04	3.19	9.67	2.44	32.85	0.01	0.008	3.41	0.80
0.90	2.33	31.75	0.05	3.17	9.65	2.45	32.89	0.01	0.009	3.42	0.85
1.00	2.33	31.67	0.05	3.17	9.63	2.46	32.93	0.01	0.010	3.43	0.89

Notes:
In the initial situation, x_1 and x_2 equal q_1 and q_2.
[a] Fraction of second-best; 0 = first-best, 1 = second-best.

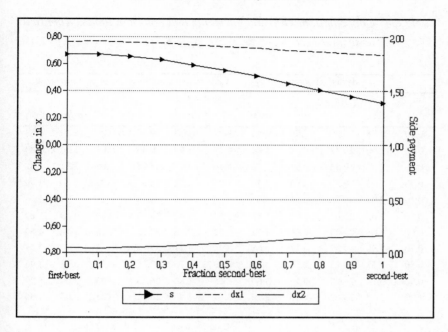

Figure 6.5 Coordination with side payments: emission limits, from first- to second-best; $R_1 = R_2 = 30$, $\mathbf{q_1} = 8$, $\mathbf{q_2} = 10$

Table 6.4 Coordination with side payments and emission limits, from first-to second-best; $R_1 = R_2 = 30$, $q_1 = 8$, $q_2 = 10$

	Initial situation				Cooperative equilibrium with side payments					
					Country 1					
frc[a]	tx1	y_1	ty1	px/py	x_1	tx1	y_1	ty1	px/px	Side
0.00	2.88	31.00	0.00	3.88	8.77	2.39	29.70	0.00	3.39	1.84
0.10	2.90	30.77	0.02	3.82	8.77	2.43	29.33	0.02	3.36	1.84
0.20	2.93	30.53	0.03	3.82	8.76	2.47	28.98	0.05	3.31	1.82
0.30	2.96	30.30	0.05	3.77	8.76	2.52	28.65	0.08	3.26	1.79
0.40	2.99	30.07	0.06	3.76	8.74	2.57	28.33	0.10	3.24	1.74
0.50	3.02	29.83	0.08	3.72	8.73	2.62	28.02	0.13	3.20	1.69
0.60	3.05	29.60	0.09	3.72	8.72	2.66	27.71	0.15	3.18	1.57
0.70	3.08	29.37	0.11	3.68	8.70	2.71	27.44	0.18	3.14	1.51
0.80	3.11	29.13	0.13	3.64	8.69	2.76	27.15	0.20	3.13	1.45
0.90	3.14	28.90	0.15	3.60	8.68	2.80	26.88	0.23	3.09	1.39
1.00	3.17	28.67	0.16	3.59	8.67	2.85	26.61	0.25	3.08	1.35

					Country 2					
frc[a]	tx2	y_2	ty2	px/py	x_2	tx2	y_2	ty2	px/py	Side
0.00	2.00	30.00	0.00	3.00	9.23	2.36	31.30	0.00	3.36	1.84
0.10	2.03	29.67	0.02	2.97	9.23	2.38	31.10	0.01	3.35	1.84
0.20	2.07	29.33	0.05	2.92	9.24	2.41	30.88	0.03	3.31	1.82
0.30	2.10	29.00	0.07	2.90	9.25	2.43	30.65	0.04	3.30	1.79
0.40	2.13	28.67	0.09	2.87	9.26	2.45	30.40	0.06	3.25	1.74
0.50	2.17	28.33	0.12	2.83	9.27	2.47	30.15	0.07	3.24	1.69
0.60	2.20	28.00	0.14	2.81	9.28	2.49	29.89	0.09	3.20	1.57
0.70	2.23	27.67	0.17	2.76	9.30	2.51	29.60	0.10	3.19	1.51
0.80	2.27	27.33	0.20	2.73	9.31	2.53	29.31	0.12	3.15	1.45
0.90	2.30	27.00	0.22	2.70	9.32	2.55	29.02	0.14	3.11	1.39
1.00	2.33	26.67	0.25	2.66	9.33	2.57	28.72	0.16	3.08	1.35

Notes:
In the intial situation, x_1 and x_2 equal q_1 and q_2.
[a] Frc is the fraction of second-best; 0 = first-best, 1 = second-best.

6.4 SUMMARY OF THE SIMULATION RESULTS

Instead of a damage function, exogenously determined emission limits, that is consumption quotas for x, can be introduced into the model. The Pigouvian tax will then be equal to the shadow price of this emission limit divided by the shadow price of taxation. The exogenously determined emission quotas of the two countries can be interpreted either as the result of uncoordinated policies or as the outcome of policy coordination. The countries can achieve higher welfare levels when they jointly implement their reduction of emissions (and consequently consumption of good x). Under joint implementation, one country makes a side payment to the other country which in turn will reduce its emissions further. The Pigouvian taxes are then equal in both countries.

The simulations show that, *ceteris paribus*, both in a first-best and in a second-best setting, the country which has the lower initial quota of x and therefore has the highest tax on the polluting commodity or the lower revenue requirement will be the country which makes the side payment. This country will lower tx and therefore increase consumption of x while the other country will raise tx and reduce consumption of x. The side payment will be larger in the second-best world when revenue requirements differ because it has the additional benefit of reducing overall deadweight loss of distortionary taxation. This benefit does not occur when only the quotas differ and the revenue requirement is equal in both countries. In that case the side payment is lower the more distortionary is taxation.

There is a noticeable difference between the results from the model analysed in Chapter 5 (with a damage function) and the model considered here (exogenously determined emission ceilings) in the case where marginal damage or emission ceilings are equal and revenue requirements differ. In the damage model, the country with the lowest revenue requirement receives a side payment from the other country in the first-best case, while in the second-best case it pays the side payment. With exogenous emission limits, the country with the low revenue requirement makes the side payment in both the first-best and the second-best case. This is summarized in Table 6.5.

Two remarks can be made concerning this difference. First, there is a difference between the non-cooperative Nash equilibrium in the damage model and the initial situation in the emission limit model. In the damage model, the Nash equilibrium is the result of the interaction between the two countries. Therefore, this interaction influences the welfare levels in the non-cooperative equilibrium and therefore the threat points in the Nash bargaining solution. In the emission limit model, the initial situation is not influenced by actions in the other country. Consequently, comparing the two models is not straightforward.

Table 6.5 Overview of results

	First-best	Second-best
Damage function	High revenue country makes side payment	Low revenue country makes side payment
Emission ceiling	Low revenue country makes side payment	Low revenue country makes side payment

Second, it should be realized that there is a difference between equal marginal damage coefficients and equal emission ceilings. In the latter case, the country with the lower revenue requirement and therefore higher real income has to tax *x* considerably more to limit emissions. In the former case, equal marginal damage coefficients means that Pigouvian taxes will be equal, *given a total consumption of* x *in both countries*. The difference in relative abatement effort is therefore determined by the difference in revenue requirement and not by initial abatement efforts which differ considerably, as is the case in the model with equal emission targets. The two situations, equal ceilings and equal marginal damage functions, are not comparable. The emission ceiling case is more comparable with the case in the damage function model where one country has a higher marginal damage coefficient. That country abates more in the non-cooperative equilibrium and in the cooperative equilibrium without side payment.

6.5 THE INSTITUTIONAL SETTING

In this section we are concerned with the institutional settings which make the optimum possible. Deriving the formulas for an optimum might be an interesting exercise in itself, but it is also important to study how such an optimum can be achieved and what the real-world obstacles to such an optimum are. Two types of instrument will be considered: taxes and tradable emission permits. The cooperative equilibrium studied here is the equilibrium from the quota case of the previous section. This case is more realistic in that countries formulate their greenhouse policies not on the basis of damage functions but by setting emission limits. This implies that we study a world in which the benefits of coordination consist of two elements: reduction of the opportunity costs of sacrificed consumption of *x* (abatement costs) and, second, reduction of the costs of raising revenue.

Taxes

In order to achieve (one of) the range of cooperative equilibria determined by the first-order conditions of equation (6.7) (for example, the Nash bargaining equilibrium), countries will have to use specific instruments. In the previous section, both countries used taxes in order to achieve the agreed emission targets. In the cooperative equilibrium of the quota case, this means that countries agree on a distribution of the abatement effort between themselves, given their initial reduction quota, and on the necessary side payment. Simultaneously, both countries will have to change their tax rates in order to realize their respective emission targets. As has been shown, the new taxes on good x in both countries consist of a (changed) Ramsey tax and a Pigouvian tax which is uniform in both countries.

One way to realize the optimum is to specify in detail in an agreement how countries should change their taxes. It is, however, difficult to envisage countries accepting such an interference in their sovereignty (see Hoel 1993). A much more acceptable agreement would be to specify the emission reduction targets and the side payment, leaving it to the countries themselves to set the tax rates necessary to realize their targets. It is easy to see that both countries, maximizing welfare subject to their new emission constraints and revenue constraints (including the side payment), will choose the optimal tax rates.[1]

Tradable Permits: National System

In the agreement mentioned above it is not necessary to specify that countries use taxes to realise their emission targets. Another possibility is for countries to use a national tradable emission permit system instead of taxes. The number of permits available is determined by the emission quota. Of course, countries will have to levy taxes as well because they have to raise revenue. Their optimization problem is:

$$\max V_i' + \mu_i(x_i t_{xi} + y_i t_{yi} - (R_i + S)) - \eta_i(x_i - q_i) \qquad (6.21)$$

where S is the agreed side payment to be made ($S > 0$) (or received, $S < 0$). From the first-order conditions for (6.21) (see equations (6.2)–(6.5)), the optimal tax t_{xi} will consist of a tax determined by the Ramsey tax rules, t_x^R, and a tax equal to η/μ. This second, Pigouvian, part of the tax, η/μ, is the price of the permits which the consumer would be willing to pay *if the authorities levy the Ramsey taxes and auction the permits.*

Another option is to grandfather the permits. This alters the analysis. In the case of auction, the consumer's optimization does not change compared with the taxation case: the price he or she pays for the permits plus the revenue-raising tax on x is equal to the tax that would have to be paid if emissions were limited by means of a tax. However, when the consumer is given permits free with the right to consume a limited amount of x, the maximization problem will change:

$$\max \ U(x,y,l) \text{ subject to } x(1+tx) + y(1+ty) + l = M \qquad (6.22)$$

$$q - x = 0$$

The quantity of x is fixed at q by the number of permits grandfathered, as long as the constraint on x is binding. This is the case as long as tx, the tax which the government levies in order to raise revenue, is not higher than the Ramsey tax plus the price which the consumer is willing to pay for the permits (the Pigouvian tax).[2] This tax, $tx^R+\eta/\mu$, is denoted tx^*. The first-order conditions are:

$$U_x - \lambda(1+t_x) - \rho = 0 \qquad (6.23)$$

$$U_y - \lambda(1+ty) = 0 \qquad (6.24)$$

$$U_l - \lambda = 0 \qquad (6.25)$$

$$y(1+ty) + l = M - q(1+tx) \qquad (6.26)$$

ρ is the shadow price of the constraint on x. Conditions (6.24) and (6.25) can be combined, yielding the standard result:

$$U_y/U_l = (1+ty)/1 \qquad (6.27)$$

Condition (6.27) is the budget constraint. A higher tax on x means a lower real income for the consumer which he can spend on y and on leisure l. With x fixed at q, the tax on x has the character of a lump-sum tax, reducing real income directly. From these first-order conditions demand functions can be constructed for y and l, $y(ty,tx)$ and $l(ty,tx)$. The authorities maximize the indirect utility function $V'(tx,ty)$ (denoted V' because it differs from the indirect utility function V used in the tax model) subject to the revenue constraint $q \ tx + y \ ty \geq R+S$. The permit price does not enter as a variable in the indirect utility function which the government maximizes: the permits are grandfathered, not sold. The government only has the two taxes on good x and good y as variables.

Two cases can be distinguished. The first possibility is that at $tx = tx^*$, where

tx^* is the maximum tax which can be levied without reducing consumption of x below q, the revenue of the tax on x, $(q \cdot tx^*)$ is lower than $R+S$. In order to fulfil the revenue requirement, a positive tax ty must be levied next to the tax on good x. In this case, the optimal tax tx is equal to the maximum tax tx^* which can be levied because it is a lump-sum tax which is levied directly on income; a Pigouvian tax is non-distortionary. Setting tx at a lower level means that ty must be raised. Tax ty is a distortionary tax because it is only levied on y and does not affect l, it is not a 'lump-sum' tax like the tax on good x which affects income and therefore the consumption of both y and l. Raising ty and reducing tx below tx^* reduces welfare: less is consumed of good y when $q \cdot tx^* \leq (R+S)$.

Table 6.6 Grandfathering in a one-country second-best model, I

tx	x	y	ty	l	U
2.58	9.30	27.37	0.22	33.33	20.395
2.55	9.40	27.27	0.22	33.33	20.443
2.51	9.50	27.17	0.23	33.33	20.490
2.47	9.60	27.07	0.23	33.33	20.537
2.44	9.70	26.97	0.24	33.33	20.582
2.40	9.80	26.87	0.24	33.33	20.627
2.37	9.90	26.77	0.25	33.33	20.671
2.33	10.00	26.67	0.25	33.33	20.715
2.30	10.00	26.50	0.26	33.50	20.706
2.27	10.00	26.34	0.28	33.66	20.697
2.24	10.00	26.18	0.29	33.82	20.688
2.21	10.00	26.03	0.31	33.97	20.678
2.17	10.00	25.87	0.32	34.13	20.669
2.14	10.00	25.72	0.33	34.28	20.659

This is illustrated in Table 6.6, which presents the result of a simulation carried out using the Cobb–Douglas function introduced in section 6.3. The revenue requirement is set at 30 (S is assumed to be zero) and the emission limit is 10. At a tax on good x of 2.333, the consumer will consume exactly this limit quantity; at a higher level of the tax, he or she will reduce the quantity of x consumed and welfare will decline. Lowering the tax on x will not increase the quantity of x consumed because of the limit set on consumption by the permits. The tax on good y will rise, and less will be consumed of good y (and slightly more of leisure l). The consequence is that welfare declines.

Under the condition that $q \cdot tx^* \leq R + S$) the optimal tax rate on good x is therefore tx^* and tax ty will be equal to the tax levied in the tax case or when permits are auctioned. *In effect, grandfathering permits to the consumer does not differ from selling them: the tax on* x *will be raised up to the point where it is equal to the combined price and Ramsey tax in the auction (or tax) case.* The income transfer to the consumer of the grandfathered permits will therefore be fully taxed away. In other words the (shadow) price of tradable permits is zero.

Table 6.7 Grandfathering in a second-best model, II

tx	x	y	ty	l	U
2.40	9.80	36.86	-0.09	33.33	22.922
2.36	9.90	36.76	-0.09	33.33	22.979
2.33	10.00	36.66	-0.09	33.33	23.035
2.20	10.00	36.00	-0.05	34.00	23.046
2.15	10.00	35.75	-0.05	34.25	23.049
2.10	10.00	35.50	-0.03	34.50	23.051
2.05	10.00	35.25	-0.01	34.75	23.052
2.00	10.00	35.00	0.00	35.00	23.052
1.95	10.00	34.75	0.01	35.25	23.052
1.90	10.00	34.50	0.03	35.50	23.051
1.85	10.00	34.25	0.04	35.75	23.049
1.80	10.00	34.00	0.06	36.00	23.046

The other possibility is that the revenue of the maximum tax tx^* exceeds $R+S$. The excess revenue could be returned to the consumer either by means of the tax on good y (which would be negative, a subsidy) or by lowering tax tx. A subsidy on good y would distort the price ratio between good y and good l and therefore reduce welfare compared with grandfathering: grandfathering raises the income of the consumer directly and therefore affects consumption of both y and l. Therefore, when $q \cdot tx^* > R+S$, the tax on x should be lowered while ty is set at zero. A simulation similar to the one presented above illustrates this (see Table 6.7). The simulation is the same except that the revenue requirement is now set at 20 instead of 30. Consequently, tax tx^* (2.333) now raises excess revenue which has to be refunded to the consumer through a subsidy on good y of .091. Welfare is 23.035. Increasing the tax on x reduces consumption of x, consequently welfare decreases. Decreasing the tax on x does not increase consumption of x because of the limit imposed by the permit system. It does increase welfare because more of l is consumed and less of y. The optimal tax on x is such that no excess revenue is raised. At this point, the tax (or subsidy) on good y is zero and equal quantities of y and l are consumed.

The conclusion is that (under the condition that $q \cdot tx^* > R+S$*) grandfathering permits is more attractive than a full tax on good* x *because the excess revenue which would be raised by the tax needed to reduce emissions can be avoided.* Instead, a lower tax can be levied on x to raise revenue because the quantity of x which is consumed is now limited by the number of permits made available.

Which of the two situations occurs depends on emission ceiling q and the revenue requirement R. In the case of carbon emission reduction, it is plausible to assume that the revenue of the carbon tax needed to achieve the emission targets which have been accepted by several countries (stabilization of emissions) will not exceed their budgets. *Consequently, there is no difference between selling the permits or grandfathering them and charging the full tax.*[3]

Tradable permits with Auctioning: an International System

Instead of a national system of tradable permits, trade in permits can be allowed between countries. International tradeability means that the government in each country sells a number of permits equal to its internationally agreed quota. The consumer of one country can buy permits in both its own and in the other country.[4] In that case the price of the permits will be equal in both countries. An optimal solution is that both countries levy taxes on the consumption of x equal to the taxes which they would levy in a national system (these taxes on x are equal to the Ramsey taxes in a tax system). In that case the permit price is equal to the Pigouvian tax, which, as was shown above (p. 140) is equal in both countries (see equation (6.17)).

How would such an equilibrium come about? A first possibility is that countries cooperate and agree on the following items: (a) side payments to be made and received; (b) (redistribution of) quota; (c) the level of Ramsey taxes for each country. Since the permit price would equal the Pigouvian tax level in separate national permit markets, the same permit price would be realized if the two markets were integrated into one international market. We shall compare this outcome with a second possible solution in which both countries make an agreement on side payments and quotas, but make no binding agreement on the level of their respective (Ramsey) taxes.

The question arises whether in this second case there would be an incentive to levy a tax which is different from the optimal Ramsey taxes. To explore this question, assume that the two countries cooperate in limiting emissions and agree on quota and side payments but are left free to set their own taxes. Let q_1 be the quota allotted to country 1 and S the side payment it will receive (or pay if it is negative). Consequently, country 1 will maximize:

$$W_1(tx1,ty1,P(tx1,tx2,q_1+q_2))$$

$$+ \mu_1[x_1 \cdot tx1 + y_1 \cdot ty1 + P(tx1,tx2,q_1+q_2) \cdot q_1 - (R_1+S)] \qquad (6.28)$$

Country 2 will maximize a comparable welfare function, given its agreed quota and side payment. The indirect welfare function has changed, because welfare will also be a function of P, the permit price. An increase in P will decrease demand for the permits and for good x, and consequently influence the welfare level. The revenue constraint includes the side payment and the revenue of the sale of the permits, $P \cdot q_1$. The price of the permits, P, is determined by the demand and supply for the permits:[5]

$$x_1(tx1,P) + x_2(tx2,P) = q_1 + q_2 \quad x_P < 0 \qquad (6.29)$$

From this implicit function, price P is determined as a function of the emission limit and the taxes levied in both countries on good x, $tx1$ and $tx2$. Differentiating the market equilibrium condition yields:

$$dP/dtx1 = - x1_{tx1}/(x1_P+x2_P) < 0 \quad (>-1) \qquad (6.30)$$

Equation (6.30) states that a rise in tax $tx1$ decreases the equilibrium permit price on the international market (see the appendix to this chapter for the necessary conditions for and proof of the existence of an equilibrium). We could view this process as a two-stage game, the first being a cooperative game yielding permit quota (to be sold by each of the governments) and side payment, the second being a non-cooperative game in which countries react to changes on the permit market resulting from changes in each other's taxes.

In order to see whether this second-stage non-cooperative game yields a different equilibrium from the first cooperative stage or not, the Cobb–Douglas utility functions from the previous section are used to simulate this two-stage game (see section 6.3).[6] Consequently, in the first stage of the game, the two countries maximize:

$$(V_1-T_1)(V_2-T_2) \quad \text{subject to } x_1 tx1 + y_1 ty1 \geq R_1 + S \qquad (6.31)$$
$$x_2 tx2 + y_2 ty2 \geq R_2 - S$$

$$x_1 + x_2 \le q_1 + q_2$$

with $V_i = x(tx+P)^\alpha \, y(ty)^\beta \, l^\gamma$ $\alpha=\beta=\gamma=1/3$ $i=1,2$

The demand functions for x and y are found by maximizing $U(x,y,l)$ subject to the consumers' budget constraint $x \cdot (1+tx+P) + y \cdot (1+ty) + l = M$ (M is set at 100). This optimization yields the cooperative (Nash Bargaining) equilibrium analysed on p. 158, given the welfare levels in the non-cooperative Nash equilibrium T_1 and T_2.

In the second stage, both countries maximize their own welfare, given the emission quota $q_1{}^*$ and $q_2{}^*$ and the side payment S^* agreed upon in the cooperative equilibrium in the first stage (see equation (6.28)):

$$\max V_1 = x(tx1, P(tx1, tx2))^\alpha \, y(ty1)^\beta \, l^\gamma \tag{6.32}$$

$$\text{subject to } x_1 tx1 + q_1{}^* P + y_1 ty1 \ge R_1 + S^*$$
$$x_1 + x_2 \le q_1{}^* + q_1{}^*$$

The second constraint is the permit market equilibrium condition (see equation (6.29)). For the Cobb–Douglas function used here, $x_1 = M/(1+tx1+P)$. The permit market equilibrium becomes:

$$M_1/(1+tx1+P) + M_2/(1+tx2+P) = q_1{}^* + q_2{}^* \tag{6.33}$$

Equation (6.33) is an implicit function which determines P as a function of $tx1$ and $tx2$. Therefore, changing tax $tx1$ will have consequences for the permit price, as described above (p. 158). Governments do not set the permit price directly; it is a result of the tax level they choose and the level of the tax on good x in the other country. Each country maximizes welfare by choosing the level of taxes tx and ty, given the level of tx in the other country. The non-cooperative Nash equilibrium is at the point where neither country can improve welfare, given the other country's tax on good x.

Table 6.8 shows the results of the first simulation, in which initially (before the first cooperative stage) $R_1=40$, $R_2=20$, $q_1=q_2=10$. With cooperation, the side payment S is -3.01: country 1 is paid to reduce consumption of x further (see section 3). The first column for each country gives the values for x, tx, P, y, ty and the welfare level U in the initial non-cooperative Nash equilibrium. The second column shows the results in the cooperative (Nash bargaining) equilibrium, the first stage of the game defined above. In these first two equilibria there is no international permit market. In both countries, either a tax is levied or permits are sold. Tax tx is the full tax on x (the Ramsey tax and the Pigouvian tax) or the Ramsey tax and the permit price P

(which is equal to the Pigouvian tax). Necessarily, cooperation increases welfare as can be seen in the table; country 2 pays country 1 and increases its own consumption of x while country 1 reduces the quantity of x consumed.

The third column shows the consequences of allowing trade in permits between the two countries after they have agreed to cooperate (the last column for each country is explained below). This is the second (non-cooperative) stage, in which countries maximize welfare, given the agreed emission quota and the side payment of the first cooperative stage. *The final equilibrium does not differ from the first-stage cooperative equilibrium.* Both countries consume the same amount of x and the combined tax and permit price equals the tax on good x which they levied in the first stage. Welfare achieved is equal to the welfare level in the first stage. Tax competition by means of the influence of their taxes on the permit price does not lead to lower welfare levels. Consequently, agreements on emission reduction in a second-best world can include a system of international tradable permits without welfare loss. (It should, however, be noted that there is no incentive to trade: the consumer in each country uses a number of permits equal to the quota of its own country, and the price of the permits is equal in both countries without the need of arbitrage between the permit markets.) Allowing trade in permits between the two countries might not decrease welfare, but neither does it increase it.

Table 6.8 Simulations of international tradable permit systems, I

	Country 1: R_1=40 q_1=10				Country 2: R_2=20 q_2=10			
	Initial Nash equilib.	First stage coop.	Second stage noncoop.	Permit market no coop.	Initial Nash equilib.	First stage coop.	Second stage noncoop.	permit market nocoop.
x	10.00	8.08	8.08	8.85	10.00	11.92	11.92	11.15
t_x	2.33	3.12	1.45	1.24	2.33	1.80	0.13	0.46
P	–	–	1.67	1.53	–	–	1.67	1.53
y	16.67	21.60	21.56	19.59	36.67	31.75	31.75	33.75
t_y	1.00	0.54	0.54	0.70	-0.09	0.05	0.05	-0.01
U	17.71	17.98	17.98	17.94	23.03	23.28	23.28	23.24
Transfer	–	-3.01	-3.01	-1.76	–	3.01	3.01	1.76

Why is the non-cooperative equilibrium of the second stage of the game equal to the cooperative equilibrium of the first stage? First of all, when the permits are tradable, countries have an incentive to lower their tax on good x. This increases the price of the permits (see equation (6.29)), reducing consumption of x in the other country. The impact of the tax decrease on revenue outweighs the price increase:

$$d(tx1+P)/-dtx1 = -(1+dP/dtx1) = -(1 - x1_{tx1}/(x1_P+x2_P)) < 0 \quad (6.34)$$

Consequently, x_1 increases and, up to a certain point, welfare increases. The burden of limiting the consumption of x (and emissions) can be further shifted towards the other country by reducing the tax on x. An *increase* in tx would have the opposite effect: it would reduce x and therefore reduce welfare.

However, there is a limit to the welfare increase which can be realized by reducing the tax on x. This limit occurs here because of the revenue which has to be raised through taxes and the auctioning of the permits. At a certain point, a further reduction in $tx1$ increases x_1 above the permit quota of the own country, q_1^*. Consequently, the revenue raised by the tax on x and the auction will fall not only because of the fall in $(tx1+P)$,[7] but also because some permits have to be bought from the other country: $P \cdot (x_1 - q_1^*)$ is going abroad. This loss of revenue has to be compensated by higher taxes on y and a lower consumption of y, which will have a negative influence on welfare. In the simulation presented above (and in those presented below) this negative welfare consequence is such that reducing the tax on x beyond this point decreases welfare and therefore is not attractive.

It is now evident why the first stage cooperative equilibrium is the point at which it is no longer attractive for either country to reduce its tax on x further. In the first stage cooperative equilibrium, the permit market is in equilibrium and each country consumes the quantity of x which is covered by the quota agreed upon for that country. Reducing tx would increase consumption of x above this quota and result in a loss of revenue to the other country. Therefore neither country can increase its welfare level by reducing tx at this point. Increasing tax tx also reduces welfare, therefore neither country can improve welfare at this point, given the tax on good x levied in the other country. The first-stage cooperative equilibrium is therefore also the second-stage Nash equilibrium.

In the two-stage game described above, countries first agree to cooperate in realizing the combined emission limit, while subsequently trade is allowed, given the agreed upon emission quota and side payment. Another option is that, instead of cooperating first on quota and side payment, both countries simply allow trade in permits between the two countries. In a first-best analysis, emission trading will minimize abatement costs (and maximize welfare) in both countries. This option is simulated as well, using the same functions and procedure as above with this difference: that the emission quotas are the initial non-cooperative quotas and that there is no side payment. In the simulation presented above, $q_1 = q_2 = 10$. The results are shown in the last column (for both countries) in Table 6.1. In both countries, the welfare levels achieved are higher than without trade (the first columns) but neither country realizes a welfare level as high as in the coordinated equilibrium (second and third column). In this equilibrium, country 1 consumes less than its initial quota while country 2 consumes more. As a result, there is a side payment from country 2 to country 1: country 2 consumes 11.15 of x and therefore has to buy 1.15 permits in the other country. At the price of 1.53 per permit this is a transfer of 1.76 from country 2 to country 1. This transfer, however, is less than the side payment in the cooperative agreement (which is -3.01). Allowing trade in permits is an improvement on no trade, but it does not realize the welfare increase which is achievable under a cooperative agreement.

Tables 6.9 and 6.10 present the results of two other simulations which underwrite the conclusions from the first. The initial quotas, revenue requirements and the transfer (side payment) between the countries are shown in the tables. A positive side payment or transfer means that the country pays the other country, a negative transfer indicates the receipt of a side payment.

Table 6.9 Simulations of international tradable permit systems, II

	Country 1: R_1=30, q_1=10				Country 2: R_2=30, q_2=8			
	Initial Nash equilib.	First stage coop.	Second stage noncoop.	Permit market no coop.	Initial Nash equilib.	First stage coop.	Second stage noncoop.	Permit market no coop.
x	10.00	9.33	9.33	9.59	8.00	8.67	8.67	8.41
l_x	2.33	2.57	0.50	0.37	3.17	2.84	0.77	0.86
P	–	–	2.07	2.10	–	–	2.07	2.10
y	26.67	28.73	28.73	27.93	28.67	26.61	26.61	27.40
l_y	0.25	0.16	0.16	0.19	0.16	0.25	0.25	0.22
U	20.72	20.75	20.75	20.74	19.70	19.74	19.74	19.73
Transfer	–	-1.39	-1.39	-0.86	–	1.39	1.39	0.86

Table 6.10   Simulations of international tradable permit systems, III

	Country 1: R_1=40, q_1=10				Country 2: R_2=30, q_2=8			
	Initial Nash equilib.	First stage coop.	Second stage noncoop.	Permit market no coop.	Initial Nash equilib.	First stage coop.	Second stage noncoop.	Permit market no coop.
x	10.00	8.29	8.29	9.02	8.00	9.71	9.71	8.98
l_x	2.33	3.02	1.50	1.17	3.17	2.43	0.91	1.19
P	–	–	1.52	1.52	–	–	1.52	1.52
y	16.67	20.91	20.91	19.13	28.67	24.43	24.43	26.20
l_y	1.00	0.59	0.59	0.74	0.16	0.36	0.36	0.27
U	17.71	17.94	17.94	17.92	19.70	19.92	19.92	19.89
Transfer	–	-2.53	-2.53	-1.49	–	2.53	2.53	1.49

6.6 CONCLUSIONS

In the second-best two-country model of the previous chapter, the optimal level of consumption of the polluting good, and therefore of pollution, was determined endogenously, given the damage function. Another approach, followed in this chapter, is to assume exogenously set emission ceilings for both countries instead of damage functions. The only way in which welfare can be increased is by joint implementation: the countries jointly implement their emission targets. One country makes a side payment to the other country which in turn will further reduce consumption of the dirty good (and therefore its emissions). The Pigouvian taxes, which in this model are based upon the shadow price of the emission limit, are equal in both countries when they use joint implementation. It is shown that, as in the case of welfare maximization, the Pigouvian taxes will be equalized but total tax on the polluting good will differ in a second-best world.

Again, simulations have been used to analyse the consequences of different revenue requirements and different initial emission quotas on the side payment and the tax structure. These simulations show that, *ceteris paribus*, both in a first-best and in a second-best setting the country which has the most stringent emission limit and therefore the highest tax on the polluting commodity is the country which makes the side payment. This country will lower the tax on the polluting good and therefore increase consumption, while the other country will raise its tax and reduce consumption and pollution.

When only the revenue requirements differ, the country with the lower revenue requirement and the highest absolute tax on the polluting good will pay the other country, both in the first-best and in the second-best case. In both cases, realizing the same emission limit is more costly in welfare terms in the country with the lower revenue requirement. Given the higher real income in this country, a higher tax on good x is needed to realize the emission limit. It is therefore more attractive for this country to pay the country with the higher revenue requirement and to consume more of good x itself. In the second-best world, the side payment will be larger because it has the additional benefit of reducing the overall deadweight loss of distortionary taxation. This benefit does not occur when only the quotas differ, therefore in that case the side payment will be lower the more distortionary the taxation is.

Our main objective in this study of international coordination of environmental policy in a second-best world is to establish which institutions are necessary to realize the optimal tax structures. Can taxes and systems of tradable emission permits be used, either alone or in combination, and be designed in such a way that the optima are realized? The analysis of the institutional requirements for an optimal agreement yields several insights. The first is that both in national and international systems of tradable emission permits there is no difference between auctioning or grandfathering of the permits. In the case of grandfathering the optimal tax on the polluting good equals the tax plus the price of the permits when they are sold. Put in a different way, the rent obtained by the gift of the permits is fully taxed away and the permit price is zero under grandfathering. Therefore, the welfare effects of either grandfathering or auctioning are similar in this second-best model. One qualification should be mentioned: this conclusion only holds as long as the revenue from the maximal tax which can be levied on the dirty good without reducing consumption below the consumption limit does not exceed the total revenue requirement of the government. When the revenue from auctioning (which is equal to the revenue from the maximal tax) exceeds the revenue requirement, welfare can be increased by grandfathering the permits and taxing the polluting good at a lower rate. However, in the case of carbon taxes (and other environmental taxes) this reservation will not be a problem.

Second, it suffices to specify the side payment and emission targets in a cooperative agreement; it is not necessary to specify the taxes which each country has to levy. It can be left to the countries themselves to set taxes or to use a national system of tradable permits. Given the emission targets and the side payment agreed upon, each government will set the optimal tax rates and the national permit markets will be in equilibrium at the optimal permit price. This is one of the attractive points of specifying emission limits in international agreements. Countries will 'automatically' set optimal taxes as long as they fulfil their treaty obligations.

In the second-best model considered here, an international permit system can be used which allows trade in permits between the two countries. It has been shown that with internationally tradable permits countries have to agree only on the side payment and (redistribution of) quotas and can be left free to set their revenue-raising tax. Although tax competition is allowed, governments will set the tax at the level of the (optimal) Ramsey tax. Allowing trade in permits between two countries does not reduce welfare. However, it should be noted that in each country the quantity of the polluting good consumed is equal to that country's emission limit. Allowing transboundary trade in emission permits may not be harmful, but neither is it useful in reducing the welfare costs of pollution abatement.

Instead of this two-stage approach, trade in permits between two countries could be allowed, starting with national emission limits for each country without first agreeing on emission limits and side payments. Simulations show that, as might be expected, this will increase welfare in both countries compared with the situation in which countries neither coordinate their emission reduction policies nor allow trade in permits. However, in neither country does it achieve the welfare levels which are realized when countries explicitly cooperate. In the second-best model studied here, an international system of tradable emission permits without initial coordination might therefore be termed a second-best policy, second-best to explicit coordination of emission reduction policies.

NOTES

1. Levying a higher tax would be suboptimal. The consumer would take into account the price of good x as the constraint is no longer binding. In that case, the optimal tax is the combined Ramsey and Pigouvian tax determined in the tax model.
2. It should be noted that both countries in deciding and agreeing on optimal quotas and transfers, have simultaneously decided for themselves (given their tax regime) what their optimal tax rates (t_x and t_y) will be.
3. In a first-best world, it doesn't matter whether permits are auctioned or grandfathered. If auctioning yields excess revenue, it can be returned through either a lump-sum tax or proportional excise taxes on goods y and l. If the revenue from auctioning is less than the government revenue requirement, or if the permits are grandfathered, revenue can be raised through lump-sum or excise taxes. In each instance, the optimal levels of y and l will be consumed.
4. They can either be bought directly from the other government on the primary market, or indirectly from the consumer in the other country, the secondary market (see Chapter 2).
5. It is assumed that demand is independent, therefore a change in tax t_{y1} does not affect demand for x_1.

6.   The sign of the reaction curves can be either positive or negative (see appendix). It is not possible to determine analytically if the two equilibria differ.

7.   Revenue increases with a rise in taxes t_x and t_y (see appendix).

APPENDIX: TWO-STAGE PERMIT GAME

Sign of the Reaction Curve in the Two-stage Coordination and Permit Market Game

The reaction curve for country 1 can be determined by looking at the effects on the first-order conditions for problem (6.28) of a small change in tax tx_j. The optimization problem (equation (6.28)) is:

$$W_1(tx1, ty1, P(tx1, tx2, \Sigma q)) + \mu_1[x_1 \cdot tx1 + y_1 \cdot ty1 \qquad (A6.1)$$

$$+ P(tx1, tx2, q_1 + q_2) \cdot q_1 - (R_1 + S)]$$

The first-order conditions (assuming independent demand) are:

$$W_{tx1} + \mu_1[x_{tx1} \cdot tx1 + x_1 + P_{tx1} \cdot q_1] = 0 \qquad (A6.2)$$

$$W_{ty1} + \mu_1[y_{ty1} \cdot ty1] = 0 \qquad (A6.3)$$

$$x_1 \cdot tx1 + y_1 \cdot ty1 + P \cdot q_1 - (R_1 + S) = 0 \qquad (A6.4)$$

Totally differentiating the first-order conditions yields the Hessian matrix:

$$H = \begin{bmatrix} a & x & b \\ y & c & d \\ b & d & 0 \end{bmatrix} \qquad (A6.5)$$

with the following notation (for the signs see above):

$a = W_{tx1tx1} + \mu(2x_{tx1} + x_{tx1tx1} \, tx + P_{tx1tx1q1}) < 0$
$c = V_{ty1ty1} + \mu(2y_{ty1} + ty1 \, y_{ty1ty1}) < 0$
$b = x + x_{tx1} \, tx1 + P_{tx1} \, q_1 > 0$
$d = y + y_{ty1} \, ty1 > 0$
$x = W_{tx1ty1} > 0$
$y = W_{ty1tx1} > 0$

$x^1_{tx2} > 0, \; x^1_{tx1tx2} < 0, \; P_{tx1} < 0, \; P_{tx1tx2} = P_{tx1tx1} > 0$

Assuming concavity of both the utility function W_1 and the revenue function $x_1 tx1 + y_1 ty1 + Pq_1$ in $tx1$ and $ty1$; a and c are negative and b, d, x and y are positive. The determinant of the Hessian is $bd(x+y) - (ad^2 + b^2c)$, which is positive (as it should be if the optimum is to be a maximum).

Differentiating the first-order conditions with respect to $tx2$ yields:

$$[W_{tx1\,tx2} + X_{tx1\,tx2} + x_{tx2} + P_{tx1\,tx2}\,q_1]\ dtx2 = p1\ dtx2 = 0 \qquad (A6.6)$$

$$[x^1_{tx2}\cdot tx1 + P_{tx2}\cdot q_i]\ dtx2 = p2\ dtx2 = 0 \qquad (A6.7)$$

$$W_{tx1\,tx2} = U_{x1}\,[x_{tx1}\,x_P\,P_{tx2} + x_P\,P_{tx2}\,P_{tx1} + x_P\,P_{tx1\,tx2}] < 0 \qquad (A6.8)$$

Using comparative statics, the effect of a change in $tx2$ on $tx1$ is given by:

$$dtx1/dtx2 = [(dx - bc)p2 - d^2 p1]/\,|\,H\,| \qquad (A6.9)$$

$p1$ and $p2$ can be either positive or negative. It can therefore not be established whether $dtx1/dtx2$ is positive or whether it is negative.

Existence of the Market Equilibrium

Under certain conditions the non-cooperative Nash equilibrium exists in this second game. Following the theorem formulated by Debreu, Glicksberg and Fan (Fudenberg and Tirole 1985), sufficient conditions for the existence of a Nash equilibrium are that the payoff functions, the utility functions of each player, are continuous in the strategies which can be played (the taxes on good x and y in both countries) and quasi-concave in each country's own strategies txi and tyi. Furthermore, the strategy spaces should be compact and convex.

It was assumed above that the utility functions are concave. Moreover, they will be continuous. The strategy space will be compact and convex if it is closed and bounded. Or there should be an upper and a lower bound to the possible strategies. Let the revenue function ($x_i txi + y_i tyi$) be concave with $\partial R/\partial t > 0$ up to a certain point and $\partial R/\partial t < 0$ for higher taxes. Consequently, at a certain tax level a further tax increase decreases the revenue raised. There will therefore be tax levels which are so high that they cannot be best responses. Moreover, there will also be a lower limit because if taxes are set too low, neither will the revenue constraint be met. The strategy space is therefore closed and bounded.

7. Conclusions

Economists have pointed out the suitability of economic instruments such as taxes and tradable emission permits for reducing CO_2 emission because with these instruments emissions are abated at minimum costs. Less attention has been paid to the practical design of instruments, in particular to the design of a system of tradable carbon permits. One of the aims of this study has been to fill this gap, describing in detail the requirements of a feasible system of tradable carbon permits for the European Union. In addition to the design of a system of TCPs, the consequences of implementing such a system have been studied, concentrating on the effect which TCPs might have on entry into industries, a subject which so far has received little attention in the literature.

The enhanced greenhouse effect occurs worldwide, therefore the problem of coordination of policies arises. As a third subject we have analysed whether and how countries can cooperate in reducing emissions and what the role of taxes and TCPs can be in an international setting, taking into account the complication that fossil fuels are already taxed in most countries. Moreover, we have studied how this might affect the optimal design of a system of TCPs.

Two themes recur in this study. The first is the choice between grandfathering and auction of the permits. This is important in designing a feasible system of TCPs: it can affect entry barriers and it has consequences for the revenue which governments raise when they use tradable permits. The other theme is the comparison between, on the one hand, TCPs and, on the other hand, carbon taxes and command-and-control type regulation such as emission standards.

A major conclusion is that it is possible to design a feasible system of TCPs. An important element of such a system is the distribution of the permits. From a political economy point of view it is attractive to grandfather permits to sources of CO_2 because the negative impacts on the cash flow of firms will be considerably smaller with grandfathering than with auction of the permits or emission charges. With grandfathering, firms as a group will only have to incur expenditure on the abatement costs. For the energy-intensive sectors of industry in particular, permit expenditure will be several times larger than abatement costs. Therefore, tradable carbon permits will be politically more acceptable than a tax or an auction of permits, making a system more feasible. However, a distinction is made between industrial and other sources. The permits for the other sources are auctioned by the government. In order that households and other small fuel users are not burdened with the necessity to buy permits, these can be sold instead to suppliers of fossil fuels, who can subsequently mark up their fossil fuel prices with the price of the permits.

A system of tradable permits, and indeed any other instrument, is only feasible when there is adequate monitoring and enforcement. Our system of TCPs can be monitored and enforced by obliging importers and producers of fossil fuels to hand over carbon permits to the authorities for the carbon contained in the fossil fuels which they bring on to the market. This considerably limits the number of firms to be monitored and makes it possible to use existing procedures for levying excise taxes on fossil fuels.

Within the context of the EU, the question arises whether TCPs can be implemented in one Member State (MS) of the EU or whether it should be implemented at the European level. Introducing the TCP system at the European level poses no problems. It also seems to be possible to implement a system in one MS because so far there is no European CO_2 reduction policy. TCPs will probably fall under the 'rule of reason' which allows exemptions to article 30 EG dealing with free movement of goods.

The second question dealt with in this study is whether tradable permits would create entry barriers. The conclusion is that entry barriers could occur when tradable permits are introduced. Three types of entry barriers have been identified which would in theory be affected. First, transaction costs on the permit market can have consequences for entry in the limit-pricing model. Second, capital markets might not work perfectly, in which case grandfathering puts incumbent firms at an advantage. Third, firms can try to make it more expensive for entrants to acquire permits by driving up the price of the permits, thereby reducing entry.

It should be noted that grandfathering permits to the established firms does not necessarily create entry barriers in the sense of creating a cost advantage for those firms. Grandfathered permits have an opportunity cost when they are used. These opportunity costs are equal to the price for which they can be sold, and therefore established firms do not have a cost advantage over entrants just because they received permits free.

Transaction costs, which can occur on the permit market (and are borne by either the buyer or the seller of permits or by both), can affect entry barriers in the limit-pricing model. The limit-pricing model is a two-period (Stackelberg) game in which the incumbent firm invests in the first period, taking into account how the potential entrant will react in the second period. In this way the incumbent influences the output of the entrant in the second period. It might also be profitable for the incumbent to deter entry completely. The occurrence of transaction costs on the permit market can make it more attractive for the established firm to deter entry or it can reduce the size at which the entrant will enter.

An extreme form of entry barrier can occur when a firm or group of firms controls a vital input and excludes other firms from the use of this input. This forces these firms to use less-optimal and more-expensive substitutes and reduces their competition, or even excludes them completely from the market. Exclusionary manipulation can also occur on the permit market when one or a small group of established firms controls the price of permits and thereby drives up the costs of potential entrants.

Neither the transaction cost barrier nor exclusionary manipulation seem to be very relevant to our system of TCPs. The main reason for this is that the market for carbon permits is large and has many potential actors from most sectors of industry. It is therefore probable that a well-functioning market will develop with low transaction costs, reducing the effect that transaction costs might have on entry barriers. Moreover, it will be very costly for a firm to use the permit market to drive up the costs of rivals because of the large size of the market.

The most relevant type of entry barrier with respect to our system of TCPs occurs when capital markets do not work perfectly and established firms receive their permits through grandfathering. According to the long purse theory, an incumbent firm can drive a potential entrant out of the market by means of a price war if its financial resources are larger. *Ceteris paribus*, grandfathering permits to established firms and selling them to newcomers means that the incumbent has larger financial resources because grandfathering permits is in effect equal to making a capital gift. Therefore an incumbent firm can outlast the entrant in a price war. Given imperfect capital markets, grandfathering can effectively reduce entry.

In empirical studies it has been found that capital requirements are a significant determinant of entry barriers. Using the Dutch economy as an example, it has been estimated how much a system of tradable carbon permits will increase the capital requirements of new firms, assuming that entrants acquire at least one year's stock of permits before they enter a market. As is to be expected, energy-intensive industries are most affected although the increase in their capital requirements is modest, at most 1.7 per cent (in the petroleum industries). Entry might be reduced when capital markets do not work perfectly and permits are grandfathered, but probably only to a small extent.

The last question posed at the beginning of this study was how countries could cooperate in reducing transboundary pollution such as CO_2 emissions and how the coordination of environmental policies would influence the optimal design of instruments such as taxes and TCPs. A two-country model was used which takes into account the complicating problem that countries already tax fossil fuels for reasons other than reducing CO_2 emissions. The simple economy modelled consists of one consumer who can consume two goods, one of which causes pollution when it is consumed. In addition, the consumer chooses how much time will be spent at work (and earning income) and how much at leisure. The government must raise an exogenously determined amount of revenue and reduce pollution by means of taxes (or tradable permits) on the two goods. This second-best model is used to establish which combinations of instruments will maximize welfare in the two countries.

Two variants of the model have been used. In the first variant a damage function is included, and therefore the optimal emission reduction level, the optimal level of CO_2 abatement, is determined endogenously. The two countries can increase their welfare when they cooperate in reducing emissions. Cooperation can be extended further when they use side payments: one country pays the other country and reduces its emissions less. The other country diminishes its emissions further. An interesting conclusion is that including side payments in agreements on emission abatement can actually increase pollution compared with agreements which do not include side payments.

In the second variant it has been assumed that emission ceilings are set exogenously. In this variant countries can only cooperate when they use side payments. This form of cooperation, where one country pays another country for reducing its emissions, is called joint implementation. The model with exogenously determined emission ceilings has been used to establish which institutions are necessary to realize the optima and to determine the role of taxes and tradable permits. This analysis yields several insights.

First, in the second-best model used here, there is no difference between grandfathering and auctioning of the permits in either national or international systems of tradable emission permits. In the case of grandfathering, the optimal tax on the polluting good equals the tax plus the price of the permits when they are sold. To put it a different way, the rent obtained by the gift of the permits is fully taxed away and the permit price is zero under grandfathering. Therefore, the welfare effects of both grandfathering and auctioning are similar in this second-best model.

Second, it is sufficient to specify the side payment and emission targets in a cooperative agreement; it is not necessary to specify the taxes which each country has to levy. It can be left to the countries themselves to set taxes or to use a national system of tradable permits. Given the emission targets and the side payment agreed upon, each government will set the optimal tax rates and the national permit markets will be in equilibrium at the optimal permit price.

Third, instead of taxes, an international permit system can be used which allows trade in permits between the two countries. Given agreed emission ceilings and side payments, countries can be left free to set revenue-raising taxes. Although tax competition is allowed, both countries will set (welfare) optimal taxes. In this case, in each country the number of permits used is equal to that country's emission ceiling.

Fourth, it is not welfare optimal to allow trade in permits between the two countries without first agreeing on emission limits and side payments. Simulations show that, as might be expected, this will increase welfare in both countries compared with the situation in which countries neither coordinate their emission reduction policies nor allow trade in permits. However, in neither country does it achieve the welfare levels which are realized when countries explicitly cooperate. In the second-best model studied here, an international system of tradable emission permits without initial coordination might therefore be termed a second-best policy: second-best to explicit coordination of emission reduction policies.

Throughout the book, the choice between grandfathering and auction of permits has been part of the analysis. Surveying the results, is it possible to give a final verdict on this choice, given our central question of how to design a feasible system of TCPs? Our conclusion in Chapter 2 is that grandfathering would be preferable for industrial sources, or at least for the energy-intensive sectors of industry, while permits for the other sources should be sold. The main reason is that this makes a carbon-reduction policy more acceptable to these sources than would be the case if permits were auctioned or a tax levied. The choice between grandfathering or auction does not affect the relocation decisions of industries, therefore from this point of view there is no preference for either of the two methods. Grandfathering could increase barriers to entry, but even for the energy-intensive sectors the increase in entry barriers appears to be small. In contrast to the conclusion that a policy of grandfathering should be applied when the government's aim is to increase the political acceptability of tradable carbon permits stands the conclusion from our second-best analysis, which indicates that when welfare maximization is the aim, grandfathering is of no use because the authorities would tax this capital gift away completely. Therefore, different criteria lead to different policy advice. It should also be realized that the second-best model used is very simple and only focuses on the revenue aspect of taxes and permits.

The second recurrent issue in this study is the comparison between TCPs and other instruments such as taxes and direct regulation. A system of TCPs seems to be just as feasible as a carbon tax. Monitoring and enforcement would not pose larger problems than would a tax, although in a European-wide system insufficient enforcement might lead to larger excess emission when TCPs are used compared with a tax (or standards). Tradable permits have the advantage over a tax that permits can be grandfathered to (some of) the sources of CO_2 emissions, which would reduce their expenditures. Furthermore, the emission reduction level is set, which is not the case with a tax or with standards.

Tradable permits can increase entry barriers through imperfect capital markets. This problem does not arise with taxes or standards; however, the problem is relatively small and seems to be more theoretical than practical. Both taxes and tradable permits can be used in international agreements on emission reduction. Whichever instrument is used, cooperating countries should first agree on emission reduction ceilings and monetary compensations in order to realize maximum welfare gains. In this respect there is no difference between the two instruments.

Our final conclusion is that a system of TCPs is an attractive and feasible instrument for reducing CO_2 emissions, at both national and international levels. The system described in this study can be implemented at the European Union level; it might also be possible to introduce it in one Member State. Entry barriers might be affected by TCPs when capital markets do not work perfectly, but the effect is small and limited to a few sectors of industry.

Bibliography

Allers, M. (1994), *Administrative and Compliance Costs of Taxation and Public Transfers in the Netherlands,* Groningen: Wolters-Noordhof.

Atkinson, S. and T. Tietenberg (1991), Market failure in incentive-based regulation: the case of emission trading. *Journal of Environmental Economics and Management,* 21: 17–31.

Auerbach, A. (1987). Excess burden and optimal taxation. In: A. Auerbach and M. Feldstein (eds), *Handbook of Public Economics,* Vol. 2, Amsterdam: North-Holland.

Bain, J. (1965), *Barriers to New Competition,* Cambridge, Mass.: Harvard University Press.

Barrett, S. (1992), Reaching a CO_2 emission limitation agreement for the Community: implications for equity and cost-effectiveness. *European Economy,* special edition no. 1: 3–24.

Baumol, W. and R. Willig (1981), Fixed costs, sunk costs, entry barriers and sustainablity of monopoly. *Quarterly Journal of Economics,* 95: 405–31.

Benoit, J.-P. (1984), Financially constrained entry in a game with incomplete information. *Rand Journal of Economics,* 15: 490–99.

Blok, K., R.A.W. Albers, E. Worrell, and R.F.A. Cuelenaere (1990), *Data on Energy Conservation Techniques for the Netherlands,* Utrecht: University of Utrecht.

Bohm, P. (1988), Second best. In: *The New Palgrave Dictionary of Economics,* vol. 3, London: Macmillan.

Bovenberg, A.L. and F. van der Ploeg (1992). *Environmental Policy, Public Finance and the Labour Market in a Second-best World,* Center for Economic Research discussion paper no. 9243, Tilburg.

Case 6–7/93 (1974), *Instituto Chemioterapico Italiano and Commercial Solvents Corporation* vs. *Commission of the EC,* ECR: 22.

(CBS) (1990), *Luchtverontreiniging: Emissies door Verbranding van Fossiele Brandstoffen in Vuurhaarden* [Air pollution: emissions from burning of fossil fuels in furnaces], Voorburg: CBS.

(CBS) (1991), *Samenvattend Overzicht van de Industrie* [Industry Overview], Voorburg: CBS.

(CBS) (1992), *Kapitaalgoederenvoorraad* [Capital Stock], Voorburg: CBS.

Central Planning Bureau (CPB) (1992). *Economische Gevolgen op Lange Termijn van Heffingen op Energie* [Economic long-term consequences of taxes on energy], Den Haag: Staatsdrukkerij.

Cnossen, S. and H. Vollebergh (1992), Towards a Global Excise on Carbon, *National Tax Journal*, 45 (1): 23–36.

Dales, J.H. (1968), *Pollution, Property and Prices*, Toronto: University of Toronto Press.

Demsetz, H. (1982), Barriers to entry. *American Economic Review*, 72: 47–57.

Dijkstra, B. and A. Nentjes (1994), The political economy of instrument choice in environmental policy. Faure, M., Vervaele, J. and Weale, A. (eds), *Environmental Standards in the European Union in an Interdisciplinary Framework*, Antwerp: Maklu.

Dixit, A. (1980), The role of investment in entry-deterrence. *The Economic Journal*, 90: 95–106.

Downing, P.B. and J.L. White (1986), Innovation in pollution control, *Journal of Environmental Economics and Management*, 13: 18–24.

Dunne, T. and M.J. Roberts (1991), Variation in producer turnover across US manufacturing industries. In P.A. Geroski and J. Schwalbach (eds) *Entry and Market Contestability*, Oxford: Basil Blackwell.

Dwyer, J.P. (1992), California's tradable emissions policy and its application to the control of greenhouse gases. In *Climate Change – Designing a Tradable Permit System*, Paris: OECD.

Eaton, B.C. and R.G. Lipsey (1980), Exit barriers are entry barriers: The durability of capital as barrier to entry. *Bell Journal of Economics*, 12: 593–604.

Edwards, C. (1955), Conglomerate bigness as a source of power. In *Business Concentration and Price Policy*, NBER Conference report, New York: National Bureau of Economic Research.

Europe Environment (1994), 445 (20 December).

Fudenberg, D. and J. Tirole (1984), The fat-cat effect, the puppy-dog ploy and the lean and hungry look. *American Economic Review, Papers and Proceedings*, 74: 361–8.

Fudenberg, D. and J. Tirole (1985), *Predation without Reputation*, Working Paper no. 377, Cambridge, Mass,: Massachusetts Institute of Technology.

Gale, D. and M. Hellwig (1985), Incentive compatible debt contracts: the one-period problem. *Review of Economic Studies*, 52: 647–64.

Geroski, P.A. and J. Schwalbach (eds) (1991), *Entry and Market Contestability*, Oxford: Basil Blackwell.

Gilbert, R.J. (1989), Mobility barriers and the value of incumbency. *Handbook of Industrial Organization*, Vol. 1, R. Schmalensee and R.D.

Willig (eds), Amsterdam: North-Holland.

Hahn, R.W. (1989), Economic prescriptions for environmental problems: How the patient followed the doctor's orders. *Journal of Economic Perspectives,* 3 (Spring): 95–114.

Hahn, R.W. and G.L. Hester (1989), Where did all the markets go? An analysis of EPA's Emission Trading Program, *Yale Journal on Regulation,* 6: 109–53.

Hahn, R.W. (1984), Market power and transferable property rights, *The Quarterly Journal of Economics,* 99 (4): 735–65.

Hanley, N. and I. Moffat (1993), Efficiency and distributional aspects of market mechanisms in the control of pollution: an empirical analysis, *Scottish Journal of Political Economy,* 40 (1): 69–87.

Hoel, M. (1991). Global environmental problems: the effects of unilateral actions taken by one country, *Journal of Environmental Economics and Management,* 20: 55–70.

Hoel, M. (1993). Harmonization of carbon taxes in international climate agreements. *Environmental and Resource Economics,* 3: 221–31.

Hoeller, J. and J. Coppel (1992). *Energy Taxation and Price Distortions in Fossil Fuel Markets: Some Implications for Climate Change,* Economics department working paper no. 110, Paris: OECD.

Jeong, K.-Y. and R.T. Masson (1991), Entry during explosive growth: Korea during the take-off. In P.A. Geroski and J. Schwalbach (eds) *Entry and Market Contestability,* Oxford: Basil Blackwell.

Kete, N. (1992), The U.S. acid rain control allowance trading system. *Climate Change – Designing a Tradable Permit System,* Paris: OECD.

Klaassen, G. (1996), *Acid Rain and Environmental Degradation, The Economics of Emission Trading,* Cheltenham, UK and Brookfield, US: Edward Elgar.

Klaassen, G. and A. Nentjes (1995a), Handel in emissierechten in de VS van start (Trade in emission permits in the U.S. started). *Economisch Statistische Berichten,* 80 (3991): 18–20.

Klaassen, G. and A. Nentjes (1995b), *Emission Trading for Air Pollution Control in Practice,* IIASA Working Paper 95–21, Laxenburg.

Komen, M.H.C. and H. Folmer (1995), Vluchten bedrijven voor milieubeleid? [Do firms relocate because of environmental policy?] *Economisch Statistische Berichten,* 80 (3997): 148–52.

Koutstaal, P.R. (1992), *Verhandelbare CO_2 Emissierechten in Nederland en de EG* [Tradable CO_2 emission permits in the Netherlands and the EC], The Hague: Ministry of Economic Affairs.

Koutstaal, P.R. (1993), Verhandelbare CO_2 emissierechten: uitvoerbaar en voordelig (Tradable CO_2 emission permits: feasible and efficient). *Tijdschrift voor Politieke Economie,* 15 (4): 12–23.

Koutstaal, P.R. and A. Nentjes (1995), Tradable carbon dioxide permit for the EU, *Journal of Common Market Studies,* 33 (2): 219–33.

Koutstaal, P.R., H. Vollebergh and J. de Vries (1994), *Hybrid Carbon Incentive Mechanisms for the European Community,* OCFEB Research memorandum no. 9406, Rotterdam.

Koutstaal, P.R., H. Vollebergh and J. de Vries (1995), *Hybrid Economic Instruments for European Carbon Policy.* F. Dietz e.a. (eds), *Environment, Incentives and the Common Market,* Dordrecht: Kluwer Academic Publishers.

Krattenmaker, T.G. and S.C. Salop (1986a), Anticompetitive exclusion: raising rivals' costs to achieve power over price. *The Yale Law Journal,* 96: 209–93.

Krattenmaker, T.G. and S.C. Salop (1986b), Competition and cooperation in the market for exclusionary rights. *American Economic Review,* 76 (2): 109–13.

Mata, J. (1991), Sunk costs and entry by small and large plants. In P.A. Geroski and J. Schwalbach (eds), *Entry and Market Contestability,* Oxford: Basil Blackwell.

McGee, J. (1958), Predatory price cutting: the Standard Oil (NJ) case. *Journal of Law and Economics,* 1: 137–69.

Misiolek, W.S. and H.W. Elder (1989), Exclusionary manipulation of markets for pollution rights. *Journal of Environmental Economics and Management,* 16: 156–66.

Minne, B. and V.P.C.F. Herzberg (1992), *Nederlandse Industrie en Regulerende Energieheffing.* [Dutch industry and regulating energy taxes], Research memorandum no. 90, The Hague, Central Planning Bureau.

Mørch von der Fehr, N.-H. (1991), Domestic entry in Norwegian manufacturing industries. In P.A. Geroski and J. Schwalbach (eds), *Entry and Market Contestability,* Oxford: Basil Blackwell.

Myers, S.C. (1984), The capital structure puzzle. *Journal of Finance,* 39: 575–92.

NECIGEF (1990), *Annual Report,* Amsterdam.

Nentjes, A. (1994), Control of reciprocal transboundary pollution and joint implementation. In G. Klaassen and F. Førsund (eds) *Economic Instruments for Air Pollution Control,* Dordrecht: Kluwer Academic Publishers.

Nentjes, A. and D. Wiersma (1988), Innovation and pollution control. *International Journal of Social Economics* 15: 51–70.

Novshek, W. and H. Sonnenschein (1978), Cournot and Walras equilibrium. *Journal of Economic Theory,* 19: 223–66.

Nussbaum, B. (1992), Phasing down lead in gasoline in the U.S.: mandates, incentives, trading and banking. *Climate Change – Designing a Tradable Permit System,* Paris: OECD.

OECD (1992), *Climate Change: Designing a Practical Tax System,* Paris: OECD.

Ordover, J.A. and G. Saloner (1989), Predation, monopolization and antitrust. In R. Schmalensee and R.D. Willig (eds), *Handbook of Industrial Organization,* Vol. 1, Amsterdam: Elsevier.

Orr, D. (1974), Determinants of entry. *Review of Economics and Statistics,* 56: 58–66.

Oskam, A.J., D.D. van der Stelt-Scheele, J. Peerlings and D. Strijker (1987), *De Superheffing – is er een Alternatief?* [The superlevy – is there an alternative?], Landbouwuniversiteit, Wageningen.

Dutch Parliament (1991), *Wet op de Accijns,* Memorie van Toelichting, Kamerstukken no. 21368.

Pearse, P.H. (1992), Developing property rights as instruments of natural resource policy. *Climate Change: Designing a Practical Tax System,* Paris: OECD.

Pearson, M. (1992), Equity issues and carbon taxes. *Climate Change: Designing a Practical Tax System,* Paris: OECD.

Peeters, M. (1992), *Marktconform Milieurecht? Een Rechtsvergelijkende Studie naar de Verhandelbaarheid van Vervuilingsrechten,* Zwolle: Tjeenk Willink.

Pezzey, J. (1992). Some interactions between environmental policy and public finance, paper presented at third annual conference of the European Association of Environmental and Resource Economists, Cracow, 16–19 June.

Pisuise, C.S. and A.M.M. Teubner (1994), *Elementair Europees Gemeenschapsrecht,* 3rd edn, Groningen: Wolters-Noordhof.

Pototschnig, A. (1994), Economic instruments for the control of acid rain in Britain. G. Klaassen and F. Førsund (eds), *Economic Instruments for Air Pollution Control,* Dordrecht: Kluwer Academic Publishers.

Salop, S.C. and D.T. Scheffman (1983), Raising rivals' costs. *American Economic Review,* 73 (2): 267–71.

Salop, S.C. and D.T. Scheffman (1987), Cost-raising strategies. *The Journal of Industrial Economics,* 36 (1): 19–34.

Sandmo, A. (1975). Optimal taxation in the presence of externalities. *Swedish Journal of Economics,* 1975: 87–98.

Schuurman, S. (1992), *Verhandelbare Emissierechten* [Tradable emission permits], The Hague: Ministerie van Economische Zaken.

Scottish Agricultural College dairy test farm (1993), Interview.

Samenwerkende Electriciteits Producenten SEP (1991), *Plan van Aanpak ter Uitvoering van het Convenant over de Bestrijding van SO_2 and NO_x*

[Strategy for implementation of the voluntary agrement for reducing SO_2 and NO_x], Arnhem: Samenwerkende Electriciteits Producenten.

SkjÆrseth, J.B. (1994), The Climate Policy of the EC: Too Hot to Handle?, *Journal of Common Market Studies,* 32 (1): 25–45.

Sleuwaegen, L. and W. Dehandschutter (1991), Entry and exit in Belgian Manufacturing. In P.A. Geroski and J. Schwalbach (eds), *Entry and Market Contestability,* Oxford: Basil Blackwell.

Smith, S. (1992), Taxation and the environment: a survey, *Fiscal Studies,* 13 (4): 21–57.

Spence, A.M. (1977), Entry, capacity, investment and oligopolistic pricing. *Bell Journal of Economics,* 8: 534–44.

Stavins, R. (1994), Transaction costs and tradable permit markets. *Journal of Environmental Economics and Management,* 29: 133–48.

Stavins, R. and R. Hahn (1993), *Trading in Greenhouse Permits: a Critical Examination of Design and Implementation Issues,* Faculty Research Working Paper R93–15, Cambridge, Mass.: Harvard University.

Telser, L. (1966), Cutthroat competition and the long purse. *Journal of Law and Economics,* 9: 259–27.

Teubner, A.M.M. (1993), *Europees Recht (werkboek),* Amsterdam: University of Amsterdam.

Teubner, A.M.M. (1995), Personal communications, University of Amsterdam, Faculty of Law.

Tietenberg, T. (1985), *Emission Trading: An Exercise in Reforming Pollution Control,* Washington D.C.: Resources for the Future.

Tietenberg, T. (1988), *Environmental and Natural Resource Economics,* Glenview, Scott Foresman.

Tirole, J. (1992), *The Theory of Industrial Organization,* Cambridge, Mass.: MIT Press.

UNCTAD (1992), *Combatting Global Warming, Study on a Global System of Tradable Carbon Emission Entitlements,* New York: United Nations.

United Nations (1992), *Framework Convention on Climate Change,* New York: UN.

United Nations (1994), Climate Change Convention enters into force. *Climate Change Bulletin,* 3: 1.

Velthuijsen, J.W. (1995), *Determinants of Investment in Energy Conservation* (Diss.), Amsterdam: SEO.

Victor, D. (1991), Limits of market-based strategies for slowing global warming: the case of tradable permits. *Policy Sciences,* 24: 199–222.

Weizsäcker, C.C. von (1980), A welfare analysis of barriers to entry. *Bell Journal of Economics,* 11: 399–420.

Index